The Illustrated Guide to
Liverpool Herculaneum Pottery
1796—1840

The Illustrated Guides to Pottery and Porcelain

General Editor
GEOFFREY A. GODDEN

Already published
LOWESTOFT PORCELAIN by Geoffrey A. Godden
WORCESTER PORCELAIN by Henry Sandon

Soon to be published
MASON'S PATENT IRONSTONE CHINA by Geoffrey A. Godden
ROCKINGHAM CHINA by Dennis Rice
STAFFORDSHIRE SALT-GLAZED STONEWARES by A. R. Mountford

Frontispiece. JUG. Pearlware, polychrome enamelled decoration. Impressed HERCULANEUM. c.1805. Height $7\frac{1}{4}$". *Courtesy of The Art Institute of Chicago.*

The Illustrated Guide to

LIVERPOOL
HERCULANEUM
POTTERY

1796–1840

ALAN SMITH

PRAEGER PUBLISHERS
New York · Washington

BOOKS THAT MATTER

Published in the United States of America in 1970 by
PRAEGER PUBLISHERS, INC.
111 Fourth Avenue, New York, N.Y. 10003

Library of Congress Catalog Card Number: 72-107218

Printed in Great Britain

To the Memory of
JOSEPH MAYER
1803–1886
collector, scholar, public benefactor
and first historian of the
LIVERPOOL
POTTERIES

Contents

LIST OF ILLUSTRATIONS   ix

FOREWORD BY GEOFFREY A. GODDEN   xi

PREFACE   xiii

ACKNOWLEDGEMENTS   xv

CHAPTER I   Introduction: The Eighteenth-century Potteries
                   of Liverpool   1

CHAPTER II   Herculaneum. The Early Years 1796–1800   9

CHAPTER III   Growth and Prosperity c 1800–1820   28

CHAPTER IV   Trade Overseas   50

CHAPTER V   Problems and Change 1820–1833   62

CHAPTER VI   The End of the Road 1833–1840   73

CHAPTER VII   Methods and Management   89

APPENDIX I   Factory Marks   108

APPENDIX II   Resolutions of the Committee   110

APPENDIX III   The Tomkinson Papers   121

BIBLIOGRAPHICAL NOTE AND ADVICE TO COLLECTORS   132

INDEX   135

List of Illustrations

COLOUR PLATES

Frontispiece Jug, Pearlware c 1805
  I Creamware plaque printed with a portrait of Mary Queen of
       Scots c 1805   8
 II Bust of George Washington, Earthenware c 1800   32
III Teapot, Pearlware c 1805   40
 IV Meat Dish, Earthenware c 1805   56
  V Plate, Coalport Porcelain c 1815   64
 VI Vase, Porcelain c 1815   72
VII Covered Tureen and Stand, Earthenware c 1835   88

BLACK AND WHITE PHOTOGRAPHS

All between pages 48 and 49

  1–   2 Views of the Herculaneum Pottery
  3– 17 Pre-Herculaneum Liverpool Wares
 18– 28 Liverpool-Associated and Herculaneum Creamwares
 29– 92 Herculaneum Creamwares
 93–113 Herculaneum Stonewares
114–121 Herculaneum Modelling
122–145 Herculaneum Porcelains
146–170 Herculaneum Blue Printed Earthenwares
171–182 Herculaneum Earthenwares Between 1830 and 1840
183–191 Herculaneum Lustrewares and Other Miscellaneous Pieces

MAPS

                                    pages
Map of Liverpool and Toxteth Park about 1806   6–7
Plan of the Works of Charles Roe & Company, about 1790   16–17
Map of part of St. Helens, Lancashire, showing the Green Bank Pottery
  and adjoining premises   84–85
Plan of the Herculaneum Pottery about 1800   94–95

LINE ILLUSTRATIONS

A Flint Pan 102
Blunging the Clay 102
Sieving the Clay 103
Throwing 103
Plaster Moulds 104
Handle Making 104
Packing a Kiln 105
Applying Transfer prints 105

Editor's Foreword

One of the main objects of this series of these *Illustrated Guides*, of which I am general editor, is to give information on little understood and little known manufacturers. This present book, written by the local Museum Curator, is a case in point, as it gives for the first time a clear picture of the various Liverpool wares between 1796 and 1840.

The scope and quality of these often unmarked or unfamiliar pieces will, I am sure, pleasantly surprise collectors. We tend to forget that Liverpool closely rivalled the Staffordshire Potteries at this period, that Staffordshire wares sometimes were decorated at Liverpool and that huge quantities of Liverpool earthenware and fine porcelain were exported from this port to North America and our other Export markets; chapter IV is devoted to this overseas trade.

Mr. Smith has, in fact, found in the American collections some of his more important pieces for illustration and his book will prove to be of the greatest interest to collectors, dealers and auctioneers on both sides of the Atlantic.

Apart from the description of the wares and other material of a conventional nature the author has discovered much contemporary material, including factory records, committee reports and instructions, accounts, a price book, recipes of different bodies, etc. and a journalistic review of the factory, written in 1827. These unique records have been intelligently used, both to ensure reliability of the information given and to clothe the flesh and bones of the story, giving added interest and colour to a book which will surely be regarded as an enjoyable and helpful standard work of reference for many generations of collectors.

GEOFFREY A. GODDEN

Author's Preface

About twelve years ago the author purchased a transfer-printed creamware plate impressed 'HERCULANEUM'. At that time this name meant no more to him than that the plate was from a relatively little-known Liverpool pottery which had chosen to use this classical name in much the same way as Wedgwood had used 'Etruria' for his Staffordshire factory. Reference to ceramic literature revealed that practically everything written about Herculaneum was traceable to Joseph Mayer's *History of the Progress of the Art of Pottery in Liverpool*, first published in 1855, and that on the whole there was only a moderate enthusiasm amongst either collectors or authors for the work of this Liverpool concern. One might take this even further and say that the Herculaneum factory was completely disregarded by all except a few as being of no importance whatsoever.

Since the purchase of that plate, however, times have changed. The whole field of Liverpool ceramics has aroused as much interest in recent years as any other English pottery or porcelain-making centre, an interest which has developed in inverse ratio to the neglect which had previously been its fate. We have now not only come to realise that Liverpool has much to offer to the student of eighteenth-century ceramics, but also that its last and largest factory can stand the comparison with any of its Staffordshire contemporaries and competitors.

Herculaneum, like the Cambrian factory at Swansea, may be considered more objectively than most other potteries of the day because it existed, to some extent, in isolation. On the other hand, it was intimately tied to Staffordshire throughout its working life, not only because so many of its workpeople came from that over-crowded pottery-making area, but also because it maintained contact with the Staffordshire Potteries by acting as a commercial and forwarding agent for the overseas trade. The true relationship between Staffordshire and Liverpool over a period far longer than that of the factory itself is the subject of a study still to be written. It is hoped that this book may be regarded at least as a beginning in the analysis of the interdependence of Liverpool, as a manufacturing and exporting centre, and Staffordshire which so largely depended upon it.

The author has become increasingly aware that a full and informed interest in pottery cannot be confined exclusively to an investigation of bodies, glazes, forms, colours and designs. It must also lead to the study of the ways of life, standards of taste and manufacturing conditions of the period, which are related to and yet are as different from those of our own day as the pots we use now differ from those of the past. The book, therefore, attempts to describe the life and conditions of the people at Herculaneum as well as the pots they made.

ALAN SMITH
13 Park Road, Worsley, Manchester

Acknowledgements

In making my acknowledgements to the many people who have helped me to compile this book I would first like to thank Mr. T. A. Hume, Director of the City of Liverpool Museums. As a member of his staff I owe him a great deal for his encouragement in many ways, and particularly for allowing me freely to make use of illustrations of specimens in the museum, which total just over half of the examples shown. At the same time I also wish to thank Mr. N. Carrick and his staff at the Liverpool Public Record Office, where much of the original research work has been done. Many of the Liverpool parish church registers are now in that library, but for access to those which still remain in the safekeeping of Liverpool churches I here record my thanks. The Reverend Brian Green of St. James' Church, Toxteth, the Reverend John Barrow of St. Michael's-in-the-Hamlet, Toxteth, the Minister and Committee of the Ancient Chapel of Toxteth and Canon R. G. B. Bailey of Ormskirk Parish Church have all been most helpful in allowing me to examine at leisure their valuable parish records. As well as acknowledging these Liverpool and district sources I must also extend my thanks to the staff of the Lancashire Record Office in Preston for helping me to search for information and for giving me permission to use the plans reproduced on pages 16–17 and 94–95.

A large number of individual collectors and historians have helped me in many different ways, and I owe them my most sincere personal thanks. In this connection I would particularly like to mention Mrs. E. Blatch, Colonel B. Blewitt, Dr. Knowles Boney, Dr. J. L. Brown, Mrs. R. D. Chellis, Mr. N. H. F. Cusack, Mr. W. J. Grant-Davidson, Mr. R. Evans, Mr. and Mrs. J. K. des Fontaines, Mr. and Mrs. C. Gorely, Mr. Reginald Haggar, Mr. and Mrs. W. W. Hamilton-Foyn, Mr. L. Harrison, Dr. Lloyd Hawes, Mr. David Holgate, Mr. and Mrs. Jack L. Leon, Mrs. B. K. Little, Mr. G. P. G. Monk, Mr. Raymond Plant, Mrs. de Saye Hutton, Mr. and Mrs. A. Schaffer, Mrs. Samuel Schwartz, Mr. and Mrs. E. N. Stretton, Mr. Edward Thomas, Dr. Bernard Watney and Mr. David S. Weinstock. Last, but by no means least,

I must thank Mr. Geoffrey A. Godden, the editor of this series, for his ready help and encouragement since he first asked me to undertake the work. Many of these people have allowed me to illustrate specimens in their collections, and it has always been a great privilege to talk to them and to examine their treasures.

The resources of many of the Art Galleries and Museums both in England and in the United States have been used in compiling the material. I would particularly like to thank the following individuals and the institutions they represent for allowing me to see and handle specimens in their care, and for permission to use illustrations of examples in their collections: Messrs. H. H. G. Arthur and David Armitage, *Williamson Art Gallery, Birkenhead*; Mr. John Austin, *Colonial Williamsburg, Virginia*; Mr. H. F. Brazenor, *Art Gallery and Museum, Brighton*; Mr. J. S. Bunt, *Glynn Vivian Art Gallery, Swansea*; Mr. R. J. Charleston, *Victoria and Albert Museum*; Miss Mellanay M. Delhom, *Mint Museum of Art, Charlotte, North Carolina*; Mr. E. S. Dodge, *The Peabody Museum of Salem, Massachusetts*; Mr. John M. Graham, *Colonial Williamsburg, Virginia*; Mr. Calvin S. Hathaway, *Philadelphia Museum of Art*; Mr. Dwight P. Lanmon, *Henry Francis du Pont Museum, Winterthur, Delaware*; Mr. E. J. Laws, *Museum and Art Gallery, Nottingham*; Miss Catriona MacLeod, *National Museum of Ireland, Dublin*; Mr. Arnold Mountford, *Hanley Museum, Stoke-on-Trent*; Mr. J. Jefferson Miller, *Smithsonian Institution, Washington*; Mr. J. P. Palmer, *Fitzwilliam Museum, Cambridge*; Mr. Michael R. Parkinson, *City Art Gallery, Manchester*; Mr. J. R. Rimmer, *Museum and Art Gallery, Warrington*; Mr. Paul F. Rovetti, *The Mattatuck Museum, Waterbury, Connecticut*; Miss Vivian Scheidemantel, *Art Institute of Chicago*; Mr. H. Schnabel, *Museum of Fine Arts, Boston, Massachusetts*; Mr. David R. Shearer, *Museum and Art Galleries, Paisley*; Miss A. E. C. Simoni, *British Museum Library*; Mr. Ross E. Taggart, *Nelson Gallery and Atkins Museum, Kansas City, Missouri*; Mr. G. H. Tait, *British Museum (British and Mediaeval Antiquities)*; Mrs. M. Ward, *Sadler Collection, Myott Son & Co, Ltd, Hanley*; *The National Trust* at Upton House, Warwickshire, and Mr. H. C. Caistor, *The Central Library, St. Helens*.

I would finally like to thank Mr. G. D. Hyslop of Liverpool City Museums for taking the original photographs used for colour plates II, III, IV, V, VI, VII, and the members of his studio who took the photographs of other specimens from Liverpool Museum. Mr. Thomas Walters of Charlotte, North Carolina, took the photograph for colour plate I and I wish to extend my thanks to him also.

Chapter I

Introduction: The Eighteenth-Century Potteries of Liverpool

The Herculaneum factory was founded on the outskirts of a town which had a long tradition of potting history. Liverpool in the eighteenth century had about twenty-five potteries which made both humble wares and first-class products, and employed practically every current technique. Amongst Liverpool ceramics, therefore, we find rough earthenwares, refractories, salt-glazed stonewares, delftwares, porcelain, pearlwares and creamwares. Several techniques of lead-glazed earthenwares were employed and transfer-printing was used extensively on delftware, creamware and china. Herculaneum came of good stock in so far as it owes part of its heritage to its Liverpool father, whatever the merits of its Staffordshire mother might have been.

The earliest references to potting on Merseyside date from the seventeenth century, but most of these are concerned with the making of bricks and tiles. The Liverpool Town Records show that permission was granted for 'clay getting for bricks' as early as May 16th, 1615. There are many other references from the same source: in 1639 James Southerns was 'getting marl'; in 1659 Mr. Thomas Storie was making bricks; in 1674 Mr. Augustus Wilkins was 'permitted to get clay on the Heath'; in 1692 Mr. William Praddock was permitted to 'build a shead upon ye Common to make or mould Bricks or Tyle'. Such activities one would expect to find in a growing town, and there is no doubt that rough mugs, jugs and bowls were being made alongside the bricks, in Liverpool itself, and in small villages such as Prescot or Ormskirk only a few miles away. Numerous early lead glazed mugs and jugs with mottled glazes streaked with iron-brown stains (Plate 3) have come to light recently in excavations in what is now the centre of the city.

Slip-trailed earthenwares may well have been produced and it would indeed seem strange if this had not been the case. Over fifty years ago William Burton published an illustration of a fine slipware posset-pot* attributed to the Liverpool potters, though the pot itself no longer exists.† Further evidence

---

* William Burton, *English Earthenware & Stoneware*, London, 1904, Fig. 7, p. 36.
† Destroyed by bombing at Liverpool Museum, 1941.

was revealed when some slipware fragments were unearthed near the site of one of the Shaw's Brow potteries in 1967 when the burials at Christ Church graveyard were exhumed. Thirty to forty slip decorated pieces were discovered in a relatively small area, some with a lead glaze of a very high standard. Slipware has only, so far, been found in Liverpool in conjunction with a pottery site and this suggests that the discovery in Christ Church graveyard should not be dismissed as domestic waste. It is now well known that the Staffordshire potters were exporting slipware through the port of Liverpool; it would be unwise to assume that the Liverpool potters did not also try their hand at manufacturing it. We believe they did with considerable success.

However fragmentary our knowledge of Liverpool slipware may be, the Liverpool delftware is considered its most typical pottery, as it was made on a tremendous scale for almost a hundred years. All the pot-banks made their tin-glazed delftware, and the first of which we have any precise knowledge is the Lord Street Pothouse which began in 1710.

> The Corporation of Liverpool in Lancashire have encouraged there a Manufactory of all sorts of fine white and Painted pots and other vessels and Tiles in imitation of China, both for Inland and outland Trade, which will be speedily ready and sold at reasonable rates.*

Delftware requires as its base a light-firing clay not found locally and, in the year just mentioned, Mr. Richard Holt of London, who was granted a lease of the Lord Street works, imported his clay from Belfast. Several potters from the Southwark area appear to have come to this pottery to start the delftware trade, and under several different proprietors the establishment continued until at least 1789. A large number of shards have been discovered on the site, but delftware is found almost everywhere in Liverpool where the potters worked. Of the other potteries which made tin-glazed earthenware we may mention the Dale Street works of Samuel Poole, from about 1729 to 1779; another Dale Street factory belonging to Alderman Thomas Shaw, from 1725 to about 1784; and Patrick's Hill Pothouse (so-called from its proximity to St. Patrick's Cross), originating at an unknown date early in the eighteenth century and surviving in the hands of John Dunbibbin until at least the 1760s. The Shaw's Brow factory of John Livesley also manufactured delft in the first half of the century, and was subsequently mortgaged to Richard Chaffers who made this ware before and during the time he was producing porcelain. Another factory was established on Shaw's Brow in 1714 by Samuel Gilbody (the elder) when he was described as 'a brickmaker, potter and dealer in white earthenware'. There was also the Duke Street works of George Drinkwater & Co. in Pothouse Lane who used Irish clay in considerable quantity:

> 50 tons Potters' Clay from Belfast delivered May 27th, 1768
> 10 tons Potters' Clay from Carrickfergus delivered June 24th, 1768†

---

* *The Post Boy*, May 23rd, 1710.
† From the *Entwistle Papers*, Liverpool Public Record Office.

The full range of delftwares made in Liverpool and the detailed histories of the various factories producing it have already been published elsewhere,* and examples may be seen in Plates 4 and 5.

The names of John Sadler and Guy Green have always been famous in the history of English ceramics for their part in the introduction of transfer-printing at their Harrington Street works, first on delftware tiles and later on creamware and porcelain. A scholarly study of Sadler's life has already been published by the late E. S. Price† and Dr. Knowles Boney has also analysed the importance of his printing on Liverpool porcelain.‡ In a book which is devoted primarily to Herculaneum the writer can only add one comment to the work of these earlier authorities—that it was undoubtedly the tradition of fine printing on ceramics, begun by Sadler and continued by Green, Abbey and others (see pages 23ff) that gave the early Herculaneum-printed pots their superior quality amongst other printed wares of the day.

Lead-glazed earthenwares of a rough and humble type have already been mentioned, but some of the Liverpool potters made finer earthenwares as well. Joseph Mayer in 1855 referred to the tortoiseshell-glazed 'Whieldon' types made by Philip Christian at his Shaw's Brow factory,§ and knowledge of tortoiseshell and agate by the Liverpool potters is amply illustrated by, for example, the correspondence of John Roscoe and James Rigby with Josiah Wedgwood during the years 1761 to 1785. Wedgwood's connections with Liverpool are too well known to be repeated here. His influence, and that of other Staffordshire manufacturers, can be seen on Liverpool potting of the eighteenth century. One particularly interesting example of Wedgwood's connections may be noted in his letter to Thomas Bentley of June 25th, 1769 when he wrote about the hiring of painters¶. Thomas Bentley was Wedgwood's partner, and had formerly been a Liverpool merchant. In his letter Wedgwood refers to Mr. Wilcox, a painter who served his time in Philip Christian's factory, then went to Worcester and was later taken on by Wedgwood. Mrs. Wilcox, the daughter of Thomas Frye of Bow, was also a highly accomplished painter, perhaps better than her husband, and both eventually worked on part of the famous Wedgwood Russian service, Mr. Wilcox painting the borders and his wife doing the 'landskips'.

The foregoing mention of Philip Christian's pottery on Shaw's Brow, where Wilcox was apprenticed, brings us to the porcelain makers of Liverpool. There were far fewer potters who attempted to work with this difficult material than those employed making delftware, and their careers and products are perhaps the best documented in the whole field of Liverpool

* See F. H. Garner, *English Delftware*, London, 1948.
Anthony Ray, *English Delftware Pottery in the Robert Hall Warren Collection*, London, 1968.
† E. S. Price, *John Sadler, A Liverpool Pottery Printer*, West Kirby, 1948.
‡ Dr. Knowles Boney, *Liverpool Porcelain of the Eighteenth Century*, London, 1957.
§ Joseph Mayer, *History of the Progress of the Art of Pottery in Liverpool*, Liverpool, 1855 and 1873.
¶ See Ann Finer and George Savage, *The Selected Letters of Josiah Wedgwood*, London, 1965, p. 75.

potting.* William Reid was the first porcelain manufacturer whose factory lasted a few years on Brownlow Hill.† He was closely followed by Richard Chaffers whose agreement with Robert Padmore (or Podmore) of Worcester was published in full by Dr. Boney in 1957, and whose excursion to Cornwall to search for soaprock for his porcelain was first told by Mayer in 1855.‡ Other porcelain makers included Philip Christian who was Chaffers' partner and successor in the Shaw's Brow factory; Samuel Gilbody (the younger) who for a short time made excellent china and whose work has been firmly identified by Dr. Bernard Watney and the author following a successful excavation in 1966.§ The Pennington brothers, Seth, James and John, were all engaged in porcelain-making in various potteries, and William Ball of Ranelagh Street was also employed in this field. The early wares of Chaffers, Christian, Reid, Gilbody and Ball are perhaps the most exciting and are certainly the rarest of Liverpool porcelains. However, the later products of the Penningtons have a good deal less charm and quality, with their under-glaze printed blue, standardised porcelain bodies and suitably christened 'thunder cloud' glaze (Plates 6, 7, 8, 9 and 10).

By the closing decades of the eighteenth century, when delftware was declining and creamware was taking its place, cream and pearlware bodies were also made by the Liverpool potters. More will be said about creamware in Chapter II, but little has ever been written about Liverpool pearlware, a type not so demanding in terms of colour of body and glaze. Of the examples illustrated here (Plates 14 and 15) the pearlware punchbowl, decorated with the 'Liver Bird' from Liverpool Corporation coat-of-arms and a border used on Pennington's porcelain is particularly important. Another piece from the same factory is the jug inscribed 'Success to the Watchmakers' which reminds us that the horological trade was for long of unique importance in the economy of Liverpool and district (Plate 14). It is of interest to note that in the sale advertisement of Seth Pennington and John Part's factory of August 12th, 1799 the following detail is included:

> There are three spacious Hovels or Outbuildings containing Kilns, well adapted for the manufacturing of China, *or any kind of Earthenware* and there is also a spring of excellent water on the premises [author's italics].

Amongst the various types of pottery made by the older Liverpool factories we must not overlook salt-glaze (Plates 12 and 13). For many years this method of potting was never seriously considered in Liverpool, but as further

---

* Knowles Boney, *ibid.*
R. J. Charleston, *English Porcelain 1745–1850*, London, 1965.
Bernard Watney, *English Ceramic Circle Transactions*, Vol. 4, Part 5, pp. 13–25.
Vol. 5, Part 1, pp. 42–52. Vol. 5, Part 5, pp. 269–282.
  † For a full account of the bankruptcy of William Reid and his association with John Baddeley of Shelton see John Mallet, *English Ceramic Circle Transactions*, Vol. 6, Part 2, p. 124ff. Part 3, p. 181ff.
  ‡ Joseph Mayer, *ibid.*
  § Bernard Watney and Alan Smith, *Samuel Gilbody—some recent finds at Liverpool.* *English Ceramic Circle Transactions*, Vol. 7, Part 2.

evidence has come to light we have begun to realise that not only was salt-glaze made but produced by more than one factory. The dated and inscribed salt-glaze tea caddy (Plate 12) has been shown to be of Liverpool manufacture and is closely related to the teapot now in Truro Museum.* The following advertisement from *The Public Advertiser* of April 7th, 1761 suggests that salt-glaze was made at Dunbibbin's works:

> Whereas the Co. partnership with Messrs. JOHN DUNBIBBIN & CO. Potters at Liverpool is dissolved, debts are to be paid to Samuel Dunbibbin at the Liverpool Warehouse, St. Margaret's Hill, Southwark. The said warehouse is continued by JOHN DUNBIBBIN where persons may be supplied with all sorts of Delft ware and Gally Tiles from their own manufactory, likewise white stoneware and Nottingham ware.

A teapot (Plate 13) in Liverpool Museum is sprigged with the usual vines and also incorporates a 'Liver Bird'. The 'plumper' mug, now lost, made on behalf of Sir William Meredith in the Liverpool parliamentary election of 1761† is closely related to the Chaffers porcelain mug, formerly in the collection of the late Ernest Allman of Bootle and now in the British Museum. *Williamson's Liverpool Advertiser* of June 18th, 1756 refers to a pottery which produced humble stonewares, refractories and almost certainly salt-glaze. I quote this in full because it is important to realise that Liverpool was not an isolated pottery-making centre; there were other neighbouring towns contributing to the industry:

> '*Mould Works near the Infirmary*
> The Proprietors of the Mould Works near the Infirmary, Liverpool, acquaint the public that they continue to make all sorts of sugar moulds, and drips, chimney moulds, large jars for water, black mugs of all sizes, crucibles, and melting pots for silver smiths, founders &c. and sell them on the same terms as from Prescot, Sutton and other places. Direct to the proprietors of the Mould Works, Wood & Co.'

Prescot, Sutton and Ormskirk were all towns involved in the pottery production of S.W. Lancashire, and manufactories in these places have been amongst the last to disappear. When the complete history of potting in this area is written it may prove that they had a greater part to play in the Lancashire ceramic tradition than has been previously recognised.

The remaining potteries of eighteenth century Liverpool are referred to in greater detail in Chapter II. The Flint Mug Works in Parliament Street, The Park Lane Pothouse, The Islington China Manufactory of Mason, Wolfe and Lucock and The Haymarket Pottery of Zachariah Barnes were amongst the last survivors of the old established potteries of the town, and it

---

* Knowles Boney, *Documentary Liverpool Saltglaze, Apollo*, December 1960.
† See *The Liverpool Bulletin*, March 1954, p. 39. Published by the Libraries, Museums & Arts Committee, Corporation of Liverpool.

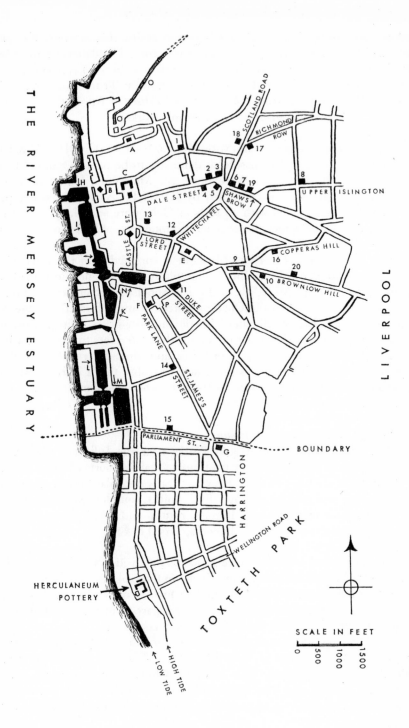

THE RIVER MERSEY ESTUARY

LIVERPOOL

SCOTLAND ROAD

RICHMOND ROW

18

17

2 3

6 7 19

DALE STREET

4 5

SHAWS BROW

UPPER ISLINGTON

8

A

C

H

B

13

D

12

CASTLE ST.

LORD STREET

WHITECHAPEL

COPPERAS HILL

E

9

16

20

10 BROWNLOW HILL

N

11

DUKE STREET

F

P

J

K

L

PARK LANE

14

ST. JAMES'S STREET

M

15

PARLIAMENT ST.

BOUNDARY

G

HARRINGTON

WELLINGTON ROAD

HERCULANEUM POTTERY

TOXTETH PARK

HIGH TIDE

LOW TIDE

SCALE IN FEET

0   500   1000   1500

showing the situation of the Harculaneum Pottery, the lay-out of the streets of Harrington (not completely built at this date), the docks, some of the principal streets and churches, and the sites of the eighteenth-century potteries of Liverpool.

1. PATRICK'S HILL POTHOUSE John Dunbavan (sometimes given as Dunbibbin) from c. 1750. Thomas Deare & Co. from 1760.

2. DALE STREET POTTERY Samuel Poole from c 1729; apprentices listed 1760–1767; works offered for sale in 1779.

3. DALE STREET POTTERY Begun by Samuel Shaw (d 1725) and succeeded by Alderman Thomas Shaw; sold to John Chorley 1774 and continued until c 1784.

4. DALE STREET/PRESTON STREET POTTERY Richard Hillary & Co. from 1753 until possibly 1769.

5. HAYMARKET POTTERY Leased to John Livesley 1751; Zachariah Barnes and James Cotter until early in the nineteenth century.

6. SHAW'S BROW POTTERY John Livesley, mortgaged to Richard Chaffers 1747; Phillip Christian partner with Chaffers 1755–1765; about 1775 Seth Pennington and John Part until 1799; Pennington and Edwards until c 1805.

7. SHAW'S BROW POTTERY Samuel Gilbody the elder and Thomas Morris from 1714 until 1752; Samuel Gilbody the younger until his bankruptcy in 1761.

8. ISLINGTON CHINA MANUFACTORY Leased to Thomas Shaw 1743; in the hands of John Pennington by 1779; Thomas Wolfe, Miles Mason and John Lucock about 1795–1800.

9. RANELAGH STREET POTTERY Beginnings unknown but occupied by William Ball about 1755–1770.

10. REID'S CHINA WORKS William Reid 1756–1761.

11. DUKE STREET POTTERY George Drinkwater & Co. c 1757 until c 1774.

12. LORD STREET POTHOUSE Richard Holt 1710; Josiah Poole 1714; Thomas Seel and Robert Thyer 1748, continued possibly until c 1789.

13. PRINTED WARE MANUFACTORY, HARRINGTON STREET John Sadler and Guy Green from c 1750, Sadler retiring in 1770 and Green retiring in 1799.

14. PARK LANE POTHOUSE John Eccles & Co. 1775; Richard Thwaites & Robert Willcock c 1766; James Pennington working in 1769; closed by 1780.

15. FLINT MUG WORKS Known to have been in existence prior to 1772 in the hands of John Okill & Co.; 1773 Rigg & Peacock, then John Sykes & Co. until the 1790s.

16. COPPERAS HILL POTTERY Thomas and John Mears then James and John Pennington, 1771–1785.

17. MUG WORKS, RICHMOND ROW AND SCOTLAND PLACE John Livesley in occupation in 1779.

18. CANNING STREET POTTERY Archibald Mansfield, 1824–1840; see pages 66, 67.

19. SHAW'S BROW POTTERY John Roscoe and James Rigby from c 1761 to c 1770.

20. BROWNLOW HILL POTTERY Joseph Brooks working about 1778; 1788 Thomas Pendleton—still in existence as a pottery in 1790.

A. ST. PAUL'S CHURCH.
B. ST. NICHOLAS' CHURCH.
C. TOWN HALL AND EXCHANGE FLAGS.
D. ST. GEORGE'S CHURCH.
E. ST. PETER'S CHURCH.
F. ST. THOMAS'S CHURCH.
G. ST. JAMES'S CHURCH.
H. DRY BASON.

I. GEORGE'S DOCK.
J. OLD DRY DOCK.
K. SALTHOUSE DOCK.
L. KING'S DOCK.
M. QUEEN'S DOCK.
N. OLD DOCK.
O. LEEDS–LIVERPOOL CANAL.
P. CLIEVELAND SQUARE.

is to them that we must turn in tracing the roots of Herculaneum at Toxteth.

Samuel Worthington's Herculaneum Pottery was the first and only Liverpool factory to use a trade name to identify itself, for all the others were known by the names of the roads in which they stood or the names of their owners. The significance of this is interesting, for Worthington was a business man of insight, and he foresaw the possibilities in the appeal of a well-chosen name. He was not the first to do so, he clearly followed the lead of Wedgwood who had used the classical name of Etruria for a similar purpose. Although Wedgwood's Etruria was deservedly more famous on an international scale than Herculaneum could ever have been, Herculaneum is still thought of first when Liverpool potting is discussed by the present inhabitants of that town.*

* For a complete list of books on the history of pottery in Liverpool see the Bibliographical Note, page 132.

I. PLAQUE. Creamware, set in a black basalt frame. Polychrome printed with a portrait of Mary Queen of Scots. Plaque and frame impressed HERCULANEUM. c.1805. Height $6\frac{1}{8}$". *Courtesy of The Mint Museum of Art, Charlotte, North Carolina.*

Chapter II

Herculaneum. The Early Years 1796–1800

On December 15th, 1796 a Liverpool journal announced the following particulars which give us the precise date of the foundation of the Herculaneum Pottery:*

> On Saturday last the NEW POTTERY (formerly the Copper Works) near this town, was opened, and a plentiful entertainment given by MR. WORTHINGTON, the PROPRIETOR, to upwards of SIXTY PERSONS employed in his manufactory, who were preceded by a Military Band from the Works, along the Docks and through Castle Street. TWO COLOURS were displayed on the occasion—one representing a Distant View of the Manufactory. We have the pleasure to say, these Works are very likely to succeed, which, if they do, from their extent and situation will be of infinite advantage to the Merchants of Liverpool.

From a long and somewhat romanticised description by Joseph Mayer† we know that many of the workpeople had come directly from the pottery centres of Staffordshire, having landed at the site on November 11th, 1796 after a journey along the Mersey–Trent Canal. At that time the canal entered the Mersey estuary down a long flight of locks at Runcorn which are now filled in, and the journey from Runcorn to Toxteth was completed on a Mersey 'flat', a flat-bottomed boat of the type used in the estuary and in coastal waters in those days. Mayer tells us that there were about forty potters who made the journey with their wives and children, hoping to find a more secure life than was possible in their native Staffordshire. It is ironic to realise that the canal on which they travelled was the route pioneered by Wedgwood to carry the exports of Staffordshire—one of the factors which contributed to the decay of the eighteenth century Liverpool potteries.

* *Gore's General Advertiser.*
† Joseph Mayer, *History of the Progress of the Art of Pottery in Liverpool*, Liverpool 1855 and 1873.

9

Emigration of potters from Staffordshire to Liverpool does not appear to have been unusual during the eighteenth century. It is reasonably clear that there were, at that time, too many potters at work in Staffordshire to be supported by the trade, and many must therefore have sought employment in the coastal towns of Liverpool, Bristol and Swansea, where transport costs for materials and finished goods were considerably less than in the Staffordshire districts. Contacts between the Staffordshire Potteries and these places were well established at least as early as the 1750s and from Liverpool alone, in 1770, as many as 492,980 pieces of earthenware were exported, most of which were presumably of Staffordshire origin.*

For Samuel Worthington, therefore, to have drawn on Staffordshire sources for his skilled labour force was not a new idea, though the *scale* on which he did it was probably unprecedented. It must not, however, be assumed that all the members of the factory were Staffordshire people; many of the potters had long associations with the earlier Liverpool factories, some of which were still in existence when Herculaneum came on the scene. Apart from those factories mentioned in Chapter I there were several coming to the end of their days on the outskirts of the rapidly growing town. Even some of the more centrally placed 'banks' were still conducting their affairs in one form or another, though perhaps becoming more involved as dealers in pottery than as manufacturers. Guy Green of Harrington Street does not appear to have retired from business until about 1799, and the Flint Mug Works at the corner of Flint Street and Parliament Street, almost on the borders of Toxteth, appears on a map dated 1806, though not necessarily still in production. Little enough is known about the later years of this pottery but in the *Liverpool Advertiser* of October 29th, 1773 the factory was advertised as follows:

> To be sold, the assignment of a term in lease (14 years whereof are unexpired) of a valuable established pottery, conveniently situated on the south side of the town of Liverpool, together with the stock-in-trade, consisting of several materials necessary for carrying on the said business; as also a large assortment of cream colour or Queensware, manufactured at the said work, which is now carried on in great perfection, and a set of workmen and customers fixed. Such persons as are desirous of treating for the same are requested to apply to Mr. J. Okill in Liverpool. N.B. There are a few apprentices to the said business, who have considerable part of their time to serve, which may be assigned over to any purchaser.

The J. Okill mentioned in this advertisement was James, the nephew of the famous Liverpool ship-builder Mr. John Okill who had died suddenly on August 20th, 1773.† Amongst his other effects his pot-house is mentioned in his will with James as beneficiary, but it is clear from the advertisement

---

* William Enfield, *An Essay towards the History of Leverpool*, London, 1774.
† R. Stewart-Brown, *Liverpool Ships in the Eighteenth Century*, London, 1932.

that James did not wish to own it. In the following year 1774 another advertisement appeared. It is quoted by Mayer, and shows that the works continued in other hands:

> Flint Potworks. Rigg and Peacock beg leave to acquaint their friends and the public that they have taken and entered on the Flint Potworks, upper end of Park Lane, near the Pitch-house, lately belonging to Mr. Okell [sic], deceased, where they intend carrying on the business of making all kinds of cream-coloured earthenware, &c. Those who are pleased to favour them with their orders may depend upon being well served, and on the lowest terms, by their most humble servants.
>
> RIGG AND PEACOCK

One final reference which gives us a clue to the continued ownership of these works following Rigg and Peacock, is again quoted by Mayer and suggests that it was still a going concern in the hands of John Sykes and Co. as late as 1790. There are also several potters' names recorded in the parish registers of St. James' Church, Toxteth (which is only a few hundred yards from the pottery site) of dates carrying well into the 1790s.

Another pottery not far from the Flint Mug Works which must be mentioned was the Park Lane Pothouse. Park Lane was, and still is, the main road into Toxteth, and the pottery was sited in an area now dominated by nineteenth century warehouses, at the corner of the present Blundell Street alongside what was the 'White Ropery'—a rope-making works. Dr. Knowles Boney* has shown that this factory, in the hands of John Eccles and Co., was making black 'Jackfield' type wares in the middle of the eighteenth century, and almost certainly salt-glaze, of which an important documented piece has been acquired by Liverpool Corporation (Plate 12). Blue and white earthenwares also seem to have been made at Park Lane and there is no doubt that creamwares were made there once they had come into fashion. There has been some confusion in the past about the ownership of these works. Some authorities state that Rigg and Peacock took them from Mr. Okill, but this must surely be mistaken if one takes into consideration the entries already quoted for the Flint Mug Works which were not far away. Charles Gatty, in his book on the Liverpool potteries,† mentions Richard Thwaites and Robert Willcock and Co. as being in possession in 1766 and most authorities are agreed that James Pennington, the porcelain manufacturer, worked here for a time about 1769. By 1780 the site of the Park Lane Pottery was occupied by a brewery and our last documentary evidence of potters working there is the directory entry of David McCreary as a potter and victualler at 46 Park Lane in 1777. It is of some interest to note that one David McCrery, by profession a potter, was married at St. Nicholas' Church on June 13th, 1798. By this date he could have moved to the Flint Mug Works or, as seems more likely, taken employment at Herculaneum.

---

* Knowles Boney, *Apollo*, March and July 1955, December 1960.
† Charles T. Gatty, *The Liverpool Potteries*, Liverpool, 1882.

Both the potteries considered above were involved in the manufacture of creamware, a type of pottery produced in large quantities at Herculaneum, but we know from other evidence that creamware was also being made on the site of Pennington's Shaw's Brow factory on the eastern edges of the town. In the late 1850s when the foundations of the present library and museum were being excavated on Shaw's Brow, (now William Brown Street, named after the benefactor who provided the money for the library and museum) a vat of clay was discovered, some of which was taken to Stoke-on-Trent and made into commemorative vases, duly inscribed, one of which may still be seen at the Museum and Art Gallery, Hanley. This vase is a typical example of creamware, and the site where the clay was found was formerly occupied by the potter Seth Pennington. He worked there from 1778 or thereabouts, until 1799, with his partner John Part. John Part left the business in 1799 but Seth carried on until he retired in 1805, almost ten years after the founding of Herculaneum. The large number of potters and pot-painters who were living in the vicinity during the last ten years of the eighteenth century clearly testifies to the continuance of pottery-making in the area and it is certain that many workpeople sought employment at Herculaneum when the older potteries closed. One such man was Thomas Walls, who is reputed to have fired the first porcelain oven at Herculaneum, and who previously lived on Shaw's Brow.

Another of the older factories which continued until about 1800 was that of Zachariah Barnes, a Liverpool merchant who owned the business but, like Samuel Worthington, was not a working potter. Barnes is listed in the directories as a 'China Manufacturer' and there is still much difference of opinion as to whether or not he made porcelain as well as the delftware and tiles, for which he is well-known. Barnes' factory was known as 'The Haymarket Pottery', and was situated at the corner of Dale Street in an area now occupied by the eastern end of the Mersey road tunnel. Since the works were still producing until about 1800 it is possible that creamware was made, and some evidence to support this view has recently been excavated near the site of the works. Creamware shards of engine-turned and slip banded baluster-shaped jugs and bowls were found, as well as teabowls and plates in under-glaze 'Pratt-type' colours, also some fragments of creamware decorated with a dense black glaze outside, on which 'cold' enamels were applied. The types found have for long been associated with Leeds and Staffordshire, particularly the sgraffito chequer-board designs, but nothing of this kind has been found in Liverpool before. However, since one sugar bowl cover, from this site, has been proved to be Herculaneum, this suggestion may not be warranted and the finds may simply be the discards of a pottery dealer.

The last of the eighteenth century potteries to be considered in the present context is that which was working a little further east than Pennington's, in Folly Lane, now called Islington. This factory, known in its later years as 'The Islington China Manufactory', had a history going back to the first half of the eighteenth century, the site being leased to Thomas Shaw, presumably as a pot works, in 1743. In July, 1787 the lease was renewed to

Richard Gerard and described as 'China works and garden, north side Folly Lane . . .' Since Gerard was not a potter he may at this time have rented the premises to John and Jane Pennington (John being Seth's brother), who were using the factory from 1779. In that year John issued an announcement which opened as follows:

> John Pennington, China Manufacturer, begs to inform his friends and the public that he has removed from his late factory at Copperas Hill to one perfectly commodious in that part of Folly Lane called CHELSEA, where he now carries on business in the most extensive manner and makes cheap, elegant and serviceable china ware, which are for brilliancy of colour equal to any in Great Britain. . . .

John Pennington died in 1786 and Dr. Boney* is of the opinion that the works were run thereafter, until 1794, by Jane Pennington, her son John and her brother-in-law James. However, at least part of the works was leased from February 22nd, 1790 to Thomas Wolfe, a Staffordshire potter; he gained control of the whole site when he purchased the rest of the property in 1795. The advent of Thomas Wolfe from Staffordshire provides us with yet another link which at this period bound the ceramic fortunes of Staffordshire and Liverpool, and it is rather surprising that he should have embarked on a china-making venture in Liverpool when the older china-makers there were closing down. Dr. Bernard Watney has already speculated on the identification of the wares made by Wolfe† and has also recorded the full circumstances of Wolfe's partnership, at this factory, with Miles Mason and John Lucock, both Staffordshire men.‡ This partnership was broken up in 1800 and from a plan of the works dated 1801 it has recently been possible to identify, with some degree of accuracy, the precise location of the works in relation to the present roads and buildings. Although excavation in an area which has been redeveloped by later domestic buildings is a difficult, not to say hazardous business, the author and his colleagues discovered in the summer of 1968 a large deposit of unglazed porcelain shards, decorated in underglaze blue printing of various designs, but mostly of the 'willow pattern' type, and owing far more to the Staffordshire tradition than to Liverpool (Plate 11).§ Following the dissolution of the partnership Miles Mason and John Lucock returned to Staffordshire while Thomas Wolfe remained in Liverpool to supervise his Staffordshire warehouses. He is listed in the directories as an 'earthenware dealer' at the South East Corner of the Old Dock until his death in 1818.

The foregoing brief account is by no means exhaustive, but perhaps enough has been said to emphasise that the older established Liverpool potteries were fading from the scene by the time Samuel Worthington

* Knowles Boney, *Liverpool Porcelain of the Eighteenth Century*, London, 1957.
† R. J. Charleston, (Editor) *English Porcelain 1745–1850*, London, 1965, pp. 103–104.
‡ Bernard Watney, *English Ceramic Circle Transactions*, Vol. 5, Part 1, pp. 49–52.
§ See R. G. Haggar, *The Masons of Lane Delph*, 1952.

founded Herculaneum and that Herculaneum did not begin as a complete 'outsider' to the Liverpool tradition as has sometimes been suggested; it was, in fact, a continuation of a tradition which was forced to change. The reasons for the decline of the older factories are clear enough. Industry flourishes where the conditions are favourable and the capital is forthcoming. By the end of the eighteenth century there were far more profitable opportunities for investment of capital than the relatively small field of china and earthen-ware manufacture. The town of Liverpool was growing into the leading port serving the industrial areas of the north of England, with its textile, mining and engineering developments. Warehousing, docking and shipbuilding were increasing at an enormous rate and the population of the town was growing too, with speculative housing taking over the ground on the fringes of the town where the potteries had previously stood. Shipbuilding yards and timber yards were absorbing much of the Mersey river frontage, and these in their turn were ousted by the docks. By 1796 a complete system of en-closed docks had grown up, beginning with the construction of the Old Dock in 1715 and ultimately stretching from St. Nicholas' Church in the north (by the present Pierhead) to the boundary with Toxteth in the south; fortunes were being made by investors in docks, warehouses and ships, and there seemed no prosperous future for the manufacturers of pottery.

From what has been said, therefore, it would seem strange that a *new* pottery venture should be planned and developed in Toxteth in 1796. The enterprise, however, was well conceived and took into consideration factors which were not applicable on the older sites in the centre of the town. In the first place the area of Toxteth was *scheduled* for industrial development; well away from the populous town it was ideally suited for a new industry, planned on broader lines and with room for expansion. The development area was to be known as Harrington, named after the dowager Countess of Sefton, with streets to be laid out in regular form and with sites available along the river frontage on lease from the Earl of Sefton.* One of the first industrialists to take advantage of the position was the copper-smelting firm of Charles Roe (of the firm of Roe and Co. Macclesfield), and because the buildings he erected are intimately connected with the Herculaneum factory the contemporary account by John Gregson is here quoted in full:†

> In the year 1767 Messrs. Charles Roe and Co. erected a work for smelting copper ore it was situated upon the piece of land now used as a timber yard bounded on the north by the new street which leads from the bot-tom of Sparling Street to the Kings Dock on the East, by Wapping on the South by other Timber Yards and the West by the Quay of the Kings Dock. These works were opened on the 1st January, 1768 and were then upon the Banks of the River Mersey. In the year 1771 these works were removed into Toxteth Park a mile further up the River

* J. Aiken, *A Description of the Country from Thirty to Forty Miles round Man-chester,* London, 1795.
† *Holt and Gregson Mss.,* Vol. X, 303. Liverpool Public Record Office.

Mersey where smelting of copper is still continued with vigour by the same Company under the management of Mr. Wm. Roe son and successor to the late Charles Roe Esq. in 1778 Mr. Wm. Roe invented a new method of Smelting Copper Ore and extraiting (sic) Brimstone from it for which he obtained a patent. These works contain 35 Furnaces besides other necessary buildings and employ about 80 Persons and consume 10 to 12,000 Tons of Coals annually. On the account of the scarcity and dearness of this great Article of Consumption the works are under contemplation of being removed.

The above notes must have been written early in the 1790s, for by 1794 an advertisement[*] was published showing that the works were up for sale in spite of the fact that Roe's eighty-year lease from the Earl of Sefton had only run a quarter of its time. Copper in these years was in great demand for the sheathing of ships' bottoms and the ores which were used came from the Parys mines in Anglesey, in which the company had a share.[†] In 1794 or 1795 the smelting business was removed to South Wales, leaving behind a complete set of buildings with a lease to be taken up, a useful fresh-water supply (Jackson's Dam),[‡] a group of workers' cottages and most important of all, a well-found dock suitable for the import of raw materials and the export of finished goods. It is entirely typical of the business acumen of Samuel Worthington that he should not only have recognised the possibilities of this site, but that once having acquired it he should have traded for road-making and building purposes, at great personal profit, the five or six thousand tons of copper slag or dross which lay around the area. A complete plan of the copper works dating from about 1790 may be seen on pages 16, 17.

Before we consider what Worthington did at the copper works site however, a connection with these buildings for a very short period between 1794–1795 and 1796 must be mentioned. In Joseph Mayer's account of potting in Liverpool[§] he says that the works were occupied by 'Richard Abbey and a Scotchman named Graham'. Although we have been unable to find any other definite reference to confirm Mayer's statement it is important if only to establish the likelihood of *pottery printing and decorating* existing here, as perhaps it was some form of pottery activity in the old copper works which gave Worthington his ideas for the developments which he brought about later.

Richard Abbey is well known in the history of Liverpool potting, and several signed examples of his work have survived (Plate 16) though many are *attributed* to him rather than being firmly documented. According to Mayer, Abbey was born at Aintree in 1720 and died at Melling in 1801, aged 81, and was buried at Walton Parish Church. However, recent searches have shown that Mayer was mistaken, for the burial of Richard Abbey

---

[*] *Gore's General Advertiser*, July 3rd 1794.
[†] J. R. Harris, *The Copper King*, Liverpool, 1964.
[‡] Joseph Boult, *Liverpool Architectural & Archaeological Society Proceedings*, 1867–1868, p. 30.
[§] Joseph Mayer, *ibid*.

PLAN OF THE COPPER WORKS OF CHARLES ROE & COMPANY, ABOUT 1790

Adapted from a map amongst the *Molyneux Muniments, Lancashire Record Office, Preston.*

A. BUILDINGS FOR SMELTING THE ORES.
B. WAREHOUSE AND COUNTING HOUSE.
C. YARD FOR STORING THE ORE.
D. THE DOCK.
E. REFINING FURNACES.
F. THE YARD.
G. PART OF THE SHORE FILLED LEVEL WITH CINDERS.
H. POOL, ARTIFICIALLY ENLARGED.
I. GREAT SEA HEY.
J. HIGHER CROFT.
K. LOWER CROFT.
L. THE ROUGHS.
M. COPPER WORKERS' DWELLINGS.
N. DOTTED LINE SHOWING ORIGINAL EDGE OF ENCLOSURES ON THE SHORE.
O. ROCKY SHORE BETWEEN HIGH AND LOW TIDE.
P. POOL.

SCALE: 1 chain = 66 feet

Compare with plan of the Herculaneum Pottery, Chapter VII, pages 94, 95.

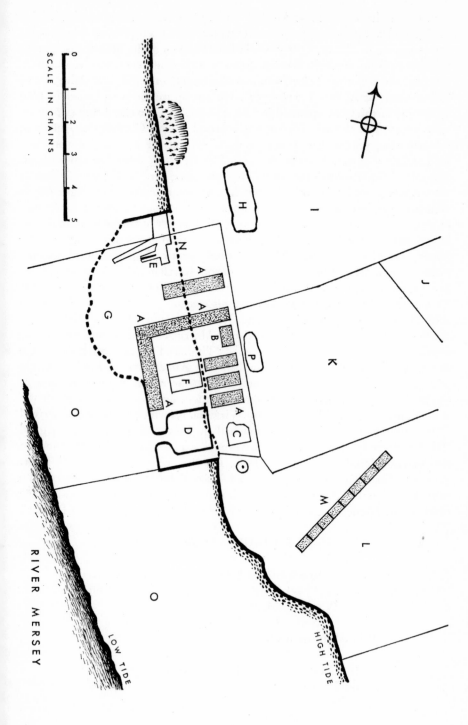

SCALE IN CHAINS

0 1 2 3 4 5

RIVER MERSEY

LOW TIDE

HIGH TIDE

c

appears in the registers at Walton on January 21st, 1819, aged 65. This evidence clears up several statements which have been difficult to reconcile, for according to Mayer, Abbey would have been 47 at the time of his apprenticeship to John Sadler.* We can now say with confidence that he was born in 1754, the son of William Abbey of Walton (1711–1786) and Alice Abbey (née Bolton) of Aintree (1715–1792). He was apprenticed to Sadler in 1767 at the age of thirteen, opened his own business in Clieveland Square, Liverpool, in 1773 at the age of nineteen, married Rachel Gardiner on July 31st the following year and probably came to work at the old copper works site in Toxteth in 1794. During the period from 1777, when he gave up his Clieveland Square business, until 1794, we have very little idea of what he was doing. Joseph Mayer says that he did some teaching of engraving in Glasgow, and later went to Paris to work for a Monsieur Potter at the 'Prince of Wales Works' in the Rue de Crussol. How much of this is true we do not know, nor do we know whether he ever worked in Staffordshire for the pottery trade. In Liverpool Museum there are two jugs bearing 'Hibernia' prints signed 'R. Abbey Sculpt. Robinson Burslem pinxt.' and there are examples bearing the same signatures of the 'Hudibras and the Bear' subject. This sort of Staffordshire connection also occurs through the prints on a creamware teapot in the Victoria and Albert Museum which has the Abbey-attributed 'Gretna Green or the Red-Hot Marriage' print on one side and an engraving of 'Conjugal Felicity' signed 'Thomas Fletcher, Shelton' on the other. These examples simply establish that Abbey was *an engraver to the pottery trade.* They provide no proof whatsoever that he ever worked in Staffordshire, particularly when one considers another teapot, now in the collections at Colonial Williamsburg, Virginia, on which both prints (derived from a moralising subject first published in 1785—see page 35) are signed 'R^d Abbey Sculp. Jp^h Johnson Liverpool'. The elusive Joseph Johnson will be considered further in the following chapter (pages 34–37). As far as Richard Abbey is concerned we can safely say that he was not a potter in the ordinary sense, but a pottery decorator, and this is confirmed by his marriage entry at St. Nicholas' Church in which he is described as a 'China Painter'.

RICHARD ABBEY
Late Apprentice to Messrs. Sadler and Green
Begs Leave to inform his FRIENDS and the PUBLIC
That he has Open'd his SHOP, at No. 11, in Clieveland Square,
Where he Manufactures and Sells all
Sorts of QUEEN'S WARE,
Printed in the neatest Manner, and in a Variety of
Colours N.B. Orders for Exportation
Also Crests, Coats of Arms, Tiles, or any other
particular Device will be completed at the shortest Notice
By their most obedient humble Servant
RICHARD ABBEY

* See J. S. Price, *John Sadler, A Liverpool Pottery Printer*, West Kirby, 1948.

In 1773 Richard Abbey published the preceding advertisement in a Liverpool paper.* From this advertisement we can assume that this was the period when Abbey printed the 'Actors' series of tiles (of which a signed example is shown in Plate 16) and he is also to be credited with prints on tiles from Aesop's fables. Other subjects attributed to Abbey which are of a later date than these appear on mugs and jugs and include 'Hudibras and the Bear', 'The Man with a Load of Mischief', 'The Death of Wolfe' of which there are several versions by other engravers after Benjamin West's famous picture, 'Gretna Green or the Red-Hot Marriage', 'Youth', 'Toby Philpot' (signed), Plate 39 'The Careless Lover', 'Hibernia' (signed) and at least one version of 'The Farmers Arms' as well as several other Liverpool 'Arms' such as the 'Bakers', 'Plaisterers', 'Bricklayers', 'Cordwainers' and including a rare version with most decided Liverpool connections—'The Watchtool Makers' (Plate 17A).

Of Abbey's reputed partner in the Toxteth copper works buildings nothing definite is known, and Mayer simply describes him as a 'Scotchman named Graham'. One or two clues, however, may throw some light on the problem: an Andrew Graham is recorded in *Gore's Directory* as a potter of 2 East Street in 1810 and 1811. Moreover, the marriage entry of Andrew Graham to Mary Grant at St. Nicholas' Church, dated January 24th, 1792, describes him as a 'painter and gilder' and it is just possible that his 'painting' and 'gilding' could have been applied to pots. On the other hand another Graham called James is also known, and listed in the directories as a 'mugman' of Chorley Street; his wife Mary was one of the unfortunate victims killed when the spire of St. Nicholas' Church collapsed on February 11th, 1810. Whether it was Andrew or James (both are Scottish names) who was Abbey's partner, we have at least some evidence to link Abbey and Graham with pottery decorating at the Toxteth works. Since Abbey did not die until 1819 he may very well have been responsible, as an experienced pottery engraver, for many of the subjects which appear on early Herculaneum wares, particularly as it was the only surviving Liverpool pottery producing creamware in large quantities in the early nineteenth century. We do not mean to suggest that Abbey was actually employed by the factory, for it is much more likely that he worked as a free-lance engraver.

The name of Samuel Worthington is always associated with those of Michael Humble and Samuel Holland in early accounts of the foundation of the Herculaneum Pottery, but there is no evidence to show that these gentlemen were directly concerned until 1800 when a lease containing their names was drawn up with the Earl of Sefton.

Samuel Worthington was a merchant with a good eye for profitable investments. He is recorded as a Liverpool corn merchant for the first time in 1800 at 2 Covent Garden, while later entries extending up to the 1860s show that his family was running a grocery and provision business in Toxteth for many years after the closing of the pottery. There appear to have been

* *Liverpool Advertiser*, December 10th, 1773.

two Samuels, father and son, and it was presumably the father who was the corn merchant mentioned above, and who came from Bangor in North Wales to found the pottery. Samuel Worthington the younger married Mary Lee of Flixton, near Manchester, on June 18th, 1802, at St. Michael's Church in that town. The Rector of St. Michael's has informed me that by marrying Mary Lee the Worthington family allied itself to a wealthy Lancashire family in the Flixton area, a move which would be completely in keeping with the senior Samuel's acquisitive nature—a side of his character which we shall meet again in his later associations with Herculaneum.

Shortly after the beginning of the Herculaneum factory three advertisements were published which are worth quoting in full since they show something of what was made in the early days and bring to our attention the advantages of the site:

Samuel Worthington & Co. Herculaneum Pottery
(Late the Copper Works) near Liverpool

Manufacture all kinds of Earthen-ware, and will supply Merchants, Captains and Wholesale Dealers at the regular trade prices. From the situation of their works, they will have it in their power to ship goods without either pilferage or breakage; the evils, which are of such magnitude, when crates are conveyed by inland navigation.*

HERCULANEUM POTTERY
(Late the Copper Works) near Liverpool

SAMUEL WORTHINGTON & CO. having by great pains and attention established their Manufactory of EARTHENWARE, take upon themselves in the first place, to acknowledge their obligation for the favours of their friends. They have, and mean always to keep by them a large assortment, consisting of useful Cream coloured, Enamelled, Painted and Printed Ware, which will enable them to execute large orders on the shortest notice.

Exclusive of all other advantages to Merchants, Captains and others, they trust those derived from their situation, are such as must give peculiar pleasure and satisfaction, for without expense, Goods may be inspected, approved and packed, under the eye of the Merchant's Clerk.

Other advantages will be explained on application.†

HERCULANEUM POTTERY WAREHOUSE
The East side of Salthouse Dock.

Where the Herculaneum Pottery Company will be glad to receive orders for Cream Colours, Enamelled, printed and Fancy Ware Services, Enamelled in any pattern.

* *Billinge's Liverpool Advertiser & Marine Intelligencer*, March 6th and 20th, 1797.
† *Gore's General Advertiser*, December 28th, 1797.

A constant Supply of Bangor slates, for home consumption and exportation.*

The last of these advertisements mentions the supply of Bangor slates, which were used for roofing and brought from the Penrhyn quarries near that town. It is of interest to know that Worthington and his friends Michael Humble, Samuel Holland and Nicholas Hurry were involved in enterprises in North Wales which were in no way concerned with the pottery venture at Toxteth. One branch of their activities, however, was to provide ground flints for the clay bodies and glazes, from a grinding mill at Nant Gwreiddiog on Lord Penrhyn's estates near Bangor. The flint in this case was derived from the chert found in the limestones of North Wales, whereas most flint for the pottery industry came from nodules found either in the chalk beds of the south-east of England or on the sea-shores of that part of the country.

In a lease negotiated with the Earl of Sefton dated October 31st, 1800, Samuel Worthington (whose address at this time is given as Llwynan, near Bangor), Michael Humble of Shooters Hill near Bawtry, Samuel Holland and Nicholas Hurry, both of Liverpool, came to an agreement to take the Toxteth site including the works, cottages and a considerable area of ground on a fifty-year basis, for a rent of £94 10s. due on the 29th of September each year. At the same time as this lease was negotiated we find that the same gentlemen were establishing no less than four separate agreements with Lord Penrhyn dated March 24th, 1800, March 25th, 1801, August 1st, 1801, and November 1st, 1802, to exploit both the mineral and agricultural assets on Lord Penrhyn's Caernarvonshire estates.† The importance of the influence of such merchants in opening up the natural resources of North Wales at this time is fully discussed by A. H. Dodd in his book on this subject,‡ and the activities in which Worthington, Humble, Holland and Hurry took part included corn-milling, ochre-grinding, flint-grinding, quarrying of slates and other stones (including quartz in the Conway valley), and supplying agricultural produce to the Merseyside area.

It is, then, clear that pot-making was only one of the business activities in which the original proprietors of the Herculaneum factory were engaged. Michael Humble, originating in Bawtry near Doncaster, and perhaps related in some way to the Humble of Humble, Green and Co., founders of the Leeds Pottery, seems to have combined ship-building with his other investments, and in this field alone we find him in partnership with Hurry and Holland in 1800. They were also involved in selling such hardware as hemp, rope, oil, corn, hogshead staves, sail canvas and other ships' chandlers' materials. Clearly, these men had remarkable foresight, enterprise and energy and were fully capable of taking advantage of the opportunities of their day. The name Samuel Holland will always be associated with the opening up of the North Wales slate quarries. In particular he is remembered as the father

* *Gore's General Advertiser*, June 7th, 1798.
† *Penrhyn Castle Papers*, Library of the University College of North Wales, Bagnor. Nos. 2032, 2033, 2034, 2035.
‡ A. H. Dodd, *The Industrial Revolution in North Wales*, Cardiff, 1933.

of the Samuel Holland who pioneered the vast slate works at Festiniog in the middle of the nineteenth century. His address at the time of his death is given as Plas yn Penryn, Merioneth, and he was buried at the Ancient Chapel of Toxteth on October 2nd, 1851, aged 83.

It has already been stated that Samuel Worthington brought a group of Staffordshire people to work his factory at Toxteth in 1796. Before proceeding to review the wares which they made it might be useful to record some of their names. The senior member of the group was Ralph Mansfield (d. 1810) who brought his wife Anne and their sons Ralph and Archibald. It is clear that Mansfield was much respected by his employers and in a comfortable position. Not only did he marry Margaret Keightley, the daughter of the company's solicitor, after Anne's death in about 1802, but he held a £500 share in the company in 1806, and christened his third child by Margaret, Samuel Worthington, out of respect for his worthy employer! His illness and death are recorded in the *Minute Book* of the Committee of Proprietors in 1810 when Mrs. Mansfield was presented with the sum of forty guineas 'as a token of respect which the Proprietors bear to his memory'. Only a few months earlier in the same year Mansfield's sons Ralph and Archibald were recognised by the proprietors for their 'improving abilities . . . in the art of painting, and wishing to encourage and reward their rising Merit, they have order'd that they be paid each 10/6 by Mr. Holden, the Cash Keeper'. It was Mrs. Mansfield's eldest son Archibald who started a pottery on his own account in Canning Street, off Bevington Bush, Liverpool, about 1825, of which more will be said later (pages 66, 67).

Another family bearing the well-known Staffordshire name of Till arrived at Toxteth in 1796. Of this family the name Eli Till (1772–1828) is recorded in the two signed pieces of his work which were presented by his wife to Joseph Mayer and are now in the Liverpool Museum (Plate 118). It is likely that Thomas and Elizabeth Till who worked for many years at the pottery were Eli's son and daughter-in-law.

Ralph Cordon (1768–1834) and his wife Elizabeth were amongst the early Staffordshire immigrants to Herculaneum. According to Mayer, Ralph Cordon was a native of Gravelly Bank near Lane End, and he appears to have occupied a position of some importance at the works; perhaps he and his son Sampson were the final managers (see page 81). In the Liverpool Museum a blue-printed frog mug (Plate 158) bears the initials S.M.C. which are reputed to be those of Sampson Cordon (b. May 31st, 1797) and his wife Myrah. Ralph became Clerk of St. Michaels-in-the-Hamlet Church, Toxteth, and after his death in 1834 the office passed to his son. Many records of the Herculaneum potters are to be found in the registers of this parish church—a building of some architectural importance for its early use of cast iron, its graceful columns, beams and Gothic arches.

At least fourteen members of the Ibbs family (without counting their children) are to be found amongst the earliest potters at the Toxteth factory. The four senior members of the group were Joseph (1739–1826), William (1762–1821), James (1769–1837) and Isaac (1784–1825). William, James and

Isaac appear to have been brothers, probably sons of Joseph; all four are listed as potters. It is known that James in later years became the 'biscuit foreman' and a particular reference to him is to be found in Chapter V (page 63).

One other family is worthy of note amongst the Staffordshire immigrants to Toxteth, the Tomkinsons. James and Joseph Tomkinson seem to have been brothers and of the two Joseph (1784–1836) is the better known. He appears to have been a well-educated man and was appointed as Clerk of the concern in 1818 and was temporarily manager after William Smith's resignation in 1821 (see page 63). Of particular importance in this account is the fact that many of Joseph Tomkinson's notes and pocket books concerning factory matters, prices and recipes have survived. About 1826 Tomkinson left Merseyside to become a preacher in the United States and in 1924 his descendants, the Misses Martha and Ellen Tomkinson of Harrisburg, Pennsylvania, returned to Liverpool Museum the papers referred to above, which are practically the only original documents extant concerned with wares made at the factory. In the absence of pattern books or published price lists they have provided a wealth of information, some of which is listed in Appendix III. Joseph Tomkinson died in New York in 1836.

Other names such as Clewlow, Clues, Bourne, Buxton, Dale, Edwards, Harrison, Hood, Rogers, Seddon, Shaw, Simpson, Ware and Wood appear as potters in the early years of the factory's existence and all have links with Staffordshire.

The Wares

The first productions at Herculaneum were entirely of earthenware. This is not only stated by Mayer but is confirmed by the advertisements of 1797 and 1798 already quoted (pages 20, 21), which specifically mention cream colours and other earthenwares but contain no mention of china. Amongst the cream-coloured pottery one would expect to find a continuing tradition from the older Liverpool factories, and the difficulty has been to sort out which are from the earlier Liverpool works, which are of Staffordshire or other origin printed in Liverpool, and which are Herculaneum. Marked pieces of Liverpool-associated creamwares in the period under discussion are extremely rare. However, a fine baluster-shaped jug in the National Museum of Ireland in Dublin, which has typical Liverpool printing and enamelling (Plate 18) does bear the impressed mark 'Wilson', proving that it comes from the Church Works, Hanley, which were managed by Richard Wilson between 1795 and 1801. The body is a fine cream colour with a rich uncrazed glaze, and the prints and enamels are also of very good quality. A jug of this sort could have been decorated either at Guy Green's establishment or by Richard Abbey, and it might have been done at the Herculaneum site, since the dating would confirm this attribution. Another jug of barrel shape in Liverpool Museum is decorated with a print of Colonel Tarleton (after Reynolds' painting and signed I. Iohnson, Liverpool) and is impressed 'Wedgwood &

Co.' showing that it was brought to Liverpool for decoration from the Ferry-bridge Pottery in Yorkshire. Two other jugs illustrated here (Plates 19 and 20) from the Liverpool and Brighton Museums may fall into the category of 'outsiders' decorated in Liverpool, or might very likely be Herculaneum. They are both characterised by a 'Farmers Arms' print and by floral sprays which accompany the main designs. These floral sprays were no doubt copied from a contemporary botanical work and we have traced many different versions. That these sprays can be firmly linked with the Liverpool decorators is undoubted, and many were used on early documented Hercu-laneum pieces. The designs of the flower sprays themselves must have been copied from such delightful little works as *The Florist or Poetical Nose Gay and Drawing Book* published in London about 1780, and they can be found again and again on Herculaneum wares dating long after 1800. Another baluster jug, of which there are two identical versions, one in the Victoria and Albert Museum and one in Liverpool Museum, dated 1798 (Plate 21), is engraved with a 'Farmers Arms' print and a scene of peasants in a farmyard. The 'Farmyard' print occurs in one form or another in at least ten different versions, mostly on jugs but in one rare case on a Liverpool opal-glass beaker (Plates 24A and B) which, incidentally, has one of our floral sprays on the other side; the 'Farmyard' print also appears on the outside of a bowl in the Peabody Museum, Salem, Massachusetts (Plate 27).

The use of the 'Farmyard' print mentioned above is of the utmost im-portance in the identification of Liverpool printed creamwares. The earliest version of this subject we have seen is that illustrated in Plate 22A, and this popular theme may be seen illustrated in several versions in Plates 22A 23, 24B, 27, 28B, 30B, 32, 45A and 68A. The most important specimen of all in the present context is the one printed on a creamware jug presented to Liverpool Museum in 1964 (Plates 30A and B) by a citizen of Wallasey. This jug is decorated with a beautifully engraved version of the 'Farmyard' but the print was too large to fit the available space between the horizontal mouldings on the jug, and had to be clipped short at top and bottom. Im-pressed on the base of this jug is the word HERCULANEUM. From a careful comparison of the prints on this jug with those on other pieces it has been possible to identify with certainty other wares from the factory's early years. Two jugs in the Bethune Morgan collection at Brighton (Plates 31 and 32) are linked to our marked piece by *exactly matching* 'line for line' prints, and it is fascinating to discover that the names 'Wm. & M. Crosby' enamelled on one of them can be identified as referring to the marriage of William and Mary Crosby at St. Nicholas' Church, Liverpool, on October 7th, 1799.

Careful study of the designs on the creamware transfer-printed jugs of the period from about 1785 to about 1810 will show that the Herculaneum factory continued to use ideas which had become part of the Liverpool tradition long before the factory had opened. We have already seen this in the use of the 'Farmyard' print, and two other such examples may be shown. The creamware jug in the Grant Davidson collection (Plate 29) is a Hercu-laneum piece decorated with one of the typically Liverpudlian versions of

Masonic emblems which was probably engraved well before 1796. An impressed marked Herculaneum jug in the collection of Mr. Edward Thomas of Concorde, Massachusetts, has a print of Diana and the 'Bricklayers Arms', the Diana print being based on another print of Diana on a marked Wedgwood cream-ware jug of about 1780 belonging to Mr. C. P. G. Monk of Wigan, Lancashire (Plates 33 and 34). Many other pieces linked with this group will be mentioned in Chapters III and IV, particularly as several made for the American market bear the mark of Herculaneum, either printed or impressed, a rare feature on wares of this type and period made for home consumption.

The jug illustrated as the frontispiece of this book is a rare marked specimen now in the Art Institute of Chicago. This jug is in pearlware and is similar in shape to the jugs already described (Plates 29, 30A, 30B and 31) but the floral decoration here is entirely hand-applied in on-glaze enamels, of very fine quality. That this and several of the pieces mentioned in the last two paragraphs were amongst the best of the early Herculaneum wares there can be no doubt, but the factory must have made many more humble goods, largely indistinguishable from contemporary Staffordshire and Leeds types, in cream and pearlware bodies.

In his statement concerning the early wares of Herculaneum, Mayer* says that 'the first ware made here, November 11th, 1796, was blue printed'; he goes on to say that the first piece was a chamber-pot, made by Edward Roberts, who also made a punch bowl and used it at the christening of his second child (probably Mary Roberts, baptised May 8th, 1799). Unfortunately neither the chamber-pot nor the bowl have survived, but other pieces of blue-printed wares of this early period show that the Herculaneum factory was using this process at its inception just as the older Liverpool potteries had done in the years preceding. Of exceptional interest, since it is a great rarity, is the jug in the collection of Mrs. Samuel Schwartz of New Jersey (Plate 146). Links with the American trade are described in Chapter IV and there can be little doubt that this jug came from Herculaneum. Of creamware body and baluster shape, it is under-glaze printed in blue with portraits of President Washington and the inside edge of the lip has a printed border. Printing in blue on this kind of ware is most unusual, but both under-glaze printing and painting is to be found on a very large punch bowl in the Liverpool Museum which has all the qualities of Herculaneum earthenware and is quite unlike the earthenware associated with the older established factories such as Seth Pennington's. Chinese prints adorn the outside of the bowl, a printed neo-classical border follows both the outer and inner edges, and a painted inscription fills the centre in a delightfully spaced and lettered hand (Plate 148):

A Wonder!

An honest Lawyer!!!

Mrs. Miller's Good Health

One Bowl more and then.

.1796.

* Joseph Mayer, *ibid.*

In *Gore's Directory* for 1794 an Aaron Miller appears as an attorney at 39 Edmund Street, Liverpool, but in 1796 his name is missing. In all likelihood the bowl was commissioned and presented to Mrs. Miller by a satisfied client after her husband's death. Marked specimens of *early* blue-printed wares are by no means common, but three such pieces are illustrated (Plates 153, 154 and 155), all marked with the name impressed in very small capital letters about one eighth of an inch in height; they are a mug from the National Museum of Ireland, a jug from the collection of Dr. Lloyd Hawes of Boston, Massachusetts, and a covered bowl and stand in the Liverpool Museum. The type of stylised Chinese landscapes and borders used on these pieces are very similar to those found on the porcelain shards from the Wolfe factory site (see page 13) and the influence tends to be that of Staffordshire, not Liverpool. It is difficult to understand Mayer's assertion that the earliest mark for our factory was 'Herculaneum' printed in blue, for although blue-printing, as we shall see, eventually became the stock-in-trade of the Herculaneum factory and was in constant use to the very end in 1840, we have never found a single early piece identifiable in this way.

The manufacture of porcelain is reputed to have started about 1800, and to turn to Mayer yet again he tells us that Ralph Cordon was responsible for mixing the bodies. Identification of the earliest of the Herculaneum porcelains is by no means easy, but we should look for items which have a link with such potteries as Pennington's, where porcelain was made until the end of the eighteenth century, and the only examples known which might conceivably be Herculaneum is an enamelled teabowl and saucer (Plate 122), which has the monogram HP in blue, under the glaze. Although we would accept the opinion of many authorities that the style of this piece suggests a much earlier date than 1800, it does not seem impossible that it was made in Toxteth perhaps *before* 1800, in any case the specimen is generally agreed to be of Liverpool manufacture. No one has, as yet, explained the significance of the letters H P which form the monogram. These letters were certainly used as an impressed mark on two known Herculaneum pieces of 1809 (Plates 147 and 150) which will be considered later, and we find it perfectly reasonable to suppose that an older craftsman, coming from Shaw's Brow, would continue to work in the manner to which he had been accustomed.

Staffordshire-associated Herculaneum porcelains are firmly identifiable during the early period, around 1800, though marked examples are not at all easy to find. A marked jug in the Philadelphia Museum of Art (Plate 124) reminds us of New Hall shapes and decoration; the jug is from a tea service design matched by two teapots, one at Hanley Museum and one recently acquired by Liverpool Museum (Plate 123). The shapes of the knops and handles of these teapots show them to be Herculaneum, while Mr. David Holgate (who kindly drew my attention to one of them) affirms that they are definitely not of the New Hall hard paste body. Other porcelain tewares which must date from the very early years of the nineteenth century marked Herculaneum in impressed capitals, may be seen in Plates 127 and 128. These pieces are enamelled in various colours and in black. The teapots from

these services, like New Hall ones, are rather heavily potted, but the tea and coffee cups are very thin and delicate. More than one type of porcelain body appears to have been used, for the florally decorated jug, teacup and saucer (Plate 127) are characteristically of a creamy bone china, while the other pieces are harder and colder to the touch. The black enamelled scenes on the teapot are comparatively primitive when seen against the wares of such factories as Pinxton, Coalport, Spode and Flight and Barr Worcester, which they were no doubt seeking to emulate.

Although these examples of porcelain may well date from the very early years of the nineteenth century it has been thought reasonable to include them in the present chapter as they are the first positively identifiable examples of Herculaneum china. We also include here the porcelain plant-pot (Plate 129), with its gilded edging and mask-head handles, partly because the impressed mark is in very small capitals, like the early marked blue-printed earthenwares, and partly because in body and glaze it is hard and compact like the teapots discussed above. Unfortunately the stand is missing but it is interesting to note what must be a comparatively early use of the mask-headed handles, as the date cannot be later than about 1810.

Chapter III

Growth and Prosperity c 1800–1820

Samuel Worthington's initiative and foresight at the copper works site in Toxteth was completely justified, for by 1806 the business was in a sufficiently thriving state to attract the attention of many investors. During the early years considerable alteration in the factory buildings had taken place, and extra cottages for the potters had been added, as will be seen by comparing the plan of the copper works made about 1790 with another plan of the pottery drawn about 1800 (see plans pages 16, 17 and 94, 95). An interesting sidelight on Worthington's activities in developing his factory may be seen from a document dated March 5th, 1800.* It appears that about this time Worthington was hoping to expand the premises by requesting an extension of his lease from the Earl of Sefton, for the extra buildings. Lord Sefton, on whose estates, as we have seen, the pottery was sited, did not apparently wish this lease to go through and it is both amusing and informative to see the methods used by Worthington to press his case:

> . . . Mr. Roe and others have since left off the said business (copper smelting) and have sold and conveyed the Premises to Messrs. Worthington and others for the remaining Term in the Lease, who have for some time carried on the pottery business there but who now threaten Lord Sefton, that they will smelt Copper and other Ore at the said demised premises, and carry on other Offensive Business there unless Lord Sefton will grant them a lease of some premises adjoining. . . . But in case of Lord Sefton complying with that their request they will tie themselves not to smelt Copper or other Ore, or to carry on any other noisome or offensive business at the premises or any part thereof. . . .

The above quotation shows that Worthington was using what amounts to blackmail to gain the extra buildings, and since Sefton under the original lease with Roe had agreed *not to object to smelting* Worthington clearly had

* *Molyneux Muniments DDM 13/11*, Lancashire Record Office.

the upper hand. In the event Worthington got his way because Sefton did not want to discourage other possible tenants on his land through the proximity of a 'noisome and offensive' business. From the details of this transaction it would seem that only part of the original copper works buildings were leased in 1796 (perhaps the part occupied by Abbey and Graham) for there were no other premises in the area other than the copper workers' buildings that Worthington could possibly have taken.

Real growth and development of the pottery began in 1806 when on November 24th the first meeting of a group of new proprietors took place at the Star and Garter Tavern in Paradise Street, Liverpool. At this meeting it was decided that the capital of the concern should consist of fifty £500 shares and that each proprietor should have as many certificates as they held shares. A new lease was drawn up with Lord Sefton and the original terms of this lease may be seen in Joseph Mayer's account.* Three of the share certificates, printed on vellum and decorated with George Codling's vignette engraving of the factory (Plate 1), are still in existence.† This engraving is most valuable, for it shows the number of the ovens and their size, the windmill, the long low line of buildings with regularly-spaced chimneys typical of copper works of those times, the freshwater reservoirs, the workers' dwellings, the chapel with its lancet windows, the spars and rigging of a ship in the factory dock, the River Mersey with the Cheshire Wirral shore and the actual siting of the works on the water's edge surrounded by open fields. Another picture of the factory, which is only known through an old photograph, is J. Edmondson's water colour painted in 1808. It shows substantially the same view as the engraving, but is drawn in closer perspective (Plate 191).

The share certificates were purchased by some twenty-eight shareholders and the details of their names and holdings have survived.‡ They were Samuel WORTHINGTON, merchant (4 shares); Michael HUMBLE, merchant (4 shares); Samuel HOLLAND, gentleman (1 share); Archibald KEIGHTLEY, the company's solicitor for many years (4 shares); Samuel BEREY, merchant (4 shares); John MENZIES Junior, gentleman, son of the merchant banker who carried on the banking business of John Wyke, clock-maker and tool factor (2 shares); Edward BLACKSTOCK, gentleman (2 shares); William FAUCETT, merchant, of the famous firm of Liverpool marine engineers (1 share); Adam STEUART, merchant (1 share); William FRENCH, merchant (2 shares); Robert JONES, silversmith (1 share); John HARDING, merchant (1 share); George ROWE, gentleman (1 share); George ORRED, gentleman (1 share); Richard SUTTON, gentleman (6 shares); Richard HOLDEN, silversmith and probably the father of the Mr. Holden who was company clerk in 1808 and rose to become correspondent and commercial agent by 1822 (1 share); Latham HANMER, gentleman

---

* Joseph Mayer, *History of the Progress of the Art of Pottery in Liverpool*, Liverpool, 1855 and 1873.
† Liverpool Museum.
‡ Liverpool Record Office, *Herculaneum Account Book 1806–17*.

(1 share); Henry LAWRENCE, merchant (1 share); William CART-
WRIGHT, book-keeper (1 share); William HARDING, merchant (1 share);
Anna HIRD, spinster (1 share); William HUTCHINSON, (occupation unknown) (2 shares); Benjamin RAWSON of Darley near Bolton, merchant
(1 share); John HOLLAND of Bolton, merchant (1 share); John MOORE
of Halsall, gentleman (2 shares); John HOLLINS of Knutsford, gentleman
(1 share); Ralph MANSFIELD, Herculaneum Pottery manager (1 share);
James PARR, (occupation unknown) (1 share).

The investment of £25,000, represented by this total of fifty shares, must
have been a tremendous stimulus to the output and labour force of the factory.
The Herculaneum Minute Book* shows that on December 3rd, 1806, the
value of the utensils, fixtures, horses, carts, gears and the Flat (ship) *Hopewell*
was set at £4,106 4s. 4d. while the stock of earthenware and china on hand
was £5,117 0s. 0d. Some idea of the improving state of the company may
be gauged through such items as the following, also recorded in the Minute
Book:

March	1807	10 new cottages at a cost of £470
May	1807	New Oven and Sagger House at £180.1.6.
May	1807	Opening of the new Warehouse in Duke Street (see Chapter IV)
August	1809	China oven to be enlarged.
February	1811	Consideration of building a steam engine, but post-poned until 1817 (see Chapter VII).
February	1812	Opening of another new warehouse at the East Side of the Dry Dock, bottom of Redcross Street.
March	1813	New Flat (boat) to be built at £1,000.
May	1814	Two additional cottages at £63 each.
July	1814	Additional room to the enamelling shop.
December	1814	Two additional cottages at £113.4.0.
May	1815	Additional biscuit oven.
June	1815	Rebuilding of the Packing Room at £160 and three additional cottages at £172.10.0.
October	1815	New cottage, bakehouse and bread ovens for the workmen.
November	1815	New buildings and improvements for a sum not to exceed £1,000.
December	1815	New Slip House at £350.

A complete list of all the buildings constituting the premises and the insurance value thereon in 1815 is given in Appendix II, the total value being
£10,250.

Not only do the extracts given above indicate the increasing size and im-

* Liverpool Record Office, *Minute Book of the Committee of Proprietors Herculaneum Pottery* (see Appendix II).

portance of the works from about 1806 to 1815, but the balance sheets of
annual profits show a sound financial position except for a slight drop during
the years 1810 to 1812, caused through the wars with France and the American
embargo on trade (see Chapter IV). The profits for the 'Earthenware Account'
are given in the table below up to 1817 while the last column shows the total
business transacted:

	Profit & Loss Account					*Total Business*
1806– 7	amount gained by earthenware				£4,785. 6. 4¼	£32,393. 5. 2½
1807– 8	,,	,,	,,	,,	£4,653.12. 7	£36,217.19. 3
1808– 9	,,	,,	,,	,,	£4,340. 7. 2¾	£44,872. 7. 1¾
1809–10	,,	,,	,,	,,	£5,346. 0. 4	£39,982.10.11
1810–11	,,	,,	,,	,,	£3,748.14.10	£33,634. 0. 5
1811–12	,,	,,	,,	,,	£4,914.11. 1	£35,205.10. 0
1812–13	,,	,,	,,	,,	£8,089.16. 3½	£38,228. 1. 5
1813–14	,,	,,	,,	,,	£8,082.17. 5	£41,842.11. 4
1814–15	,,	,,	,,	,,	£8,285.15. 4	£41,427. 8. 1
1815–16	,,	,,	,,	,,	£7,201. 6. 9	missing
1816–17	,,	,,	,,	,,	£8,505.18.11	£38,928.17.10

Further details of the nature of the trading are given in Chapter IV, particularly to the overseas markets, but it will be seen from these figures alone
that a quite remarkable quantity of pottery was handled. They do not tell us,
however, how much of this pottery was actually *made* at Herculaneum, and
how much was due to Staffordshire trading. We must keep very much in
mind the fact that many Staffordshire potteries were selling their goods at
the Herculaneum warehouse, in some cases in very large quantities. A list
of the Staffordshire firms from which Herculaneum purchased goods for
retail or export is given in Chapter IV (pages 55, 56) and although this trade
appears to have died away somewhat towards the 1820s it was continued on a
lesser scale until at least 1833.

It is not easy to assess the number of workpeople who were engaged at
Herculaneum from 1806 onwards. As well as the potters many were employed
as blacksmiths, crate-makers, packers, customs officers, sailors, joiners,
labourers—and even a cordwainer for repairing the potters' clogs and shoes.
The pottery had its own clay-pipe maker, Henry Lyons, and an entry in the
accounts for '3 casks of military cleaning balls' indicates that white pipe-
clay was sent to the British Army on campaigns abroad. Although engraved
plates for transfer-printing on pottery were sometimes purchased from outside, the factory had its own engravers, some of whom are listed below:

John Brown, William Cope, William Davies, Archibald Edgar, Joseph
Fairclough, Nathaniel Johnson, George Martin, John Naylor, James
Podmore, Joseph Simpson, Joshua Seddon.

Several enamellers and painters would appear to have worked as 'outsiders',

some of whom we shall meet again when we consider their work, and the following were employed during the period under review:

> Sampson Cordon, William Dixon, John Driver, John Edwards, Abraham Floyd, Robert Evans, James Gore, William Hartley, Samuel Williams, William Potter, William Prince, William Lovatt.

By about 1806 at least a hundred and fifty people would have been working at the factory, increasing to about two hundred and fifty by 1820, and we know from an eye witness account published in 1827 and quoted in full in Chapter VII, that about three hundred people were at the works at that time.

'Outside' work at Herculaneum included the firing of figures and other modelled wares for such Liverpool sculptors as S. and J. Franceys, Frederick Lege, William Bullock, George Bullock, Charles Plinth and Solomon Gibson. Solomon Gibson was a Liverpool sculptor whose works were well-known in the town, and who made a biscuit figure of a seated 'Mercury' which is in the Liverpool Museum. Gibson's early career was much advanced by the kind patronage of William Roscoe (1753–1831) who made it possible for him to visit Italy and study the classical masters in Rome. Roscoe was a great man who did an enormous amount to encourage the arts in his native town which had its effect, albeit indirectly, on the pottery made there. He was a poet, man of letters, philosopher, humanist and in his later days a botanist of international repute. This is not the place for a full account of Roscoe, but it is interesting in this context to note that he was the nephew of John Roscoe, a potter on Shaw's Brow, and that as a young boy he frequently visited William Reid's china factory on Brownlow Hill, only a few yards from the Old Bowling Green Tavern where he was born. His own words tell us of this event in his life:*

> The numerous occasions of leisure during this period of my life were devoted to other employments. Adjoining to my father's property was a considerable manufactory of British chinaware. With the painters employed in these works I became intimate, and frequently assisted them in their labours, in which I was tolerably expert. Among these was Hugh Milligan, an engraver of copper plates, as well as a painter, who some years afterwards published a collection of his own poetical compositions in a quarto volume, some of which are not without merit. He became a kind of mentor to my youthful years. . . .

Roscoe was a central figure linking together many other personalities, of whom several had direct and others indirect links with designs on Liverpool pottery towards the end of the eighteenth century. In 1773, in the company of others, he was responsible for the formation of a 'Society for the Encouragement of Designing, Drawing, Painting &c.' in Liverpool, and on December 13th of that year he read an 'Ode' dedicated to it which was published

---

* Henry Roscoe, *The Life of William Roscoe*, London, 1833, Vol. 1, page 10.

II. BUST OF GEORGE WASHINGTON. Earthenware, polychrome
enamelled decoration. c.1800. Height 9¾". Impressed HERCULANEUM.
Courtesy of The City of Liverpool Museums.

by Joseph Johnson in London in 1774. The society did not prosper as its initiators had hoped, but in the early 1780s Roscoe revived the idea on a somewhat different plan and founded an 'Academy for Promoting Painting and Design'. The inauguration address was given by Roscoe, to be followed by specialist lecturers including Dr. Matthew Turner, friend and physician to Josiah Wedgwood when he was sick for some weeks on a visit to Liverpool. In 1784 an exhibition was arranged in Roscoe's fine Georgian residence in Rodney Street; on the committee for this exhibition we find Guy Green, the well-known Liverpool pottery printer and former colleague of John Sadler, and the same Dr. Turner. Artists of national fame were invited to exhibit, and paintings by Henry Fuseli, Sir Joshua Reynolds, Paul Sandby (who frequently came to Liverpool in the company of Roscoe's friends and painted sunsets over the Irish Sea), Joseph Wright of Derby and Angelica Kauffman (Mrs. Zucchi) were among those shown. This exhibition was such a success that in 1787 another was held which included works by Thomas Gainsborough, George Stubbs, Thomas Stothard and Francis Wheatley, as well as those who had shown previously.*

The relevance of this academy to the student of Liverpool pottery is, of course, that we now find in Liverpool a cultivated élite, interested in art and making available, for those to whom it was useful, a fund of ideas which were applicable to pottery decoration.

Some examples of this influence may be quoted. Dr. Bernard Watney has recently discovered that a Liverpool print of a lady and two children in a garden, which appears on a plate, jug and mug in three versions, was taken directly from figures in a landscape by Paul Sandby. On a jug which will be mentioned again (Plate 17B) there is a print (touched up with hand enamelling) depicting Colonel Tarleton, a local celebrity, standing with his left foot on a cannon. This print, which is seen on several Liverpool pieces, was taken directly from Sir Joshua Reynolds' portrait which was exhibited in Roscoe's 1784 Exhibition. It is more than possible that some of the other typical Liverpool engraved subjects such as the 'Farmyard' (Plate 22A) came from Gainsborough, and a 'Country Alehouse Door' (Plate 22B) may well have been inspired by a Stothard, Morland, Wheatley or Stubbs original. This was the manner and fashion of the day, and Liverpool, with its new artistic connections, provided an opportunity for the engravers to the pottery trade to know and use some of the best designs available. It is this *quality* of late eighteenth century Liverpool engraving which separates it from the cruder and more naive styles found in much of the printing of Staffordshire, Leeds or the pottery-making areas of the North-east. We must remember, of course, that Liverpool had a tradition for good engraving going back to Sadler's time and before, and indeed the art of engraving and producing fine metalwork supported the very important industry of watch-making, for which Liverpool and its environs will always be famous.

A Herculaneum mug directly connected with William Roscoe is illustrated

---

* Joseph Mayer, *Roscoe and the Influence of his Writings on the Fine Arts*, Historic Society of Lancashire and Cheshire, Liverpool, 1853.

in Plate 39. The print is entitled 'The MOTHER, From Roscoe's Nurse' and its subject was inspired by a long poem which Roscoe published in 1798; this was translated from an Italian poem by Luigi Tansillo.* The engraving is a delicate one, though the name of the engraver is unknown, and the mug has black lining round the neck and foot which is typical of the creamwares of about 1795–1810.

Liverpool is also indebted to Roscoe for introducing to his city a man whose influence in literary and artistic matters was of considerable importance, Henry Fuseli. Fuseli was a painter of very great talent, a professor of painting at the Royal Academy and a close friend of Roscoe in whose house he stayed on his visits to Liverpool. Amongst his other projects Fuseli was persuaded by Roscoe to undertake a series of pictures to illustrate Milton's *Paradise Lost* which have since unfortunately vanished. This series was known as 'The Milton Gallery' and one purpose of the pictures was to illustrate a new edition of Milton being contemplated by Joseph Johnson, the London publisher and uncle of another Joseph Johnson who was a friend of both Fuseli and Roscoe. In Liverpool Museum a Herculaneum porcelain plaque (Plate 138) is enamelled with a very competent if somewhat sentimental version of 'Adam and Eve', with the stanza from *Paradise Lost* which it illustrates enamelled on the back. The plaque is signed and dated 'William Lovatt, November 1817'. It is perhaps the only remaining one of a series inspired by the current interest in Milton, and as it was done in the year following Roscoe's bankruptcy sale of 1816 it may have been based on one of Roscoe's prints or illustrated books. The composition of the figures is very similar to an engraving by Bartolozzi published in Thomas Tegg's edition of Milton which was published in June 1817, but Bartolozzi and Lovatt may both have been using a source very much earlier in origin. The contemporary interest in this subject is further indicated by the fact that John Flaxman, Wedgwood's chief modeller, published three illustrations to Joseph Johnson's edition of Milton edited by Cowper. George Stubbs, R.A., the painter commissioned by Wedgwood to do several enamelled plaques and his portrait, was another of Roscoe's friends who would frequently visit him.

Among the personalities involved in the identification of late Liverpool and Herculaneum-associated pottery the name of Joseph Johnson occurs again and again in connection with pottery printing, but it has proved impossible to establish with certainty anything about the elusive bearer (or bearers) of this name. We can, however, supply some interesting clues. Dr. Knowles Boney has already attempted to sort out the members of the Johnson family.† Several were engravers and potters (including four recorded Johnsons at Herculaneum—James, married to Phoebe Till April 13th, 1800; John, 1817–1841; Nathaniel, married to Alice Sanderson September 19th, 1791; William, married to Ruth Ibbs April 18th, 1797) and perhaps we might begin to throw

* See Dr. G. Chandler, *The Published and Unpublished Poems of William Roscoe*, Liverpool Bulletin, published by the Libraries, Museums & Arts Committee, Vol. II, Nos. 1 and 2.
† Knowles Boney, *Liverpool Porcelain of the Eighteenth Century*, London, 1957, pp. 160–163.

some light on this problem by listing some of the more important Johnson-signed prints:

1. *Print of Colonel Tarleton* (Liverpool Museum)
   on a jug marked 'Wedgwood & Co.' signed 'J. Johnson Liverpool' (Colonel Tarleton was a well-known Liverpool character and member of Parliament from 1790 to 1812).*
2. *Print of the Bidston Hill Signals* (Harris Museum, Preston)
   on an unmarked jug signed 'Printed by Joseph Johnson Liverpool' and dated in the print 1789.
   (Bidston Hill was a famous vantage point overlooking the River Mersey on the Cheshire side, notable for its use of flags for signalling to the Liverpool docks).†
3. *Print of the Death of Wolfe* (Liverpool Museum)
   on an unmarked jug signed 'Richard Walker Joseph Johnson' (Richard Walker was a Liverpool engraver at 25 Edmund Street in 1790, Bevington Bush in 1794, Castle Street in 1803, Harrington Street in 1805, Temple Street in 1808 and presumably retired as a 'gentleman' in Rose Place as late as 1839. It is probably purely a coincidence that he was in the same premises at 25 Edmund Street as one Joseph Johnson, tallow chandler and soap-boiler in 1790.)
4. *Two prints entitled 'Fear God'* (Colonial Williamsburg, Virginia)
   on a teapot signed 'R. Abbey sculpt. Jp^h. Johnson Liverpool' (Plate 26).
5. *One* of the same prints as No. 4 (British Museum)
   on a crudely made unmarked jug with the same Johnson signature but Abbey's signature removed (Plate 25).
6. *Print of a Farmyard* (Liverpool Museum)
   on an unmarked Herculaneum jug signed 'Joseph Johnson Liverpool' (Plate 68).
7. The same *Farmyard print* as No. 6 and a *'Farmers Arms' print* (William Rockhill Nelson Gallery of Art, Kansas City) on an unmarked jug, both prints signed 'Joseph Johnson Liverpool' (Plates 28A, B).
8. *Print of 'Box the Compass'* (Private collection, Connecticut)
   on a canary yellow jug with the name 'J. Johnson Liverpool' in the centre.

This is not a complete list of Johnson signed pieces, but there are sufficient examples to justify a few conclusions. Except for identical prints (4 and 5), (6 and 7) the signatures on no two are alike and in two cases the name is accompanied by that of a known engraver, Richard Abbey, whom we have considered in detail in Chapter II, and Richard Walker. These facts would suggest that Johnson was not himself an engraver but a merchant or printer

* J. A. Picton, *Memorials of Liverpool*, London, 1875, Vol. II, pp. 86–87.
† Knowles Boney, *Bidston Hill in Pottery Decoration*, Apollo, August 1961.

who arranged for prints to be engraved by others and whose name appears because he was essentially responsible; if this were so we would expect to find him listed in some way in the Liverpool Directories or in the Town Records, but no such Joseph Johnson is to be found there.

If he was working *outside* Liverpool, but near enough to use the name on his wares, we would not find him in the town records. From the evidence of the prints and wares upon which they were applied we should look for some-one who was working between the earliest date of (perhaps) 1789 and about 1805 which would be roughly the date of the canary yellow jug (8). In *Williamson's Liverpool Advertiser* for January 21st, 1793, the following advertisement was printed:

CLAY

Lately discovered within Parbold township
sundry BEDS of CLAY, of excellent qualities
which have been proved by Joseph Johnson,
manufacturer of Earthenware, at NEWBURGH.

For further particulars apply to Mr. Leigh at Wrightinton Hall.

N.B. The above mentioned Beds of Clay are
situated and adjoining to the Canal from
Wigan and Liverpool.

Newburgh and Parbold are two small towns lying side by side about 15 miles from Liverpool and about 5 miles from Ormskirk in the low-lying area of the Lancashire coastal plain. It would seem that we have found our Joseph Johnson at last, but the punctuation does not make it altogether clear in the advertisement whether 'at Newburgh' refers to the 'beds of clay' or to 'Joseph Johnson, manufacturer of earthenware'. Rough earthenware potteries are known to have existed at Newburgh for many years, and a brickworks still produces there today, so perhaps our Joseph Johnson started his early life in that vicinity and never had his business in Liverpool at all. The only additional clue we have been able to trace is one family of potters in the Registers of the Douglas Chapel which was administered by Eccleston Parish Church, now in the Lancashire Record Office in Preston. Here we find:

Born January 3rd, 1779   Joseph, son of Edward and Ann Johnson, in the Parish of Ormskirk.
Born October 13th, 1782 Michael, son of Edward Johnson of New-burgh in the Parish of Ormskirk, *Mugman*, and Ann his wife. [Our italics]

Thereafter six other children are recorded who do not concern us here, but there is enough to show that a Joseph Johnson was born the son of a potter (mugman) at Newburgh in 1779. The date fits in well enough with the period of the prints we have listed except for the Bidston Hill print

dated 1789 which in any case seems too early a date for the actual printing and making of the jug itself. The date may well have been copied from an engraving of Bidston Hill dated 1789. One last detail must be added to this account and that is the death of Joseph Johnson listed as 'from Parbold' in the burial records of Ormskirk Parish Church on April 12th, 1805.

From the above evidence we are, then, tempted to conclude that our Joseph Johnson was born in 1779 and died in 1805 and that he was a potter, working on the outskirts of Liverpool in the Ormskirk area, who, in addition to running his own small country pottery, was concerned in the decoration of pottery made elsewhere. That the 'Farmyard' print continued to be used at Herculaneum would be easy to understand if this theory is correct since the jug (Plate 68) was made about 1805–10 and the copper printing plate could have been acquired by the Herculaneum factory at the time of his death. Of the other prints in our list 'Fear God' and 'Box the Compass' are known in other versions with Staffordshire signatures (John Aynsley of Lane End and Thomas Fletcher, Shelton) but these were popular subjects with the potters and could have been commissioned by Johnson from the Liverpool engravers. The two creamware pieces with matching prints in the British Museum and at Colonial Williamsburg (nos. 4 and 5 in our list) (Plates 25 and 26) bear all the characteristics of having been made by a not very accomplished potter seeking to emulate the sophisticated wares of Staffordshire and Leeds—perhaps they were made at Newburgh!

Before leaving the elusive Mr. Johnson we must remember that there were two other Joseph Johnsons connected with Liverpool who may have been in some way connected with the potter of that name. One was the already mentioned London publisher and friend of Roscoe, who was born in the small village of Everton (now long since absorbed into the City of Liverpool) in 1738 and died in 1809; his influence and importance in the publishing trade was sufficient to give him a long article in the *Dictionary of National Biography* and he may have been responsible for sending prints and drawings to his Liverpool kinsmen for use on pots. The other Joseph Johnson was the nephew of the publisher* and is listed as a 'gentleman' at Edge Hill, Liverpool, between 1813 and 1829. He was clearly a man of some education, and we find that Henry Fuseli painted a picture for him in 1813 and several of Fuseli's letters to him are published in John Knowles's life of Fuseli.†
Joseph Johnson is a common enough name, but who knows what connections may have existed between Joseph Johnson, potter and pottery printer of Newburgh, Joseph Johnson, Liverpool-born printer and publisher of London, his nephew, Joseph Johnson, gentleman of Liverpool, Henry Fuseli the painter and William Roscoe, patron, critic, poet and philosopher? Herein perhaps lies the key to the mystery of the name Joseph Johnson on

---

* Hugh Macandrew, *Henry Fuseli and William Roscoe*, Liverpool Bulletin, published by the Libraries, Museums and Arts Committee, Volume 8, Walker Art Gallery Number 1959–60.

† John Knowles, *The Life & Writings of Henry Fuseli Esq. M.A.R.A.*, London, 1831.

Herculaneum pottery and on pottery with Liverpool connections of pre-Herculaneum date.

The Wares

The Johnson signed 'Farmyard' printed jug (Plate 68) is a splendid example of the changing taste in the forms of hollow wares which we find in the early years of the nineteenth century. The tall, baluster form has become shorter and wider, the curves fuller and the spout more rounded. At the same time it has the earlier fashion of black lining round the lip and foot and down the edges of the handle, with one of the flower sprays of earlier usage beneath the inscribed name. The enamelled addition of names on jugs (usually within a previously printed cartouche) is referred to in the Herculaneum accounts in several places, the following extract gives us an idea of the price paid for this work and, indeed, prices for the jugs themselves:

December 9 1806 By Thomas Welsh for 2 lettered jugs . . .   7s.6d
January 27 1807   By John Serjant for Ciphering 2 jugs in Gold . . .
                  1.6d.

Another very fine example of the transition in shape between the tall baluster and the rounder, wider form may be seen in two examples from the Williamson Art Gallery, Birkenhead (Plates 69, 71 and 72). Both jugs have a print of the 'Joiners Arms' from the *same* copper plate, and the later piece is a fine example in drab, almost sage-green earthenware with a moulded handle and masked lip, inscribed with a name even more Welsh than Robert Roberts on the Johnson signed jug. The large creamware jug in the Mattatuck Museum, Connecticut, of 1814 has the print of Stonington which was used on a baluster jug at the Smithsonian Institution, Washington (Plates 64 and 65).

The manufacture of extremely large jugs seems to have been a speciality at Herculaneum and the 'Stonington' jug is a good example. Two more are illustrated here (Plates 66 and 67) which are not only very large but which have the added distinction of being entirely covered with a bright yellow glaze and subsequently decorated with black transfer prints and enamels. Tradition has it that one was decorated by Richard Abbey (Plate 66) and whatever truth there may be in this statement it is possible that Abbey engraved some of the prints. There can be little doubt that although unmarked, both were from the Herculaneum factory, for both are matched with the use of the *same* Farmers Arms print and the one in a private collection in Connecticut has a verse and cartouche 'Let the Wealthy and the Great . . .' which appears from the same engraving on the jugs illustrated in Plates 31 and 32 and which have been discussed in Chapter II. We also know that the Herculaneum potters used the yellow glaze which was made at most of the potteries in the early nineteenth century, for several recipes for this glaze appear amongst the Tomkinson papers (see Appendix III).

One of the finest specimens of Herculaneum transfer-printed earthenware

datable to about 1806 is the enormous jug illustrated in Plates 36A and B. This piece is unmarked, but is definitely from the Herculaneum factory. The handle, with its simulated riveted attachments and leaf termination and the body with its reeded neck and engine-turned base is very similar to many Turner and other Staffordshire stoneware shapes, but this body is creamware and the spout is modelled in the form of a satyr's head. There are several features which show this to be Herculaneum; some of the floral sprays exactly match those on the marked jug we have seen (page 24, Plates 30A and B), and the stipple print of Nelson occurs on several marked pieces elsewhere (Plate 35). The neck is enamelled in a rich blue which was popular on other known pieces of the period and below the Nelson portrait is the signature 'G. Martin sculpt.' George Martin is listed in the registers of St. Michaels-in-the-Hamlet Church at Toxteth as a 'Pottery engraver' in the records of the births of his children by his wife Hannah. This jug can be dated to late 1805 or 1806, for the details of Nelson's death (October 1805) are inscribed on the print. He appears in the company of his fellow officers the Earl of St. Vincent and Lord Duncan, and the whole jug is a veritable catalogue of decorative prints which can be recognised on other jugs and plates. A marked Herculaneum jug of very much the same dimensions and form with a stoneware body is illustrated in Plate 37, but this has bas-relief ornaments and a cover.

One important piece which is linked to the jug just described is a black printed one in Liverpool Museum with exactly the same verse and cartouche (From Rocks and Sand and every ill . . .) as we find inside the handle of the large 'Nelson' jug. An interesting and unusual print showing a group of merrymaking sailors entitled 'Saturday Night', seen toasting 'Sweethearts and Wives', is printed on the side and has only once been seen on another piece by the author. This is a jug in the William Rockhill Nelson Gallery in Kansas City and it has a cartouche under the spout which has helped in the identification of many other jugs. The Liverpool Museum example (Plate 40) came from the family of Miss Diane Edwards of Widnes, Lancashire, whose *completely independent* testimony was that the jug originally belonged to her ancestor John Edwards, who reputedly came from Staffordshire to Herculaneum following his apprenticeship to Flaxman at Etruria. This testimony in itself would have been valuable enough, but this is a case where complete credence can be given to such a statement, for in the catalogue of the Liverpool Sept-Centenary Exhibitions of 1907 we find that notes concerning the Herculaneum factory by John Edwards were displayed, and Joseph Mayer states that an enamelled porcelain plaque (Plate 139) was by this artist. John Edwards was born in 1774 and came to Liverpool about 1802. There is some doubt as to whether he came directly to Toxteth, but he was certainly there in 1807 and he died on April 1st, 1825, aged 51.

To return to our large creamware jug we must now look more closely at the oval stipple prints of naval heroes. These printed subjects were very popular at the time and many important portraits were rendered in this way. An excellent piece, made for the American market, is a Herculaneum

creamware plaque (Plate 38) with a stipple print of George Washington after the famous portrait by Gilbert Stewart. Four versions of this are known, one at Liverpool, one in the Victoria and Albert Museum, one in the Smithsonian Institution, Washington, and a very unusual one glazed in bright yellow in Mr. and Mrs. J. Leon's collection in Connecticut. These plaques are all exactly the same size and unframed, but the most remarkable one of all (not of Washington) is marked Herculaneum and has a marked black basalt frame.

The framed creamware plaque to which we refer is a unique piece at the Mint Museum of Art in Charlotte, North Carolina. It has a polychrome print of Mary Queen of Scots and is the only example of the use of several colours from *one* copper plate, of Herculaneum provenance which has ever been found (Colour Plate I). The Romantic novel was coming into fashion in the early 1800s and Mediaeval and Tudor subjects were attracting increasing attention with the revival of the 'Gothick' style. Queen Mary's life was enough to stimulate any imagination and numbers of portraits of that monarch were produced until Victorian times. Most, however, are based on the Zucchiro painting engraved by Sherwin and published by Thomas Cadell, Strand, in 1788 (Plate 77), who, incidentally, published Roscoe's great work on Lorenzo de Medici and Tansillo's 'Nurse'. Whoever engraved the Mary plaque and applied the print to the surface produced a work of great charm and delicacy unmatched by any other pottery workshop of that era.

Transfer-printed creamware produced in the early years of Herculaneum was amongst the best of the factory's products, and perhaps enough has been said about this Liverpool tradition, though a large number of pieces have been found for which there is no space for details here. We cannot leave this survey, however, without a brief mention of the 'Sailor's Farewells' and the 'Returning Hopes' which were, perhaps, the most popular themes for prints on plates (Plates 42, 62 and 63), nor forget to mention 'Poor Jack' (Plate 41) which was born amongst the prints on pots of pre-Herculaneum days and continued in use at the factory, but in a version with a later style of dress for both the sailor and his lady. The full verse is reproduced below, though it does not appear on the Herculaneum plates it is occasionally to be found on earlier Liverpool creamwares:

> I said to our Poll, for you see she would cry,
> When last we weigh'd Anchor for Sea,
> Whatt argufies sniveling and piping your Eye,
> Why what a damn'd Fool you must be,
> Can't you see the World's wide and there's room for us all,
> Both for Seamen and Lubbers ashore,
> And if to old Davy I should go Friend Poll,
> Why you never will hear of me more.
> What then! all's a hazard, come don't be so soft,
> Perhaps I may laughing come back,
> For d'ye see there's a Cherub sits smiling aloft,
> To keep watch for the Life of poor Jack.

III. TEAPOT. Pearlware, decorated in 'Pratt' type underglaze colours. Impressed HERCULANEUM. c.1805. Height 7½", length 11". *Courtesy of The City of Liverpool Museums.*

This is far enough removed from the cultivated taste and affectations of the kind of poetry William Roscoe wrote, but it has the warmth, humour and humanity of an English sea song, real and unaffected—part of the mariner's life.

The last transfer-printed piece in this section is a plate in the Sadler collection at Stoke (Plate 94), which brings us to another class of wares made in the early 1800s, a type of stoneware which is sometimes translucent and might be described as porcellanous. This printed plate is decorated with a drinking scene involving several rustic characters gathered round a bench and table, one with his glass aloft. This subject, reversed, is taken directly from a print of at least thirty years earlier on a Liverpool delftware tile by Sadler and Green (Plate 93) and it is often described as 'after Teniers'. Our Herculaneum potters not only used this print as a subject for engraving, but applied it (with one figure missing to improve the composition) in bas-relief on stoneware jugs. One of these is illustrated in Plate 93 and another appears on a fine jug in the Victoria and Albert Museum, dated 1803 (Plate 95). In fairness we must say that this design has been found by the author on two mugs impressed 'Adams' (Plate 96) but on this particular jug it is found in conjunction with a moulded cartouche which appears on a marked Herculaneum mug in Paisley Museum (Plate 97). The idea of using contemporary engravings as a source for bas-relief subjects is further illustrated by the modelling of 'The Death of Wolfe' on another Herculaneum jug, and yet again in a 'Gretna Green or the Red Hot Marriage' from Richard Abbey's original (Plates 100 and 101). The fact that these three particular subjects appear so closely related to Liverpool engravings suggests that they might have been actually modelled at Herculaneum. However, many subjects which one finds on Herculaneum stonewares also appear on pieces by Turner, Hollins, Elijah Mayer and Adams and this would lead us to suppose that moulds could be purchased, in several sizes, from mould-makers to the trade, probably working in Staffordshire. One very striking example of this is illustrated in Plates 102 and 103 where we compare a marked Turner buff-coloured vase, in the collection of Mr. David Weinstock of New York, with a black basalt marked Herculaneum one in Liverpool Museum. The similarity is so remarkable that one could almost believe that they came from the same workshop, but it is only the applied ornaments which are exactly alike and the measured proportions are in fact quite different.

This class of stoneware was amongst the best work produced at Herculaneum and the earliest dated specimen we have found is in the Hanley Museum, impressed 'HERCULANEUM 2' and the *painted* date December 22nd, 1802 (Plate 104). Whether or not this date is a later *opinion* we do not know, but the '2' after the mark may well denote the year. A charming little mug, marked and dated 1808 (Plate 98) in the Liverpool Museum has a square-shaped handle with acanthus moulding and simulated screw attachments which we shall find again, twenty-five years later in the closing phases of the factory's life (see page 87). Another splendidly proportioned jug, its handle like that of the mug and its shape based on a creamware form is in

the collection of Colonel Blewitt of Neston (Plate 113A and B), while the covered sugar bowl at the Glyn Vivian Art Gallery, Swansea (Plate 107), and the covered pot at Liverpool Museum (Plate 106) show that not only jugs and mugs were made in this attractive medium.

The most usual colour of the stoneware bodies is a rather drab cream or buff, and the bas-relief subjects might be in the same or a contrasting shade. Some of the jugs have a marbled slip body forming a type of solid 'agate' (Plate 111) and this style has never been noted other than on Herculaneum wares, and then only for jugs. Black basalts were made of a fairly good quality as to detailing, but there is sometimes a slight speckling which detracts from the final effect. The black basalt sugar box at Hanley Museum has the same cane-work moulded ground as the very fine teapot with coloured enamelled reserve panels in the collection of Mr. Charles and Mrs. Jean Goreley of Weston, Massachusetts (Plates 108 and 112). This latter piece is rare and has a most unusual spirally moulded spout as well as the cable moulding which will be noticed elsewhere. We must finally mention the elegant coffee pot in Liverpool Museum. The body of this pot is cream coloured with a deep maroon 'dip' ground while the bas-relief figures and ornaments are cream coloured to contrast with it. The handle has a typical Herculaneum upward curve, sweeping round to its junction with the body, which will have been noticed on other pieces. Small stars are applied all round the cover (as on the Swansea sugar bowl and on the Pratt ware teapot in Colour Plate III) and the whole piece is of the most elegant proportions. It seems very strange that matching sets of cups, saucers, bowls and jugs which must have been made have not survived and as far as we are aware this coffee pot is quite unique (Plate 110).

That some modelling of bas-reliefs was done at Herculaneum we are fully convinced, though many of the moulds may well have been purchased outside. An extremely interesting bas-relief plaque incised on the back 'July 18th, 1815 Eli Till Liverpool' survives in Liverpool Museum, having been acquired by Joseph Mayer from Eli Till's widow and presented by him, with his vast collections, to Liverpool Corporation in 1867 (Plate 118). It is decorated in Pratt-type colours and establishes firmly that colours of this range were used as much at Herculaneum as anywhere else (see Appendix III 'Colours under glaze'). By some strange chance another of Till's possessions has also survived, a small block of glazed earthenware pierced with an oval orifice and incised with his name. This is a template for use on a 'Dod-box', a simple machine in which clay is squeezed down a cylinder with a screwed plunger and is extruded below as a ribbon of the particular section determined by the shape of the aperture in the template.* From this ribbon strips were taken to form handles which are consequently known as 'extruded' handles. Individual potters made and used their own templates in clay and incised their names for identification, as was often done with smoothing tools and 'kidneys' used by the throwers.

---

* I am indebted to Mr. Arnold Mountford for pointing out the use of this tool. A.S.

Many pieces of early nineteenth-century English earthenware known as 'Pratt' types must have come from Herculaneum. A most interesting one is the moulded jug with our 'Teniers' drinking scene in bas-relief, decorated in Pratt colours, which is in the Mattatuck Museum, Waterbury, Connecticut (Plate 91). Another fine example is the impressed marked teapot now in Liverpool Museum (Colour Plate III) which has a white or pearlware body rather primitively coloured under the glaze in yellow, orange, deep blue, sage green and dark brown. The classical subjects, met on stonewares, of Venus rising from the sea and Venus with Cupid and an Eagle appear in relief on each side, while the 'stars', the curious bulbous Herculaneum knop on the cover and acanthus moulding on the handle link this to other wares already described.

Pearlwares have been the subject of much discussion in recent years but there would seem to be very little difference between the *bodies* used in pearlware and creamware, the essential difference being in the glaze. The glaze on pearlware is tinted with cobalt blue which gives a pearl-like colour to the ware; depending on the amount of blue used these wares may be found in a whole range of tints from the usual cream colour to a whitish blue. Pearlware was made at Herculaneum and two pieces will suffice as examples —a pair of identical jugs at the Art Institute of Chicago and at the Essex Institute in Salem, Massachusetts (where there is also a large Herculaneum creamware wine-cooler). Both these jugs are printed with the Washington portrait we have already met on a creamware plaque (Plate 90, page 40) and their handles have the same curved form as the coffee pot in Liverpool Museum (Plate 110). Part of a fine tea service (Plate 88) in the collection of Mr. David Weinstock in New York is decorated in under-glaze colours, the motif being a border of leaves and flowers in sepia, grey/blue of a pale tint and dark blue dots, with sepia lining on an engine-turned body. The mark on these pieces is HERCULANEUM in tiny impressed capitals, the one used on the whole range of stonewares and creamwares up to about 1810.

The modelling of busts and figures was a branch of the Herculaneum trade which we must now consider and perhaps we should begin with a glazed earthenware figure of a soldier (Plate 117). This figure, now in a private collection, has been identified by military experts as probably that of a 'Volunteer' officer. Volunteer regiments were being formed all over the country during the Napoleonic Wars and the uniform depicted suggests a date of about 1800. The suggestion has been made that this could be a 'Liverpool Volunteer' and the type of body, glaze and modelling would certainly not indicate that it comes from either Staffordshire or Leeds. We believe that a strong case can be made for this figure to be of Liverpool origin, and it might very well be our Colonel Tarleton who was so very popular at the time (see page 33). If it is indeed Liverpool ware then it must, because of its date and type of earthenware, be from Herculaneum, and the modelled portraits of military and naval heroes about to be considered will prove that the Herculaneum modellers or 'outside' sculptors working for the firm, were more than equal to producing a figure of this standard.

The range of modelled busts made at Herculaneum includes specimens in earthenware, buff stoneware, black basalt ware and porcelain. Altogether we have been able to trace eighteen of these figures, though there are probably many more still in existence. The subjects rendered are George Washington 1 (Colour Plate II); Lord Nelson 4 (Plate 114); Lord Duncan 3 (Plate 116); General Abercromby 4; Admiral de Winter 2; Count Kosciuzko 1; Admiral Earl St. Vincent 1 (Plate 115); Napoleon Buonaparte 2; though why any English factory should be making a bust of Napoleon is open to some speculation, and perhaps they were for the American market. None of the modellers of these figures is known, and marking was not invariable.

Of those listed only eight have the factory mark, nor are all the figures identified, only eleven having the name of the person depicted on the plinth or underneath. Sometimes the modellers or finishers were not over-careful in their labelling of the busts, for two *identical* models, one enamelled and one plain, bear the names Kosciuzko (a Polish adjutant to Washington) and de Winter, while another completely different figure is also labelled de Winter! Abercromby appears in several different pottery bodies which have shrunk in the firing to different sizes, and one version of Nelson has the rare mark Herculaneum in Gothic lettering as well as in the traditional form of Roman capitals (Plate 114). This Gothic mark has only been noted on one other piece (Plates 75 and 76) and it was probably used out of respect for the public mourning following Nelson's death in 1805. The bust of Washington is larger than the others and has American symbols on the plinth while the bust of Napoleon is in porcelain embellished with the republican 'Liberty Cap' design which is so frequently found in transfer-printing on American cream-wares. For a time there was some sympathy with the French cause in America, when relationships between England and the United States were not very good!

The stoneware busts described above are, generally speaking, of a very high quality and all were manufactured in two basic parts, the bust proper and the plinth or base. When Herculaneum came up for sale for the first time in 1833 (see page 74) the advertisement mentioned specifically '. . . Blocks, Moulds, &c. and all other utensils complete for carrying on the Earthenware and China manufacture, all in excellent working condition.'* Now we do not know for certain whether a sale actually took place at this time, but evidence suggests that it did, for after that date the Herculaneum factory and its wares took on a different form. It was in 1833 that Messrs. Copeland and Garrett took over the Spode works in Stoke and they may have bought some moulds for a bust of Lord Duncan. A bust of this hero (illustrated in G. A. Godden's *Encyclopaedia of British Pottery and Porcelain*) was made by Copeland and Garrett and exactly matches (except for the absence of epaulettes) another in the same volume which is marked Herculaneum. The implication is that Copeland and Garrett may have purchased from Herculaneum, or they may have had a Spode mould which was being used by Spode at a time when Herculaneum was using an identical one. In this case we perhaps ought to think of these moulds as having been supplied

* *Staffordshire Advertiser*, March 16th, 1833.

to both factories by an outside mould-maker, as was certainly done by the makers of the bas-relief moulds discussed earlier (see page 41). An amusing sequel to the whole problem is that the Copeland and Garrett figure of Duncan is exactly the same as *four* versions in Liverpool Museum, all carefully inscribed General Abercromby! The final sale advertisement of Herculaneum in *The North Staffordshire Mercury* of January 23rd, 1841 (see page 81) definitely mentions 'figure moulds' and we wonder if these were the ones to which the advertisement referred.

Of other examples of Herculaneum modelling there are but few which are positively known. The creamware modelled hand (Plate 121) by Frederick Lege is the work of an artist already listed, but he was certainly an 'outsider' for various entries in the accounts show that he paid for the firing of figures at the factory. In this case he might have supplied the finished moulds for the model to be cast in creamware, and four examples have survived to date. The subject is a curious one and in our opinion it was made as a prize for good handwriting at the Circus Street School in Liverpool, which is inscribed on the base with the date 1812. A bull-baiting group in Pratt colours with the bull predominantly yellow (Plate 119) is possibly from Herculaneum and it was catalogued as such in 1907. This identification was made by Peter Entwistle, whose researches into the history of the Liverpool potteries were sadly never published, before his death in 1939. He also classified the very crudely modelled figures of Faith, Hope and Charity (Plate 120) as from our factory, which seems more than possible; the colours compared with the marked Pratt-type teapot (Colour Plate III) and their manner of handling would certainly tend to confirm his view.

Though some of the colour decoration from the Herculaneum factory was done in a roughly finished manner this could never be said of such enamelled creamwares and white earthenwares as are illustrated in Plates 75, 84, 86 and 87. The Gothic mark impressed dish or stand is enamelled in blue and sepia with freshness and spontaneity, and the use of the Scottish thistle would suggest a Scottish client for this piece. The accounts show that several agents for the factory were in Scotland, for example, Dumfries, Glasgow, Greenock and Paisley, which were all easily accessible for the Irish Sea coastal trade. An enamelled-edged breakfast service in the collection of Dr. Lloyd Hawes of Boston, Massachusetts, printed in dusky red with a chocolate edge (Plate 74) and a splendid creamware punch bowl, enamelled with various fruits in the Victoria and Albert Museum testify to the excellence of this work. Unusual, perhaps, are the painted plate and tureen in the British Museum and at Dublin (Plates 84 and 86), all enamelled with black lining and with flowers and leaves on a deep purple ground. A basket at Warrington Museum is treated in the same way and this has the dog-mask handles which we have already seen on the porcelain plant pot (Plate 83). The author has seen examples of enamelled creamware plates which for lightness and fineness of decoration could easily be mistaken for Wedgwood were it not for the impressed Herculaneum mark (Plate 89).

Of all the enamelled creamwares from Herculaneum the most exciting are

three plates now at Hanley Museum, one in the Victoria and Albert Museum and two more in a private collection (Plate 87). From the style of painting it might be assumed that they were by the same hand as the porcelain tea service which is considered later (see pages 47 and 48); the intimate country scenes with peasants will be described more fully in that context. The pierced edges of these plates are in the same purple enamel as has been noted on the pieces described above, and the quality of the work puts them into the top class of enamelled earthenware of the day.

Vast quantities of undecorated creamware were certainly made and there is evidence to show that even transfer-printed creamwares were made well after 1820 (Plate 80, see page 69). That the Herculaneum potters sought to emulate their contemporaries in this field is certain and the pierced cream-ware cruet stand at Manchester Art Gallery (Plate 82) would easily have been taken for Leeds had it not been marked. One final example completes this section; it is the enamelled white earthenware street sign (Plate 73) now at Liverpool Museum. This enormous piece of earthenware, with its partner for Hanover Street, is lettered in black with relief mouldings on a maroon ground edge. The pair are quite unique and most unusual by any standards.

To turn now to porcelain we must first look carefully at some of the finest pieces produced, decorated with enamelling of the highest class. Of some importance is the Lovatt plaque which has already been introduced earlier in this chapter (Plate 138, page 34). William Lovatt was definitely employed at Herculaneum, for in the Minute Book of the Proprietors we see that on June 4th, 1822 they entered into

'. . . an engagement with Mr. Wm. Lovatt as Modeller & Painter for a further term of Six Months at the wages of 45s. per week.'

Now this resolution does not tell us how long his previous service with the company had been, but in 1817 when he enamelled the Adam and Eve plaque he is listed in the directories simply as a painter, at 38 Hill Street, Liverpool. Later entries, continuing until 1832 (about which time he must have died) list him as Enameller and Miniature Painter, at various addresses, and make no mention of his employment at Toxteth. From the fact that the plaque in question is Herculaneum porcelain (and where else could he have got his blanks more easily at that date?) it is likely that he had long connections with the firm, working often as an 'outsider' as well as on his own account. Lack of security as he got older may have caused him to take up his appointment on a full-time basis in the early 1820s, but at all events we must list him as one of our more important painters, working for Herculaneum as Thomas Baxter did at Worcester. Two other porcelain plaques of classical subjects have survived in Liverpool, though in a damaged state, and one is illustrated in Plate 139. These have also been mentioned before and are from the hand of John Edwards, but in this case Edwards seems to have been in the full-time employ of the factory. Apart from the very brief biographical notes on

page 39 there is nothing further known about this artist, but he was certainly a master with porcelain enamels.

A third artist concerned with enamelled porcelain is known to have worked at Herculaneum. He was William Dixon and a little more is known about this man than the others. He must have been born about 1770; he married Elizabeth Whittle on February 16th, 1797 and the baptisms of three of his daughters are recorded in a Toxteth church. Jewitt associates his name with the Sunderland firm of Dixon, Austin and Co.,* but this is clearly mistaken for Dixon was a Liverpool artist, independently known in the Liverpool scene. One of the pictures by Dixon for which we are particularly grateful is the portrait of Guy Green, the famous colleague of Sadler, now in the Liverpool Museum. In 1818 Dixon produced a splendid miniature enamel portrait of Edward Buxton (Plate 131), the salesman at the Duke Street warehouse. By some trick of fate this is the only surviving portrait of any individual person associated with our Toxteth factory, and it is curious that he should be a character known to have been removed from his post in 1815 in dubious circumstances.† By 1818, when the portrait was painted, Buxton was at 5 Clieveland Square as an earthenware dealer and the picture would suggest that he was in quite a prosperous state. Dixon's enamel of Buxton is on a piece of extremely thin porcelain. It was damaged many years ago but remains an example of the high quality of enamelling of which Dixon was capable. Another of Dixon's works is a classical painting, dedicated to the Arts (Plate 130), on a quart mug of Coalport porcelain, mentioned by Jewitt as being marked with his name on the base, an inscription which is no longer there. William Dixon was listed at the time of the Buxton portrait as an enameller at 9 Northumberland Street, Liverpool, but later in his life, like Lovatt, he was on the staff of the works for in the papers of the Herculaneum Friendly Society we find various entries concerning his membership, and his funeral expenses of £6 6s. od. are entered on November 11th, 1838.

The Coalport enamelled mug by Dixon introduces us to several pieces which might have come from John Rose's manufactory and been decorated in Toxteth. Mr. G. A. Godden has pointed out that the elaborate tea service (Colour Plate V and Plate 133) would appear to be of this group, and that the Coalport factory supplied ware 'in the white' for other decorators. A careful search in the Herculaneum accounts, however, has failed to find any purchases from Coalport until 1824 when wares were brought through the dealer Jane Smith of Chester. This search could not be conclusive, for the accounts from 1817 to 1822 are missing, and the date 1824 is considerably later than the Dixon mug or the tea service. A jug in Liverpool Museum which is proven Coalport porcelain is enamelled with military trophies and 'Success to the Liverpool Volunteers' which seems to settle the matter beyond question. The elaborate tea service, magnificently painted in reserve panels

---

* Llewellynn Jewitt, *The Ceramic Art of Great Britain*, 1877. Revised Edn. 1883.
† Edward Buxton may well have come as a potter from Staffordshire in 1796. He married Elizabeth Britain at Trentham, Staffs and was at Herculaneum by 1800. He was appointed salesman at Duke Street in 1808. (See Appendix II, page 114.)

with landscapes and figures from Welsh and English views, was enamelled by Samuel Williams from the miniatures of Thomas Griffiths. Both these artists are known in Liverpool, and Griffiths is mentioned as a painter encouraged and befriended by Roscoe, who painted a portrait of the sculptor Gibson (see page 32). The landscapes in most cases contain groups of peasants, often with children, in a style which one might associate with Rowlandson, and this quality is echoed in enamelling on a set of plates in Colonel Blewitt's collection (Plate 132) and in the figures on the mantelpiece vase illustrated in Colour Plate VI. This, and the other vases (Plates 136 and 137) are amongst the highest quality of Herculaneum porcelains of about 1815, and they were honoured with a special printed mark which has been found only on porcelain wares from the factory of the same quality, such as the spill vase (Plate 135) and the cream ewer and stand (Plate 134). The vases at Upton House (Plate 136) have splendid enamelled reserves on a claret ground, with burnished gold edging, in the style of George Morland. These vases were very much inspired by the French taste and they are definitely Herculaneum porcelain and certainly not from Coalport.

The Herculaneum factory produced vast quantities of porcelain wares as we know from the lists of prices in the Tomkinson papers (see Appendix III). Correct attribution, however, is another matter for we have seen the complications arising from the sale of Staffordshire wares at Duke Street, and we have also noted teapots in the New Hall style (Chapter II, page 26). Careful observation of knops, handles and other features helps a great deal, but what were the *moulds* that Herculaneum purchased from Machin and Baggaley of Burslem in exchange for bone ash in about 1810?* The attribution of two more tea services to Herculaneum for the period 1810–1820, therefore, is based on certain records of the pieces being in Liverpool families from the time they were made, and also having no defined characteristics which would classify them as being from another pottery. One of the services is in a fine white porcelain decorated with black transfer prints (Plate 142), while the other is printed in under-glaze blue (Plate 143). Printing in blue was the staple product of the Herculaneum works, applied more to earthenware than anything else. Increasing in popularity it was made by almost every English factory by the 1820s and a full review of the Toxteth blue-printing business will be found in chapters V and VII, however, a number of pieces from 1800 to about 1820 must be included here.

Apart from the 1796 bowl (see page 25) the earliest dated blue-printed earthenwares appear on Plate 147, a plate and a spoon tray, the latter being impressed with the year 1809. The classical garden with its fountain, figures and ornamental buildings forms a nicely balanced design, with the white areas considered as important in the decoration as the blue. This disposition of solid and void is a quality in many early blue-printed wares which distinguish them from the later designs, where often the patterns are heavy and unrelieved. At this period, before 1810, pieces made for civic or ceremonial use could be over-ornamented too, and a good example of this is the dish

* Liverpool Record Office, *Herculaneum Account Books 1806–17*, folio 283.

1. View of the Herculaneum Pottery from a share certificate of 1806, printed on vellum. The engraving is by George Codling. (See page 29.) *The City of Liverpool Museums.*

2. View of the Herculaneum Pottery from a watercolour by Joseph Mayer dated 1825. (See page 131.) *Liverpool Public Record Office.*

3. **Jug.** Rough lead-glazed earthenware excavated intact in 1965 on the site of St. John's Market, Liverpool. Early eighteenth century. (See page 1.) Height 6½ inches. *The City of Liverpool Museums.*

4. **Tile, Mug and Plate.** The tile and plate are tin-glazed earthenware, the mug is creamware. These three pieces are transfer-printed with different versions of the 'Tythe Pig', that on the plate being signed 'Sadler Liverpool'. (See page 3.) Height of mug 6 inches. Tile 5 inches square. Plate 8 inches diameter. *The City of Liverpool Museums.*

5. **Jug.** Delftware decorated with flowers in yellow, green, red/brown and dark purple. Dated 1757. (See page 3.) Height 8 inches. *The City of Liverpool Museums.*

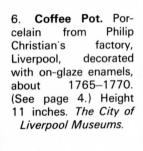

6. **Coffee Pot.** Porcelain from Philip Christian's factory, Liverpool, decorated with on-glaze enamels, about 1765–1770. (See page 4.) Height 11 inches. *The City of Liverpool Museums.*

7. **Beaker and Mug.** Porcelain from Richard Chaffers' factory, Liverpool, decorated in on-glaze enamels, about 1758. (See page 4.) Height of mug 6½ inches. *The City of Liverpool Museums.*

8. **Coffee Pot.** Porce-
lain from Seth Penning-
ton's factory, Liverpool,
decorated in under-
glaze blue printing,
about 1770–1775.
(See page 4.) Height
11 inches. *British
Museum.*

9. **Teapot, Teabowl and Saucer with Matching Shards.** Porcelain from Seth
Pennington's factory about 1775, decorated in under-glaze blue. The shards
were excavated near the factory site on Shaw's Brow, Liverpool. (See page 4.)
Height of teapot $5\frac{1}{2}$ inches. *The City of Liverpool Museums.*

10. **Jug.** Porcelain from Seth Pennington's factory, about 1785, decorated in under-glaze blue printing. (See page 4.) Height 9½ inches. *The City of Liverpool Museums.*

11. **Teabowl, Saucer and Matching Shard.** Porcelain, from Mason, Wolfe & Lucock's factory, Liverpool, 1795–1800 (see page 13), decorated in under-glaze blue printing. The shard was excavated with hundreds of others in 1968 on the site of the factory in Upper Islington, Liverpool, and it is decorated but not glazed. Diameter of saucer 5½ inches. *Mrs. Alberta Caldwell, Liverpool.*

12. **Tea Caddy.** Salt-glazed stoneware decorated in 'scratch blue' and dated 1760. This documentary piece has been identified in connection with the recorded Liverpool potter Henry Muskitt. (See page 5 and footnote *.) Height $4\frac{1}{4}$ inches. *The City of Liverpool Museums.*

13. **Teapot, Cream Jug and Stilt Rings.** Salt-glazed stoneware decorated with 'sprigging' and enamelling, about 1755–1760. The sprigged teapot includes what is perhaps a 'Liver Bird' (see page 5) and the stilt rings, used for supporting the wares during firing, were excavated in Chorley Court, Liverpool, about 1910. Height of teapot 5 inches. *The City of Liverpool Museums.*

14. **Jug.** Earthenware, probably from Seth Pennington's factory, Liverpool, decorated in underglaze painting in blue and dated 1793. The full inscription reads: 'Richard & Martha HUNT Another Jug & then. Success to the Watch makers 1793'. (See page 4). Height 8 inches. *The City of Liverpool Museums.*

15. **Bowl.** Earthenware, probably from Seth Pennington's factory, Liverpool, decorated in under-glaze blue painting, about 1790–1795. The bird in the centre is the 'Liver Bird'. (See page 4.) Diameter 11 inches. Depth 4¾ inches. *The City of Liverpool Museums.*

16. **Tile.** Delftware, transfer-printed and signed 'Abbey LiverpooL'. This is a rare 'Actors series' tile of about 1775. (See pages 15 and 19.) Size 5 inches square. *The City of Liverpool Museums.*

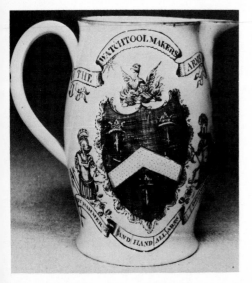

17A and 17B. **Jug.** Creamware, transfer-printed with the print of Colonel Tarleton being strengthened with hand enamelling. (See pages 19 and 33.) Height 9½ inches. *Mr. L. Harrison, Stoke-on-Trent.*

18. **Jug.** Creamware, transfer-printed and hand-enamelled painting of a ship, about 1795–1800. Impressed WILSON (Robert Wilson, Church Works, Hanley) but decorated in Liverpool. (See page 23.) Height 11¾ inches. *National Museum of Ireland.*

19. **Jug.** Creamware, transfer-printed about 1800. Possibly Herculaneum or decorated in Liverpool from Staffordshire. (See page 24.) Height 11¼ inches. *Art Gallery and Museums, Brighton.*

20. **Jug.** Creamware, transfer-printed about 1800. Possibly Herculaneum or decorated in Liverpool from Staffordshire. (See page 24.) Height 7¼ inches. *The City of Liverpool Museums.*

21. **Jug.** Creamware, transfer-
printed and dated 1798, with
green enamelled edging. Possibly Herculaneum or decorated
in Liverpool from Staffordshire.
(See page 24.) Height $9\frac{1}{4}$ inches.
The City of Liverpool Museums.

22A and 22B. **Jug.** Creamware, transfer-
printed about 1785. Possibly Liverpool or
decorated in Liverpool from Staffordshire. (See
pages 24 and 33.) Height $14\frac{1}{2}$ inches. *The City
of Liverpool Museums.*

23. **Jug.** Creamware, transfer-printed with a late version of the 'Farmyard' print about 1810–1815. Herculaneum (unmarked). (See page 24.) Height 7 Inches. *Mr.N. F. H. Cussack, Liverpool.*

24A and 24B. **Beaker.** Opal glass, transfer-printed in Liverpool and of Liverpool manufacture, about 1795–1800. (See page 24.) Height 3⅝ inches. *The City of Liverpool Museums.*

25. **Jug.** Creamware, crudely fashioned and transfer-printed with a design signed 'Jp^h. Johnson Liverpool' (see page 35) about 1795–1800. This print was published on August 16th, 1785, for Carington Bowles, No. 69 St. Paul's Churchyard, London. Height $7\frac{1}{2}$ inches. *British Museum.*

26. **Teapot.** Creamware, transfer-printed from the same engraving as Plate 25 but with the signatures 'R^d. Abbey Sculpt. Jp^h. Johnson Liverpool' about 1795–1800. (See page 35.) Height 5 inches. *Colonial Williamsburg, Virginia.*

27. **Bowl.** Creamware, transfer-printed with the 'Farmyard' and other prints, including the same festooning as on the jug in Plates 22A and 22B. Possibly Liverpool or decorated in Liverpool from Staffordshire, about 1785. (See page 24.) Diameter 12 inches. *Peabody Museum of Salem, Massachusetts.*

28A and 28B. **Jug.** Creamware, transfer-printed with the 'Farmyard' and the 'Farmers Arms', both being signed 'Joseph Johnson Liverpool', about 1800. (See pages 24 and 35.) Height $6\frac{3}{4}$ inches. *Nelson Gallery— Atkins Museum, Kansas City.*

29. **Jug.** Creamware, transfer-printed in sepia brown with Masonic emblems and enamelled in black and chocolate brown, about 1800. Unmarked. (See page 24.) Height 8¾ inches. *Grant-Davidson Collection, Swansea.*

30A and 30B. **Jug.** Creamware, transfer-printed in black with traces of gilding round the neck. The 'Farmyard' print is from the same engraved plate as Plate 32. Impressed HERCULANEUM in small capitals, about 1800. (See page 24.) Height 10 inches. *The City of Liverpool Museums.*

31. **Jug.** Buff
stoneware, transfer-
printed in puce with
enamelling on the
neck in black, green
and yellow. Un-
marked, about
1800. (See page
24.) Height 9½
inches. *Art Gallery
and Museums,
Brighton.*

32. **Jug.** Creamware, transfer-
printed in black with black lining,
about 1800. Inscribed 'Wm.
& M. Crosby'. (See page 24.)
Compare the prints on this jug
with Plates 30B and 31. Unmarked. Height 10 inches. *Art
Gallery and Museums, Brighton.*

Herculaneum
Creamwares

33A, 33B, 33C. **Jug.**
Creamware, very much
stained, transfer-printed
in black, impressed
HERCULANEUM. This is per-
haps the earliest marked
Herculaneum piece known
and in any case a mark is
rare on this type of jug.
Compare print with Plate
34. (See page 25.) Date
1796–1800. Height 10¼
inches. *Mr. Edward
Thomas, Concorde,
Massachusetts.*

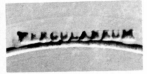

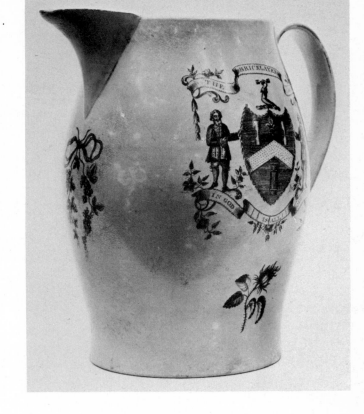

34A and 34B.
Jug. Creamware,
transfer-printed in
black, impressed
WEDGWOOD in small
capitals, about
1775–1780. (See
page 25.) Height 8¾
inches. *Mr. G. P. G.
Monk, Wigan,
Lancashire.*

35. **Soup Plate.** Creamware, transfer-printed in black with black lined edges. Impressed HERCULANEUM about 1805, following Nelson's death. Compare with Plate 36. (See page 39.) Diameter 9⅞ inches. *Hanley Museum, Stoke-on-Trent.*

36A and 36B. **Jug.** Creamware, transfer-printed in black with blue enamelling on the neck. The print of Nelson is signed 'G. Martin Sculp.' (see page 39) and the inscription indicates that it was made about 1805–1806 following Nelson's death. Height 16½ inches. *The City of Liverpool Museums.*

37. **Jug and Cover.** Stoneware, decorated with
moulded reliefs and enamelling. The dimensions and
shape are the same as Plate
36. About 1805–1810. Im-
pressed HERCULANEUM in small
capitals. (See page 39.)
Height (with cover) $19\frac{1}{2}$
inches. *Godden of Worthing.*

38. **Plaque.** Creamware,
transfer-printed in black with
a portrait of George Washington after Gilbert Stuart. No
mark, about 1800. (See page
40.) Height 5 inches. *The
City of Liverpool Museums.*

39. **Two Mugs.** Creamware, transfer-printed in black. Left: a print of Toby Philpot signed 'R. Abbey' (see page 19). Right: a print entitled 'The MOTHER From Roscoe's Nurse' (see page 33). Both unmarked, about 1800. Height of both mugs 4⅝ inches. *The City of Liverpool Museums.*

40. **Jug.** Creamware, transfer-printed in black with black lining, the main print being entitled 'Saturday Night', 'Sweethearts and Wives'. Compare the print 'From Rocks and Sands . . .' with Plate 36. Unmarked, about 1800. (See page 39.) Height 8¾ inches. *The City of Liverpool Museums.*

41. **Soup Plate.** Creamware, transfer-printed in black with 'Poor Jack' (see page 40). Impressed HERCULANEUM in medium-sized capitals, about 1805. Diameter 10 inches. *The City of Liverpool Museums.*

42. **Soup Plate.** Creamware, transfer-printed in black with 'Returning Hopes' (compare with Plate 175). Impressed HERCULANEUM, about 1805–1810. (See page 40.) Diameter 10 inches. *The City of Liverpool Museums.*

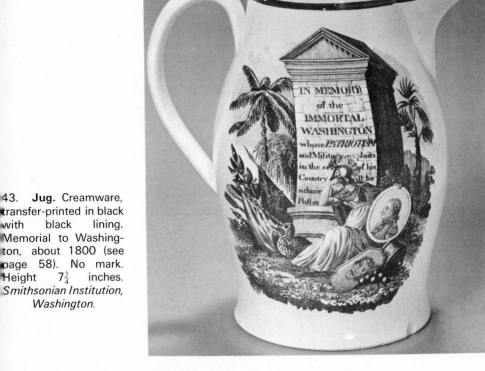

43. **Jug.** Creamware,
transfer-printed in black
with black lining.
Memorial to Washing-
ton, about 1800 (see
page 58). No mark.
Height 7¾ inches.
*Smithsonian Institution,
Washington.*

44. **Jug.** Cream-
ware, transfer-
printed in black
with the print 'By
Virtue and Valour'
(see page 58),
about 1800. No
mark. Height 9¼
inches. *Smithsonian
Institution, Wash-
ington.*

45A and 45B. **Jug.** Creamware, transfer-printed in black. This is the only 'Farmyard' print with a title added. The cartoon is by James Akin (see pages 24 and 58). Unmarked, about 1800. Height 8¾ inches. *Smithsonian Institution, Washington.*

46. **Jug.** Creamware, transfer-printed in black with traces of cold gilding. For details concerning the prints see page 59. No mark, but the 'Coopers Arms' under the spout matches that on the marked jug, Plate 56. About 1800. Height 12 inches. *Peabody Museum of Salem, Massachusetts.*

47. **Jug.** Creamware, transfer-printed, but in the view shown having a completely hand-enamelled ship and decorative border. Impressed HERCULANEUM in small capitals, about 1800. (See page 60). Height 11¼ inches. *Peabody Museum of Salem, Massachusetts.*

48. **Jug.** Creamware, completely hand-enamelled with the same border as Plate 47. The view of Mold Cotton Mill in Flintshire, North Wales, is in green, grey/blue, yellow and dark pink and the mill was first built in 1792. This jug is matched exactly by one having 'Success to Atherton, Hodgson & Co.' on the ribbon above the view. No mark, but this is probably Wedgwood decorated in Liverpool about 1795. (See page 60.) Height 9½ inches. *The City of Liverpool Museums.*

49. **Jug.** Creamware, transfer-printed in black with black lining. The prints on this fine jug match those on Plates 50 and 51, and the flower spray in the centre is the same as on Plate 30A, while the bottom left flower spray matches that on Plate 68B. About 1810, no mark. (See page 60.) Height 15 inches. *Philadelphia Museum of Art.*

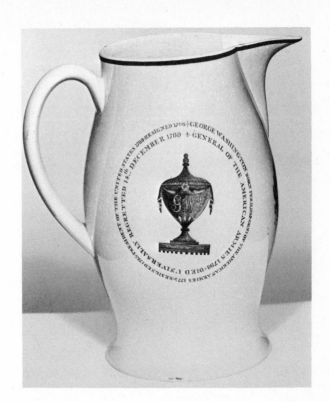

50. **Jug.** Creamware, transfer-printed in black with designs in memory of Washington, and black enamelled lining. About 1800. (See page 60. Height 9¼ inches. *Mattatuck Museum, Waterbury, Connecticut.*

51. **Two Jugs.** Creamware, transfer-printed in black with black lining. Left: printed to mark the occasion of the fiftieth Anniversary Jubilee of George III's Coronation, dated 1810. The view shows the equestrian statue of George III in Roman dress which still stands in Pembroke Place, Liverpool, and in the print the Liver Bird is engraved on the plinth. Right: another Jubilee jug with a portrait of George III. Height (left) 11 inches, (right) 7¾ inches. *The City of Liverpool Museums.*

52.   Another view of the jug shown in Plate 49.

erculaneum
eamwares

Jug. Creamware,
nsfer-printed in black
th remains of cold gild-
. The print shows a
rtrait of Commodore
ble, signed below
th a capital letter 'D'
ich may also be seen
the George III Jubilee
nt on Plate 51 left.
is letter identifies the
graver as T. Dixon
m completely signed
nts elsewhere. On the
her side is a view of
mmodore Preble's
uadron attacking the
y of Tripoli, 1804.
everal jugs with this
nt are marked as in
ate 59). Height 9
ches. *Peabody
useum of Salem,
Massachusetts.*

54. **Jug.** Cream-
ware, transfer-
printed in black with
cold gilding and
black enamelling.
The ship *The Liver-
pool Packet* occurs
amongst the records
of vessels trading
between Liverpool
and America in the
Herculaneum Ac-
count Books. About
1800–1805. Height
$10\frac{1}{4}$ inches. *Art
Institute of Chicago.*

55. **Jug.** Cream-
ware, transfer-printed
in black showing
Lafayette's Plan of
Washington supported
by symbolic figures
(see page 61). About
1800, unmarked.
Height 9 inches. *Pea-
body Museum of Salem,
Massachusetts.*

56. **Jug.** Cream-
ware, transfer-printed
in black with remains of
cold gilding. This is an
important impressed
marked Herculaneum
piece with a print of the
'Coopers Arms' match-
ing that on Plate 46
(see page 59). About
1800. Height $10\frac{1}{4}$
inches. *Smithsonian
Institution, Washington.*

57. **Jug.** Creamware, transfer-printed in black with a design dedicated to Washington surrounded by the names of the American States, and the HERCULANEUM POTTERY, LIVERPOOL version of the American Eagle. About 1800. (See Appendix I.) Height 8⅛ inches. *Mattatuck Museum, Waterbury, Connecticut.*

59. A front view of the mark on Plate 57.

58. **Jug.** Creamware, transfer-printed in black with traces of cold gilding and a print of Washington 'Ascending to Glory'. This print was first published by Simon Chaudron and John J. Barralet in Philadelphia in January, 1802. The print beneath the spout may be seen on the marked Herculaneum creamware tureen in Plate 61, and on the jug in Plate 60. About 1805. Height 12 inches. *Smithsonian Institution, Washington.*

60. **Jug.** Cream ware, transfer printed in black with cold gilding and inscribed 'Thomas & Mary Buntin'. The print below the spout appears on the Herculaneum tureen, Plate 61 (see page 59). About 1800–1805. Height 12 inches. *Peabody Museum of Salem, Massachusetts.*

61. **Tureen.** Cream-ware, transfer-printed in black un-marked, but having prints exactly as on a marked plate in the same collection. About 1800. Length $14\frac{1}{4}$ inches. Height $8\frac{1}{2}$ inches. *Philadelphia Museum of Art.*

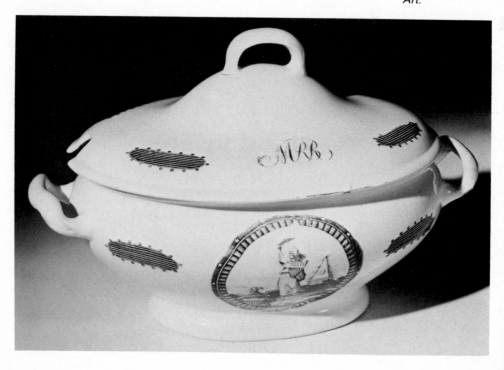

62.   **Tile.** Creamware, transfer-printed in black with a sailor's farewell subject. About 1805–1810. (See page 40.) Size 6 inches
square. *The City of Liverpool Museums.*

63.   **Jug.** Drab cream-
ware, transfer-printed
in black with the
'Sailor's Farewell' as on
Plate 62 and the
American Eagle on the
reverse as on the jug in
Plate 64. Black lining,
about 1805–1810.
(The same print may be
seen on a plate in
Hanley Museum.) (See
page 40.) Height $6\frac{1}{4}$
inches. *Mr. Edward
Thomas, Concorde,
Massachusetts.*

64A and 64B. **Jug.** Drab creamware, transfer-printed in black with 'Th Defence of Stonington' (see page 58) and an American Eagle. The Stoningto print is from the same engraving as Plate 65. Date 1814–1815. Height inches. *Smithsonian Institution, Washington.*

65. **Jug.** Creamware, transfer-printed in black with 'The Defence of Stonington' (see page 58), several flower sprays, gilding and the same printed cartouche as on Plates 49 and 51. Date 1814 or soon thereafter. Height $12\frac{1}{4}$ inches. *Mattatuck Museum, Waterbury, Connecticut.*

66. **Jug.** Earthenware, covered with a bright yellow glaze, black transfer prints and black and dark red enamelling. The prints on this jug have been attributed to Richard Abbey (see page 38) and 'The Farmers Arms' print links this to plate 67. Date about 1810. Height 16½ inches. *The City of Liverpool Museums.*

67. **Jug.** Earthenware, covered with a bright yellow glaze, black transfer prints and enamelled floral border. This view of the jug shows a late version of the 'Farmyard' print (see pages 24 and 38). Date about 1810. Height 14¼ inches. *Eleanor & Jack Leon, Connecticut.*

68A and 68B. **Jug.** White earthenware, transfer-printed in puce with the 'Farmyard' signed 'Joseph Johnson, Liverpool' and black lining (see pages 24 and 38). Date about 1810. Height $7\frac{1}{4}$ inches. *The City of Liverpool Museums.*

69. **Jug.** Sage-coloured earthenware with transfer prints in black and black lining. Inscribed 'T. & M. Hughes, Llanhassa' in a cartouche. About 1810–1815. (See page 38.) Height 7¼ inches. *Williamson Art Gallery, Birkenhead.*

70. **Jug.** Creamware, transferprinted in black with the same subject, but not the same size, of 'Commerce Revived' as on Plate 69. Black lining, about 1810–1815. Height 9 inches. *Victoria and Albert Museum, London. Crown copyright.*

71. **Jug.** Creamware, transfer-printed in black with the same 'Joiners Arms' print as on Plate 72. Date about 1810–1815. (See page 38). Height 7 inches. *Williamson Art Gallery, Birkenhead.*

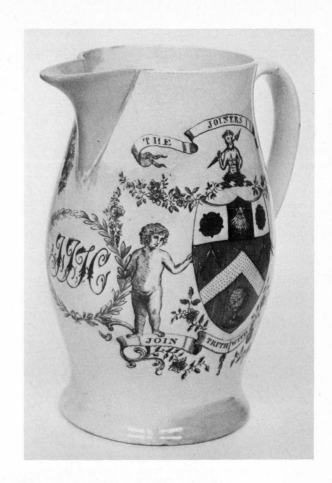

72. View of other side of Plate 69 showing 'Joiners Arms' print matching Plate 71. (See page 38.)

73. **Street Sign.** White earthenware with a moulded edge and enamelled in maroon and black. This piece is fitted with lugs on the reverse for hanging. Date about 1810. (See page 46.) Length 20½ inches. The City of Liverpool Museums.

74. **Breakfast Set.** Creamware, transfer-printed in dusky red with dark chocolate enamelled edging. Impressed HERCULANEUM 10. Date about 1810. (See page 45.) Centre dish 8 inches high. Quarter dishes 11 inches long *Dr. Lloyd Hawes, Boston.*

75. **Dish or Stand.** Creamware, enamelled in blue and sepia, about 1805. (See page 45.) Diameter 9½ inches. *Mr. Raymond Plant, Chester.*

76. Impressed mark on Plate 75 in Gothic lettering. (See pages 44 and 45). Length of mark 1$\frac{1}{10}$ inches.

77. **Print of Mary Queen of Scots.** From the painting by Zucchiro published by Thomas Cadell, Strand, January 1st, 1788. (See page 40.) *British Museum, London.*

78. **Plaque.** Creamware set in a black basalt frame, both plaque and frame impressed HERCULANEUM in small capitals. The portrait is a polychrome transfer print of Mary Queen of Scots from the print, Plate 77 (see Colour Plate I and page 40). About 1805. Height $6\frac{1}{8}$ inches. *Mint Museum, Charlotte, North Carolina.*

79. **Plaque.** Creamware, transfer-printed in puce with additional hand enamelling, pierced for hanging. No mark, about 1805–1810. Height $6\frac{1}{2}$ inches. *The City of Liverpool Museums.*

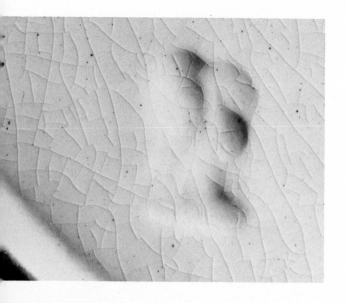

80. **Plate.** Creamware, transfer-printed in sage green, glaze very much crazed. Marked with the impressed 'Liver Bird' (see pages 46 and 69), about 1825. Diameter 10 inches. *Mr. Raymond Plant, Chester.*

81. Mark on Plate 80. The form of this mark is much obscured by the thickness of the glaze. As this mark was introduced in the mid 1820s (see Appendix I), this piece is a very late example of transfer-printed creamware. (See page 69.)

82. **Cruet Stand.** Creamware, about 1810. The individual containers are missing from the set. Impressed HERCULANEUM in small capitals. (See page 46.) Length 10½ inches. Height 6⅝ inches. *Manchester City Art Gallery.*

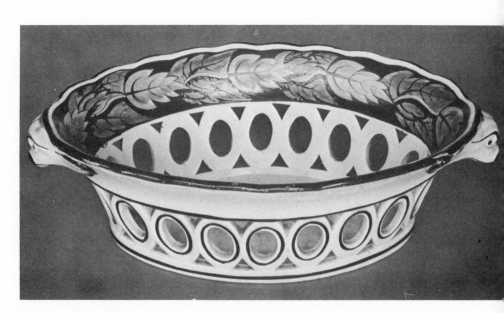

83. **Basket.** Creamware, pierced and decorated with black and green enamelling. Mark 1640 in enamels, about 1815. (See page 45.) Length 9 inches. *Warrington Museum, Lancashire.*

84. **Plate.** Creamware,
pierced and enamelled with
black lining, deep violet
ground, white roses and
green leaves. Impressed
HERCULANEUM
R , about 1815.
(See page 45.) Diameter
10 inches. *British Museum,
London.*

85.   Mark from Plate 84.

86.   **Sauce Boat and Cover.** From the same service as Plate 84 and
decorated in the same colours. Impressed HERCULANEUM
C . (See page 45.)
Height 6½ inches. Length 7½ inches. *National Museum of Ireland.*

87. **Plate.** Pearlware, enamelled in colours with a purple enamelled pierced edge, impressed HERCULANEUM, about 1810–1815. (See page 46.) Diameter 7 inches. *Hanley Museum, Stoke-on-Trent.*

88. **Teapot, Sugar Bowl and Cover and Cream Jug.** Creamware, under-glaze painted in brown lining, sepia brown and grey/blue with bright blue dots, on an engine-turned body. Impressed HERCULANEUM in small capitals, about 1805–1810. (See page 43.) Height of teapot $6\frac{5}{8}$ inches, sugar bowl $4\frac{5}{8}$ inches, jug 3 inches. *David S. Weinstock, New York.*

89. **Plate.** Creamware, the border being enamelled over the glaze in red/brown and black. Impressed HERCULANEUM in small capitals, about 1800. (See page 45.) Diameter 10 inches. *Mr. and Mrs. R. Rosborough, Massachusetts.*

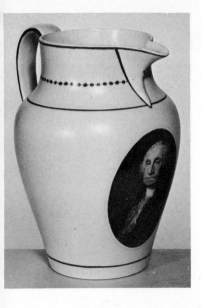

90. **Jug.** Pearlware, transfer-printed with a portrait of George Washington and black lining. This print is the one used on the plaque in Plate 38. Other examples of this jug are known in American collections. Impressed HERCULANEUM in small capitals, about 1805–1810. Height $6\frac{7}{8}$ inches. *Art Institute of Chicago.*

91. **Jug.** Pearlware with relief decoration and underglaze 'Pratt' colours. The scene depicted on this jug is related to that used on pieces illustrated in Plates 93, 94 and 95. About 1805–1810. (See page 43.) Height $7\frac{1}{8}$ inches. *Mattatuck Museum, Waterbury, Connecticut.*

92. **Mug.** Pearlware, decorated with a print of Washington and black lining, engine-turned foot. Impressed HERCULANEUM in small capitals, about 1800–1805. Height $5\frac{3}{4}$ inches. *Henry Francis du Pont Museum, Winterthur, Delaware.*

93. **Jug and Tile.** The jug is in buff stoneware with a relief decoration of a drinking party adapted from the transfer-printed delftware tile of some thirty years before. Jug impressed HERCULANEUM about 1805. (See page 41.) Height 7½ inches. *The City of Liverpool Museums.*

94. **Plate.** Creamware, transferprinted in black with a version of the drinking party on Plate 93. Impressed HERCULANEUM in large capitals, about 1810. (See page 41.) Diameter 10 inches. *Sadler Collection, Stoke-on-Trent.*

95. **Jug.** Stoneware with relief decoration against a brown ground. The cartouche design may be seen on the mug in Plate 97. No mark, dated 1803. (See page 41.) Height 7⅛ inches. *Victoria and Albert Museum, London. Crown Copyright.*

96. **Mug.** Stoneware with the same subject, but not identical moulded relief decoration as on Plates 93 and 95. Impressed ADAMS. (See page 41.) Height 6⅞ inches. *Art Institute of Chicago.*

97. **Mug.** Stoneware, with relief decoration. Impressed HERCULANEUM in small capitals, about 1805. (See page 41.) Height 6¼ inches. *Museum and Art Gallery, Paisley.*

98. **Mug.** Stoneware, with relief decoration. Impressed HERCULANEUM and dated 1808. (See page 41.) Height $3\frac{1}{4}$ inches. *The City of Liverpool Museums.*

99. Mark impressed on Plate 98.

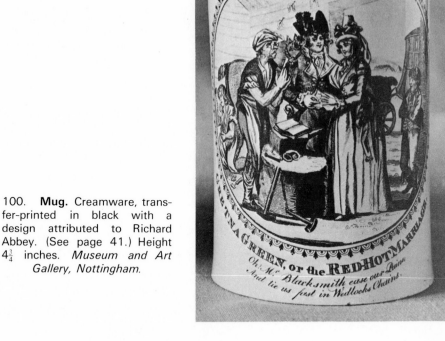

100. **Mug.** Creamware, transfer-printed in black with a design attributed to Richard Abbey. (See page 41.) Height $4\frac{3}{4}$ inches. *Museum and Art Gallery, Nottingham.*

101. **Jug.** Buff stoneware with chocolate-brown neck and foot, decorated with a relief based on the engraving on Plate 100. Impressed HERCULANEUM 1805–1810. (See page 41.) Height 10 inches. *Dr. J. L. Brown, Maidstone, Kent.*

102. **Vase.** Black basalt ware with white jasper base. Impressed HERCULANEUM about 1805. (See page 41.) Height 11½ inches. *The City of Liverpool Museums.*

103. **Base.** Buff stoneware with black basalt base. Of very similar but not identical design to Plate 102, impressed TURNER. (See page 41.) Height 12⅞ inches. *Mr. David S. Weinstock, New York.*

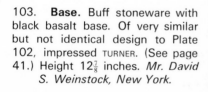

04. **Jug.** Buff
toneware with
hocolate-brown
eck and foot
ng. Impressed
ERCULANEUM 2
vith the date
ecember 22nd,
802, painted on
e base. (See
age 41.) Height
$\frac{3}{4}$ inches. *Hanley
Museum, Stoke-
n-Trent.*

105A and 105B. **Medallion of George IV.** Moulded from a coin in
white jasper and set in a dark blue jasper mount. Impressed HERCULANEUM.
Diameter $2\frac{7}{8}$ inches. *Mr. and Mrs. A. Schaffer, New York.*

106. **Pot and Cover.** Buff stoneware with dark brown inlaid decoration and applied reliefs. Impressed HERCULANEUM in small capitals, about 1805. (See page 42.) Height 7¾ inches. *The City of Liverpool Museums.*

107. **Sugar Bowl and Cover.** Buff stoneware decorated with applied reliefs of high quality, glazed interior. Impressed HERCULANEUM in small capitals, 1805–1810. (See page 42.) Height 5½ inches. *Glynn Vivian Art Gallery, Swansea.*

108. Teapot. Porcellanous stoneware with simulated basketwork body and unusual spirally moulded spout. The reserve panels are hand enamelled with a marine view. Impressed HERCULANEUM about 1805. (See page 42.) Height $7\frac{1}{2}$ inches. Overall length 10 inches. *Mr. Charles and Mrs. Jean Gorely, Weston, Massachusetts.*

109. Flower Pot. Drab-coloured stoneware with white relief decoration. This flower pot is one of a set of three made in diminishing sizes, viz. $7\frac{1}{8}$, $6\frac{3}{4}$, $6\frac{1}{4}$ inches. Impressed HERCULANEUM in small capitals, about 1805. *Museum of Fine Arts, Boston. Lent by Mr. Peter Blackman.*

110. **Coffee Pot.** Stoneware with cream-coloured reliefs on a chocolate-brown ground. Impressed HERCULANEUM about 1805. (See page 42.) Height 10½ inches. *The City of Liverpool Museums.*

111. **Jug.** Stoneware with a solid marbled slip-cast body and buff-coloured reliefs, glazed inside. Marbled bodies of this type appear to be unique to jugs of this form (see page 42). Impressed HERCULANEUM in small capitals, about 1805. Height 6½ inches. *The City of Liverpool Museums.*

112. **Sugar
Box and Cover.**
Black basalt
ware with relief
decoration and
simulated
basketwork
ground (com-
pare with Plate
108). Impressed
HERCULANEUM
1805–1810.
(See page 42.)
Height 5½ inches.
*Hanley Museum,
Stoke-on-Trent.*

113A and 113B. **Jug.** Buff stoneware with
glazed interior and classical reliefs. Impressed
HERCULANEUM in small capitals, 1805–1810.
(See page 42.) Height 7¾ inches. *Colonel B.
Blewitt, Neston, Cheshire.*

114. **Bust of Nelson.** Buff stoneware impressed twice with the name HERCULANEUM, once in Roman capitals and once in Gothic letters (compare with Plate 76), 1805. (See page 44.) Height 8½ inches. *Williamson Art Gallery, Birkenhead.*

115. (Below, left) **Bust of Admiral Earl St. Vincent.** Buff stoneware impressed HERCULANEUM but not named. (See page 44.) Height 8 inches. *The City of Liverpool Museums.*

116. (Below, right) **Bust of Lord Duncan.** Buff stoneware, inscribed with his name but not marked Herculaneum. (See page 44.) Height 7¾ inches. *The City of Liverpool Museums.*

117. **Figure of a Soldier.** Pale cream earthenware with a clear glaze. Perhaps this is a Liverpool Volunteer? (see page 43). No mark. Height 8 inches. *Private Collection.*

18. **Plaque and Template.** Both in white earthenware with a slightly tinted blue glaze, the plaque being decorated in under-glaze 'Pratt' colours. Inscribed 'July 18th. 1815 Eli Till, Liverpool'. The template is inscribed 'Eli Till' (see pages 22 and 42). Plaque $11\frac{1}{4} \times 9\frac{1}{4}$ inches. *The City of Liverpool Museums.*

119. **Bull Baiting Group.** Earthenware, decorated in under-glaze colours, yellow, blue and brown. No mark, about 1810. (See page 45.) Length of base $9\frac{1}{2}$ inches. *The City of Liverpool Museums.*

120. **Faith, Hope and Charity.** A set of earthenware figures, crudely moulded and decorated in 'Pratt' type colours. No mark, 1810–1815. (See page 45.) Height of centre figure 9 inches, side figures $8\frac{1}{4}$ inches. *The City of Liverpool Museums.*

121. **Modelled Hand with a Pen.** Creamware, incised on the base 'Designed for Circus Street School FRd. LEGE Sculpt. Liverpool 1812'. (See page 45.) Length of base 8 inches. *The City of Liverpool Museums.*

122. **Teabowl and Saucer.** Porcelain, decorated in on-glaze enamels and marked with the monogram HP in underglaze blue. (See page 26.) Perhaps 1796–1800? Diameter of saucer $5\frac{1}{8}$ inches. Height of teabowl $1\frac{3}{4}$ inches. *Miss N. Wilson, Harrogate.*

123. **Teapot.** Porcelain, decorated in on-glaze enamels and marked 189 in puce on the base, about 1805. (See page 26.) Height $6\frac{1}{4}$ inches. *The City of Liverpool Museums.*

124. **Cream Jug.** Porcelain, decorated in on-glaze enamels with the initials F. P. B. under the spout. Impressed HERCULANEUM on the edge of the base in small capitals, about 1805. (See page 26.) Height 4 inches. *Philadelphia Museum of Art.*

125. **Teapot.** Porcelain, decorated in on-glaze enamels, rather thick and heavy body. No mark, about 1810. Height 7 inches. *The City of Liverpool Museums.*

126. **Teapot.** Porcelain, decorated in on-glaze enamels and similar in weight to Plate 125. No mark, about 1810. Height $6\frac{1}{2}$ inches. Overall length $9\frac{1}{2}$ inches. *Mrs. de Saye Hutton, Blandford Forum.*

127. **Several Pieces from Two Tea Services.** Porcelain, enamelled in sepia (right) and in pale colours (left), both gilded. Teapot and left-hand cream jug impressed HERCULANEUM on the edge of the base in small capitals, 1805–1810. (See pages 26 and 27.) Overall length of teapot 10 inches. *The City of Liverpool Museums.*

128. **Covered Sugar Box and Coffee Cup.** Porcelain, enamelled and gilded, the sugar box impressed HERCULANEUM and enamelled with the pattern number 368, 1805–1810. (See page 26.) Height of sugar box 5 inches, coffee cup 2¾ inches. *Godden of Worthing.*

129. **Plant Pot.** Porcelain, enamelled and gilded against a black enamelled ground. Impressed HERCULANEUM on side of base in small capitals, 1810–1815 (compare with Plate 83). (See page 27.) Height 4½ inches. *The City of Liverpool Museums.*

130. **Mug.** Porcelain, of Coalport manufacture, enamelled with an allegorical scene connected with the Arts, by William Dixon (see page 47). No mark, about 1810. Height 5¼ inches. *The City of Liverpool Museums.*

. **Plaque.** Porcelain, ⌐ an enamelled portrait ⌐dward Buxton, signed William Dixon and ⌐d 1818. (See pages and 71. Size 3½×2⅞ ⌐es. *The City of Liverpool Museums.*

132. **Plate.** Porcelain, possibly Coalport decorated with
enamelled figures at Herculaneum. No mark, about 1810. (Compare with Plates 87, 133 and 137.) (See page 48.) Diameter
8¾ inches. *Colonel B. Blewitt, Neston, Cheshire.*

133. **Part of a Tea and Coffee Service.** Porcelain, of Coalport manufacture decorated at Herculaneum by Samuel Williams after landscapes
by Thomas Griffiths, with profuse gilding. No mark, about 1815. (See
Colour Plate V and pages 47 and 48.) Overall length of teapot 10¼ inches.
The City of Liverpool Museums.

134. **Cream Ewer and Stand.** Porcelain, enamelled with flowers on a pink ground and gilded. The mark is the same as that on Plate 135 (see Appendix I), about 1815. (See page 48.) Height of ewer 4 inches. *The City of Liverpool Museums.*

135. **Spill Vase.** Porcelain, enamelled with flowers on a yellow ground and gilded. The mark is shown on the base, printed in puce. (See page 48 and Appendix I), about 1815. Height $4\frac{3}{4}$ inches. *The City of Liverpool Museums.*

136. **Garniture of Vases.** Porcelain, enamelled with reserves after the style of George Morland, on a claret ground with gilding. Mark as in Plate 135, about 1815. (See page 48.) Height of centre vase $9\frac{1}{2}$ inches, side vases $8\frac{1}{2}$ inches. *Bearsted Collection, Upton House, The National Trust.*

137. **Vases from Garnitures.** Porcelain, the centre one being enamelled on an azure-blue ground and the side vases having floral reserves with blue neck and base, profusely gilded. The centre vase does not belong to the garniture of the flanking vases. Mark as on Plate 135, about 1815. (See Colour Plate VI and page 48.) Height of centre vase 11 inches, flanking vases $8\frac{3}{4}$ inches. *The City of Liverpool Museums.*

138. **Plaque.** Porcelain, enamelled in colours and inscribed 'W. Lovatt November 1817' and the stanza from Milton's *Paradise Lost* which it illustrates. (See pages 34 and 46.) Dimensions $10 \times 8\frac{1}{4}$ inches. *The City of Liverpool Museums.*

139. **Plaque.** Porcelain, enamelled in colours by John Edwards, depicting Telemachus and Calypso. No mark, 1815–1820. (See pages 39 and 46.) Dimensions $15 \times 12\frac{1}{4}$ inches. *The City of Liverpool Museums.*

140. **Tea Cup and Saucer.** Porcelain, enamelled with birds and flowers and edge gilding. No mark, about 1820. (See page 71.) Diameter of saucer $5\frac{1}{2}$ inches. Height of cup $2\frac{5}{8}$ inches. *The City of Liverpool Museums.*

141. **Bowl.** Porcelain, with relief decoration outside and enamelled flowers and gilding on a blue under-glaze ground inside. No mark, about 1820. (See page 71.) Diameter $12\frac{1}{2}$ inches. Height $6\frac{3}{4}$ inches. *The City of Liverpool Museums.*

142. Pieces from a Tea and Coffee Service. Porcelain, transfer-printed in black with black lining. No mark, about 1815. (See page 48.) Height of coffee pot $9\frac{1}{2}$ inches, teapot $7\frac{1}{4}$ inches. *The City of Liverpool Museums.*

143. Teapot, Sugar Bowl and Cream Jug. Porcelain, decorated in under-glaze blue with prints of animals and gilding. No mark, about 1820. (See page 48.) Height of teapot 6 inches, length $10\frac{1}{2}$ inches. *The City of Liverpool Museums.*

144.   **Teapot, Cup and Saucer.** Porcelain, decorated with 'bat' prints of animals in sepia, and gilding. No mark, about 1815. (See pages 71 and 72.) Height of teapot $5\frac{1}{2}$ inches, length 10 inches. *The City of Liverpool Museums.*

145.   **Sugar Bowl, Jug, Cup and Saucer.** Porcelain, transfer-printed on moulded forms, with landscapes. No mark, about 1825. (See pages 71 and 72.) Height of sugar bowl $5\frac{1}{4}$ inches. *The City of Liverpool Museums.*

146.   **Jug.** Creamware, transfer-printed in blue under the glaze with a portrait of George Washington. No mark, about 1800. (See page 25.) Height 7¾ inches. *Mr. and Mrs. Samuel Schwartz, New Jersey.*

147. **Plate and Spoon Tray.** Earthenware, under-glaze printed in blue, impressed HERCULANEUM on each and the date 1809 on the spoon tray. (See pages 26 and 48.) Diameter of plate 9¾ inches. *The City of Liverpool Museums.*

148. **Punch Bowl.** Earthenware, under-glaze printed in blue with under-glaze painted inscription (see page 25). No mark. Diameter 16 inches. Depth 6½ inches. *The City of Liverpool Museums.*

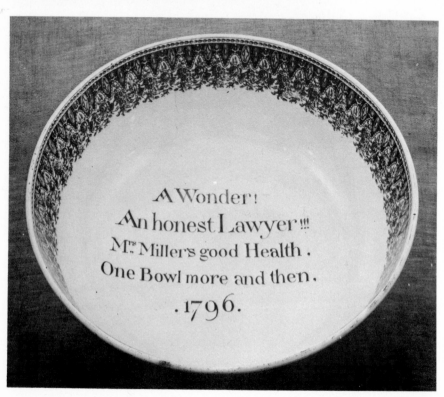

149. **Tureen.** Earthenware, under-glaze printed in blue with enamelled transfer-prints of Liverpool Coat of Arms, gilded edging. Impressed HERCULANEUM about 1815. (Compare pattern with Plate 152.) (See page 49.) Overall length 13½ inches. *The City of Liverpool Museums.*

150. **Tureen.** Earthenware, under-glaze printed in blue with enamelled transfer-printed Liverpool Coat of Arms, and gilded edging. Impressed 'H P 1809'. (See pages 26 and 49.) Overall length 9¾ inches. *The City of Liverpool Museums.*

151. **Meat Dish.** Earthenware, under-glaze printed in blue,
impressed HERCULANEUM/4, possibly about 1804. (See page 49.)
Overall length 20 inches. *The City of Liverpool Museums.*

152. **Meat Dish.** Earthenware, under-glaze printed in blue, impressed
HERCULANEUM, about 1815. (See page 49.) Overall length 23 inches. *The
City of Liverpool Museums.*

153. **Covered Bowl, Stand and Basket.** Earthenware, under-glaze printed in blue and impressed HERCULANEUM in small capitals, the bowl being marked HERCULANEUM 12, about 1810. (See page 26.) Diameter of bowl (including handles) 7¼ inches. Basket length 9 inches. *The City of Liverpool Museums.*

154. **Cream Jug.** Earthenware, under-glaze printed in blue, impressed HERCULANEUM small capitals, about 1810. (See page 26.) Height 6 inches. *Dr. Lloyd Hawes, Boston, Massachusetts.*

155. **Mug.** Earthenware, under-glaze printed in blue, impressed HERCULANEUM in small capitals, about 1805. (See page 26.) Height 5½ inches. *National Museum of Ireland.*

156. **Meat Dish.** Earthenware, under-glaze printed in blue with a
version of the Willow Pattern. Impressed HERCULANEUM about 1815.
(See page 49.) Overall length 19½ inches. *Mr. N. F. H. Cusack,
Liverpool.*

157. **Soup Plate.** Earthenware, under-glaze printed in blue with a
version of the Willow Pattern. Impressed 'H P₂ 1808'. (See page 49.)
Diameter 9¾ inches. *Sadler Collection, Stoke-on-Trent.*

158. **Meat Dish, Plate and Frog Mug.** Earthenware, under-glaze printed in blue, the dish impressed HERCULANEUM/18 . The mug has maroon edging and the initials S.M.C. (see pages 22 and 49) but no mark. The plate is impressed HERCULANEUM. All about 1815. Length of dish $18\frac{1}{2}$ inches. Diameter of plate 10 inches. Height of mug $5\frac{1}{4}$ inches. *The City of Liverpool Museums.*

159. **Bed Pan.** Earthenware, under-glaze printed in blue with the same pattern as Plate 158. Impressed HERCULANEUM about 1815. (See page 49.) Overall length $15\frac{1}{4}$ inches. Overall height 5 inches. *The City of Liverpool Museums.*

160. **Covered Breakfast Egg Dish.** Earthenware, under-glaze printed in blue with the 'Etruscan' pattern, and ochre edging. The dish contains six egg cups, a salt-cellar and spaces for six spoons. No mark, about 1810. (See page 49.) Height (with cover) 9 inches. Length 12 inches. *The City of Liverpool Museums.*

161. **Breakfast or Supper Service.** Earthenware, under-glaze printed in blue with ochre edging. No mark, about 1810. (See page 49.) Overall diameter when grouped together 21 inches. *The City of Liverpool Museums.*

162. **Jug.** Earthenware, under-glaze printed in blue, with the name of the view 'Shrewsbury' in a cartouche on the base. No other mark (compare border with Plate 165), about 1820. (See page 69.) Height to top of handle $9\frac{5}{8}$ inches. *The City of Liverpool Museums.*

163. **Cup and Saucer.** Earthenware, under-glaze printed in blue. No mark, but from the same service as a marked example in Chicago, 1810–1815. (See page 70.) Diameter of saucer $5\frac{1}{4}$ inches. *The City of Liverpool Museums.*

164A and 164B. **Plate.**
Earthenware, under-glaze
printed in blue with
pierced edge and under-
glaze painted lining. Marked
as shown on Plate 164B
(see Appendix I), about
1825. (See pages 68 and
69.) Diameter 10 inches.
*The City of Liverpool
Museums.*

165. **Meat Dish.** Earthenware, under-glaze printed in blue with the
printed mark 'Stone China' and impressed 'HERCULANEUM'/20. The view on the
dish is of Oxford. About 1820. (See page 69.) Length 21½ inches. *The
City of Liverpool Museums.*

166A and 166B. **Plate and Toy Plate.** Earthenware, under-glaze printed in blue. The plate is in a very deep blue depicting 'The Flight into Egypt'. Both pieces are marked as in Plate 166B, about 1825. (See pages 68 and 69.) Diameter of plate 10 inches, toy plate 4½ inches. *The City of Liverpool Museums.*

167A and 167B. **Plate.** Earthenware, under-glaze printed in blue with a sporting scene. Mark of a 'Liver Bird' as in Plate 167B about 1830. (See page 69.) Diameter 10 inches. *The City of Liverpool Museums.*

168.   **Bowl.** Earthenware, crudely printed in under-glaze blue with a view of Oxford inside. Marked 'Oxford' in a cartouche. No other mark, 1825–1830. (See page 69.) Diameter 13¼ inches. *The City of Liverpool Museums.*

169.   **Bowl.** Earthenware, under-glaze printed in blue with views of Cambridge.   Marked 'Cambridge' in a cartouche and impressed HERCULANEUM 1820–1825. (See page 69.) Overall length including handles 11¾ inches. *The City of Liverpool Museums.*

170A and 170B. **Tureen Stand.** Earthenware, underglaze printed in blue with a Chinese scene and with a printed mark underneath called 'Pekin Palm', about 1830. (See Appendix I and page 88.) Length 16 inches. Height of mark $1\frac{5}{8}$ inches. *The City of Liverpool Museums.*

171.   **Cake Stand, Tureen and Dish.** Earthenware, under-glaze printed in sepia, all the pieces being marked with the 'Liver Bird', about 1835. (See page 87.) Length of stand 9 inches. Height of tureen 7 inches. *The City of Liverpool Museums.*

172.   **Tureen.** Earthenware, under-glaze printed in black with views of the Duke of Bridgewater's Warehouse, Liverpool (see page 87). Mark impressed 'Liver Bird'. Overall length $12\frac{1}{2}$ inches. Height 5 inches. *Colonel B. Blewitt, Neston, Cheshire.*

173A and 173B. **Tureen Stand.** Earthenware, under-glaze printed in black with a sporting scene. The printed cartouche is shown where the print lies over the impressed 'Liver Bird', about 1830. (See page 88.) Length 13 inches. *Warrington Museum, Lancashire.*

. **Plate.** Earthen-
e, under-glaze printed
sepia with hand-
ied pink, pale green
gilding. Marked
nch Scenery' in a
ted cartouche and im-
sed with the 'Liver
'. (See page 87.)
neter 10½ inches.
'er Collection, Stoke-
on-Trent.

175A and 175B. **Jug.**
Earthenware, under-glaze
printed both inside and out
in black and incised in the
base 'February 14th. 1837
Charles Dale Maker Hercu-
laneum Pottery near Liverpool'. (See page 86 and compare Plate 179.) Height to
top of handle 13 inches. *The
City of Liverpool Museums.*

176. **Mug.** Earthenware, under-glaze printed in sepia with 'Railway' subjects and a view of Nelson's Monument in Exchange Flags, Liverpool (see page 87). Black lining. No mark, about 1833. Height $4\frac{3}{4}$ inches. Diameter $4\frac{7}{8}$ inches. *The City of Liverpool Museums.*

177. **Shaving Mug.** Earthenware, under-glaze printed in sepia with black lining, showing various 'Railway' subjects (see page 87). No mark, about 1833. Height with cover $5\frac{1}{4}$ inches. Diameter $5\frac{1}{2}$ inches. *The City of Liverpool Museums*

178. **Plate.** Earthenware, under-glaze printed in sepia with a view of the River Mersey and its shipping (see page 86). Mark impressed 'Liver Bird', about 1835. Length $10\frac{1}{2}$ inches. *The City of Liverpool Museums.*

179.   **Meat Dish.** Earthenware, under-glaze printed in black with a view of Castle Street, Liverpool (see page 86). Impressed 'Liver Bird' mark. This design is also known in sepia and blue. About 1835. Length 20½ inches. *The City of Liverpool Museums.*

180.   **Print of Castle Street, Liverpool.** Engraved by E. Wallis from the drawing by T. Harwood, from *Lancashire Illustrated* published in London in 1832. (See page 86.) *The City of Liverpool Museums.*

181. **Two Plates and Two Engravings.** Earthenware plates, under-glaze printed in sepia with scenes in Liverpool adapted from the engravings illustrated below. The scenes are 'Seacombe Slip' and 'St. Paul's Church' from *Lancashire Illustrated*, 1832. Both plates are impressed with the 'Liver Bird'. (See page 86.) Diameter of plates 10 inches. *The City of Liverpool Museums.*

182. **Bowl.** Earthenware, under-glaze printed in blue of the ferry over the River Mersey at Birkenhead (see page 86). No mark. Diameter $10\frac{1}{2}$ inches. Height $4\frac{1}{2}$ inches. *Williamson Art Gallery, Birkenhead.*

183. **Jug.** Cream-ware, Transfer-printed in black with a silver lustre decorated neck, the prints being enamelled in yellow, red and green. Probably Herculaneum, but unmarked, about 1815. Height 8½ inches. (See page 70.) *Henry Francis du Pont Museum, Winterthur, Delaware.*

184. **Vase.** Buff earthenware body with transfer-printed design in red/brown and silver resist lustre decoration. Unmarked but probably Herculaneum. (See page 70.) Height 4½ inches. *The City of Liverpool Museums.*

185. **Jug.** Earthenware with silver resist lustre decoration inscribed 'Ex Dona (sic) of T. Hatton To William Halliday Everton Coffee House' (see page 70). Probably Herculaneum, about 1815. Height 7¾ inches. *The City of Liverpool Museums.*

186. **Plate.** Pearl
ware, decorated in
under-glaze 'Pratt' type
colours and blue edg
ing (see page 61). No
mark, about 1800.
Diameter 9¾ inches. *By
permission of the
Syndics of the Fitz
william Museum, Cam
bridge.*

187. **Mug.** Earthen
ware with slip marble
and turned decoration.
Probably Herculaneum
(see page 70 and Ap
pendix III). No mark
about 1810. Height 5
inches. *The City of
Liverpool Museums.*

Herculaneum Lustrewares and Other Miscellaneous Pieces

188A and **188B. Jug.** Sage-green earthenware with added gilding, the rare mark being illustrated, about 1835. (See page 75.) Height 8 inches. *The City of Liverpool Museums.*

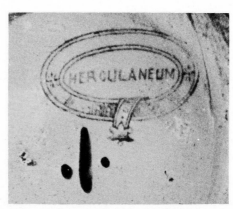

189A and **189B. Vase.** Earthenware, decorated with coloured glazes and under-glaze painting. The mark appears in Plate 189B. This piece is similar to several others in this manner and is discussed on page 88. Height 6¼ inches. *Private Collection.*

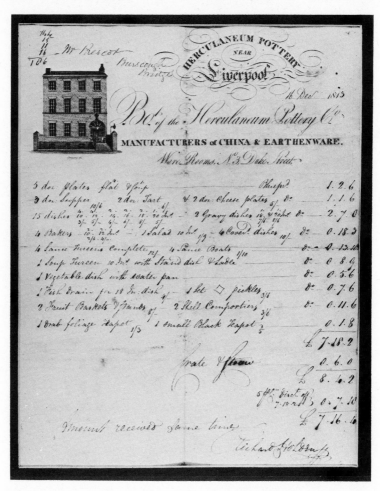

190. **Bill of Goods** sold to Mr. Prescot of Burscough Bridge, Lancashire, on December 16th, 1813, by the Herculaneum Pottery. (See page 55.) *The City of Liverpool Museums.*

191. **The Herculaneum Pottery** from a watercolour dated 1808 by J. Edmondson. The painting is only known through an old photograph of it. (See page 29.) *Liverpool Public Record Office.*

for Liverpool Corporation, dated 1809, in underglaze-blue and on-glaze enamelled red, with gilding (Plate 150). The Liverpool Coat of Arms is also included in its own reserve, printed in outline and enamelled in colours, and the same embellishment appears on another corporation tureen of a few years later (Plate 149). This in its turn is matched by the enormous 23-inch plate in Liverpool Museum, purchased from a Merseyside family (Plate 152). These large meat dishes, often with matching drainers, were amongst the best of the Herculaneum earthenwares, robust, bold and full of confidence. Some are known, in a variety of sizes, which are entirely filled with flowers and leaves in a semi-formal pattern (Plate 151), a style of design which appears on no other factory wares. An example of this pattern was recently found in western Spain, and it is interesting to note that on February 8th, 1814 the Herculaneum Committee decided, in considering a quantity of unsaleable stock, to ship

'. . . two or more parcels as may be most convenient for the Lisbon market or any other that may be thought advisable.'

Indian designs, so popular in the early nineteenth century, occur in many versions amongst the Herculaneum blue-printed, and one particular print was used on a mug, a meat dish, a dining plate and a bed pan! (Plates 158 and 159). The richest and most dynamic blue-printed Indian design the author has ever seen is on a 20-inch meat dish (Colour Plate IV). The Willow pattern, in several forms, was also used by our Toxteth potters (Plates 156 and 157).

One other under-glaze blue pattern brings this section to a close (Plates 160 and 161). It is a classical design, composed of Greek figures, chariots and other decorative motifs in white on a blue ground and is often referred to as 'Etruscan'. The only other factory producing this style was that of Josiah Spode, with whom the Herculaneum works had extensive dealings (see page 56), but on the authority of Spode experts these pieces are certainly not from that Staffordshire factory. Plates, jugs and breakfast sets are known in this manner, with a drab, almost khaki enamelled edge, but not a single piece has ever been recorded which is marked. The nearest positive identification is a jug at Liverpool with reserves bearing the arms of the City of Chester, printed and outlined in that typical chocolate brown used on other wares at Herculaneum. It may safely be said that this particular design, in a brilliant blue softened by the glaze, was used at Toxteth about 1810.

E

Chapter IV

Trade Overseas

From the circumstances surrounding the establishment of Herculaneum described in Chapters II and III it is clear that the hopes of success of the enterprise depended very largely upon the exploitation of overseas markets. The facilities afforded by the dock at the works, lying as it did directly alongside the neighbouring Liverpool docks where ships were coming and going to and from the markets of the world, gave the Herculaneum potters an enormous advantage over their Staffordshire competitors. The surviving account books give us some idea of the destinations of much of the produce, both to other English coastal towns and abroad. Supplied by the coastal trade alone we find that the factory had agents in London, Newcastle, Hull, Falmouth, Dumfries, Greenock, Glasgow, Paisley, Belfast, Dublin, Drogheda, Waterford and Sligo. In countries outside the British Isles we find such agents as John Albro, Thomas Leonard and Carritt and Alport, all of Halifax, Nova Scotia; E. le Page of Prince Edward Island; Edward Bouwman of Rotterdam; Jose de B. Lima of Oporto and Joachim Jose de Sequeira, both of Portugal; Thomas Meager of St. John's, Newfoundland; Ezekiel Hart of Three Rivers, Canada; George Pozer of Quebec; W. H. Richards of Philadelphia and Adam Omholt of Norway. These were all established agents who, to judge from the records, had settled accounts with the factory and no doubt acted as distributing dealers in their particular areas. Most pottery, however, was exported by direct negotiation with ships' captains and Liverpool export agents such as Cropper Benson and Co., who knew the markets to which goods other than pottery were traded. In certain cases the trading was carried on under the general heading of 'Speculation Account' and the following entries from 1808 and 1815 give us some idea of this type of commerce:

| January 22 | 1808 | To earthenware for 4 crates shipped per the 'Prince of Wales' for the Brazils |
| March 19 | 1808 | To earthenware for 5 crates shipped per the 'Mary' for Malta |

May 20	1808	To earthenware for 5 crates shipped per the 'Ellis' for the Brazils
May 20	1808	
August 26	1808	To earthenware for 20 packages shipped per the 'Robert' for Halifax
May 10	1815	To earthenware for 6 crates shipped per 'The True Briton' for Calcutta.

It would be tedious to list all the details of the 77 entries in the accounts of shipments abroad from Herculaneum for the single year 1806-1807 but the total quantities of these shipments are represented by 1,763 crates, 208 tierces, 31 casks, 21 packages, 12 hogsheads and 2 boxes, and the cost amounted to approximately £10,650. By a very rough calculation this figure must account for an absolute minimum of 200,000 pieces of pottery, even allowing for elaborately decorated wares which sold at about three shillings each (see page 38). One of the largest single shipments was on March 16th, 1807 when 80 crates were loaded on board the ship 'George Augustus' containing pottery invoiced at £509 18s. 4d. This vessel, according to *Lloyd's Register*, was commanded by J. Jackson and bound for Charleston in North Carolina. A shipment of 206 tierces at a value of £680 14s. 2d on May 30th, 1807 was the largest delivery for that year, carried on board the 'Addelina' which is known to have been trading between Liverpool and Massachusetts. The difficulty in tracing the records of these ships is that so many had the same names, but *The Liverpool Chronicle* for 1807 lists, amongst many others, the following vessels departing from the port with cargoes of pottery found in the corresponding entries in the Herculaneum accounts:

December 2 1806
The American Ship
RHODA & BETSY (270 tons)   for *New York*   { 1 box 2 crates
                                                      { £25 15s. 3d.

January 7 and 15 1807
The Fast Sailing American Ship
MANCHESTER PACKET (250 tons) for *New York*   { 50 crates
                                                     { £251 10s. 6d.

September 21 1807
The Fine New American Ship
WESTERN TRADER (390 tons)   for *Philadelphia* { 70 crates
                                                     { £384 5s. 10d.

February 14 1807
The American Ship
ENTERPRISE (240 tons)   for *Wilmington*   { 31 crates
                                                     { £189 1s. 10d.

March 5 1807
For Freight or Charter the Fine American Ship
GRAND SACHEM (250 tons)   for *New York*   { 3 crates
                                                     { £14 16s. 5d.

February 24 1807
The American Ship
NEW PACKET (350 tons)   for *Boston*   { 50 crates
                                                     { £218 16s. 11d.

April 30 1807
The American Ship   ⎰91 crates
AVERICK (322 tons)   for *Virginia*   ⎱£409 18s. 1d.

April 2 1807
The Fine American Brig   ⎰2 crates
WASHINGTON (170 tons)   for *Boston*   ⎱£10 4s. 11d.

September 15 1807
The Brig   ⎰2 tierces
MARIA (137 tons)   for *New Providence*   ⎱£10 6s.

June 30 1807
The Ship   ⎰17 crates 1 Hhd.
LATONA (240 tons)   First ship for *New Orleans*   ⎱£154 16s. 2d.

March 20 1807
The Fine American Ship   ⎰35 crates
ELIZA (355 tons)   First ship for *Savannah*   ⎱£127 0s. 7d.
                                             (*Georgia*)

July 31 1807
The Fine Fast Sailing American Ship   ⎰52 crates
MOSES BROWN (300 tons)   for *Charleston*   ⎱£267 5s. 10d.
(see page 59)

July 2 1807
The American Ship   daily expected from New Orleans

PERSEVERANCE (350 tons) and will immediately load   ⎰11 crates
                                       for *Philadelphia*   ⎱£56 18s. 3d.

July 18 1807
The American Ship   ⎰24 casks
JUNO (346 tons)   for *Boston*   ⎱£159 3s. 11d.

September 5 and 9 1807
The American Ship   ⎰6 crates
JOHN (no tonnage given)   for *Charleston*   ⎱£30 8s. 8d.

March 13 and 18 1807
The American Brig   ⎰44 crates
BEDFORD (200 tons)   for *New York*   ⎱£211 10s. 2d.

August 3 1807
The Fast Sailing American Ship   ⎰4 crates
ROVER (200 tons)   for *New Orleans*   ⎱£23 12s.

October 13 1807
The Ship   will take in goods for *Black River*   ⎰19 crates
ST. MARY'S PLANTER   *Blue Fields*   ⎱£132 9s. 9d.
   (no tonnage given)   and *Savannah La Mar*
                                       (*Georgia and Virginia*)

The dates given in the above entries are those provided in the account ledgers and are not the dates of sailings. From the number of times the same advertisement is given, week after week, in *The Liverpool Chronicle*, the ships must have lain in the docks in some cases for many months until complete cargoes had been gathered together and the ships prepared for sailing. The following is a typical complete advertisement for the ship 'George Augustus' and it was printed in *The Liverpool Chronicle* for March 4th, 1807:

For CHARLESTON
(To succeed the Julius Caesar)
The New American Ship
GEORGE AUGUSTUS
JOSEPH JACKSON Master

Burthen 300 tons, a ship of the first class, and a very prime sailer, is now taking on board her cargo and will positively sail the ensuing Springs; has superior accommodation for passengers. For terms apply to the Captain on board, King's Dock, or   W. LEES.

It will be noted that nearly all the ships quoted were American, sailing for America, but there are many more in the Herculaneum ledgers which it has not been possible to trace and which were, presumably, bound for other countries and plying the coastal trade of the British Isles. Shipments for the year 1808 from Herculaneum were also very high, totalling in value exactly £10,240 os. 10d. but by this time, as we shall see, hardly any of these exports were destined for the United States.

The extremely high figures for these years in all probability mark the most lucrative period for Herculaneum in the export trade, but this successful enterprise was destined to be sharply reduced from December 1807 until and during the war with America of 1812, which lasted until 1814. The reason for this loss of trade was the circumstances surrounding the Napoleonic wars. Throughout the period Britain and France waged commercial as well as military warfare against each other, by a series of Decrees and Orders in Council starting in 1806. In 1807 a British Decree forbade American trade with any country from which British trade was excluded, unless duty was paid previously at British ports! The United States' reply to this measure was to issue an embargo forbidding trade to Britain or France from its own ports, and although this embargo was clearly harmful to its own merchants and shippers it was nevertheless continued until the conclusion of the War of 1812.

As we have seen from the Herculaneum trading figures for the year 1808 the embargo must have been difficult to enforce in the first place, but the ultimate effect this had on the export of pottery from Herculaneum may be judged by the following extract from the *Committee Minute Book*. Not only does this make the position clear but by inference it also shows that the American market had been regarded as a very important outlet for the wares.

Report of the Committee to the Proprietors
Friday, November 25th, 1808

Your Committee take the liberty of observing that altho' the Hopes and Expectations which your Committee entertained at the last Annual Meeting of extending and increasing the Commercial Trade and Interest of the Herculaneum Manufactory were damped by the Embargo on the Trade and Commerce of the United States of America with this country which took place about the commencement of the present year (and which still continues) yet the exertions of your Committee were not abated by that Event and it became the study and attention of your Committee to find out and obtain Orders for the sale of the Ware through different channels of Commerce; and your Committee have the pleasure of observing that the sales at the Pottery for the last Twelve Months (notwithstanding the causes before noticed) are nearly the amount of sales made in the Preceding Year; and whenever the Intercourse and Trade with America and this Country shall be again happily renewed, the consequent advantages which the Herculaneum Pottery Company may reasonably expect to derive from such renewal of commerce are too obvious to need further remark. . . .

More will be said about the American trade later in this chapter.

By 1814 the war with America was ended and in the following year the Napoleonic wars also came to a conclusion at Waterloo. The first of the two surviving *Account Books** only continues until 1817 and we do not, unfortunately, know to what extent the foreign trade recovered in the years that followed. In 1824 the second *Account Book* begins and we can judge from the names of the pottery agents that there was still a lively trade with various towns throughout the British Isles and also with Spain, Canada, Italy, Barbadoes and Antigua. From the advertisement of the sale of the pottery of October 31st 1840† we learn that trade continued until the end with agents in the United States, Canada, South America, Africa, and the East Indies, but from the names of British agents listed in the books we can only conclude that these markets were served through the British merchants and exporters, and that the early practice of embarking consignments directly from the factory, partly on a speculative basis, had considerably diminished.

Like any large factory of the day the retailing side of the Herculaneum business was handled partly through a privately owned saleroom/warehouse and partly directly from the works. Near the docks in Liverpool there were, in fact, two warehouses, the first one being referred to in the advertisement of 1798 (see page 20) on the east side of Salthouse Dock, and the second one we know to have been opened in Redcross Street, on the east side of the Dry Dock, in 1812. The large and fashionable Duke Street Warehouse was, however, the principal 'shop window' for the factory and this establishment

* Liverpool Record Office, *Herculaneum Account Books*.
† *Staffordshire Advertiser*.

is mentioned many times in the Committee proceedings (see Appendix II). The building was a Georgian house at the lower end of Duke Street (see engraving on the Bill Heading Plate 190) in the possession of one Mr. Gregson, and it was taken by the Committee for a period of twenty-one years commencing March 3rd, 1807. Alterations to the building were immediately begun and in May of the same year the first salesman or warehouseman, Mr. William Reeves, was appointed. By November 1807 the report of the Committee to the shareholders stated that 'the Ware Rooms have been compleated and fitted up in a superior style of elegance under the direction of your Committee and opened for the Sale of China and Earthenware and a person engaged to superintend and manage that particular department, And your Committee have great pleasure in stating that the sales of China and Earthenware which have been made at the Ware Rooms since the opening on the 1st day of June last have fully answered their most sanguine expectations. . . .' The designing of the new showroom interiors and general arrangement of the building was evidently done in the most fashionable style of the day, inspired no doubt by some of the potters' showrooms in London, such as Wedgwood's or that of Abbott and Mist where Turner's wares were sold. George Bullock, a modeller and sculptor of Liverpool, undertook the work, and we can guess at the style of his designs from the address of his business at the 'Greek Rooms' in Bold Street. The Duke Street Warehouse continued as the major retailing establishment of Herculaneum until the termination of the original proprietorship in 1833 (see page 73) when a retail shop was opened in the Clarendon Buildings, South John Street. According to J. A. Picton* the warehouse and showrooms in Duke Street were subsequently occupied as a military barracks and were later demolished to make way for the storage warehouses which stand on the site today.

The business of the Duke Street Warehouse was not confined to the selling of wares made at the Toxteth factory, but it also acted as a retailing establishment for pottery from many Staffordshire manufacturers who must have found it very convenient to employ such an agency in the busy seaport of Liverpool. Business with Staffordshire potters is mentioned in Chapter III (see page 31) and from the evidence available we know that the following firms sent earthenware and china, in varying quantities, for sale through the Herculaneum warehouse:

William ADAMS & Son	Cobridge
J. & E. BADDELEY	Shelton
William BAILEY & Co	Lane End
John BARKER & Co	Lane End
William BOURNE & Co	Burslem
CHEETHAM & WOOLEY	Lane End
Samuel GINDER & Co	Lane Delph

* J. A. Picton, *Memorials of Liverpool*, 1875, Vol. II, page 267.

HACKWOOD, DIMMOCK & Co ....Hanley
HENSHALL & WILLIAMSON ....Longport
HICKS & MEIGH ....Shelton
Thomas HOLLAND ....Burslem
James KEELING ....Hanley
LOCKETT & Co ....Lane End
Miles MASON & Co ....Lane Delph
MINTON & POULSON ....Stoke
J. & W. RIDGWAY ....Shelton
John & George ROGERS ....Longport
SHORTHOSE & HEATH ....Hanley
Josiah SPODE ....Stoke
STEVENSON & GOODWIN ....Cobridge
WOOD & CALDWELL ....Burslem
John & William YATES.......................Shelton

Of these manufacturers the one sending the largest amounts of his wares to the Duke Street Warehouse was Josiah Spode, and some idea of the quantities involved may be judged by the following figures of the values of china and earthenware handled by Herculaneum over several years:

1807 Purchased from Josiah Spode by Herculaneum £126 19s. 7d.
1808   ,,   ,,   ,,   ,,   ,,   ,,   £606 7s. 1d.
1809   ,,   ,,   ,,   ,,   ,,   ,,   £1,226 10s. 9d.
1810   ,,   ,,   ,,   ,,   ,,   ,,   £1,541 6s. 1d.
1811   ,,   ,,   ,,   ,,   ,,   ,,   £892 5s. 8d.
1812   ,,   ,,   ,,   ,,   ,,   ,,   £196 17s. 5d.
1813   ,,   ,,   ,,   ,,   ,,   ,,   £286 5s. 1d.
1814   ,,   ,,   ,,   ,,   ,,   ,,   £65 15s. 3d.
1815   ,,   ,,   ,,   ,,   ,,   ,,   £98 19s. 3d.
1816   ,,   ,,   ,,   ,,   ,,   ,,   £25 7s. 10d.

Just why the trade should have reached its peak in the years 1809–1810 and then fallen almost completely away by 1816 is not fully known, but this might well be accounted for by Spode having found alternative outlets for his wares. It is equally possible that the nationwide recession in trade had its effects also, when manufacturers would prefer to reduce their costs by cutting out commission paid to outside agents. By 1820 the Duke Street Warehouse was retailing glass made by Thomas Hawkes and Co. of Dudley, Worcestershire, since business in china and earthenware alone was on the decline, and it seems that the running of the warehouse became increasingly dissociated from the factory as time went on, and their accounting became entirely separated. In *The Albion* account, however, of 1827 (see page 106) the showrooms in Duke Street were still referred to as the place to see the factory products in addition to the 'Pattern Room' at the works.

IV. MEAT DISH. Earthenware, transfer-printed in underglaze blue. Impressed HERCULANEUM. c.1815. Overall length 20″. *Courtesy of The City of Liverpool Museums.*

The Wares

No account of the Herculaneum factory would be complete without suitable reference being made to the pottery produced for the American market, and the following section is primarily concerned with these wares. Of creamware jugs or 'pitchers' as our American friends prefer to call them, there are far more in public and private collections in the United States than can now be found in England, and of much finer quality and enterprise of design. This, of course, is a natural consequence of the tremendous amount of pottery exported from Herculaneum in its early years, and no study of this type of ware can be in any sense complete without a comparison being made between this export material and pottery made for the home market.

Two of the largest collections of transfer-printed pottery in the United States are to be found in the Peabody Museum at Salem, Massachusetts and the Smithsonian Institution in Washington D.C. The Washington collection was assembled by Robert H. McCauley and his book *Liverpool Transfer Designs on Anglo-American Pottery* must remain for many years to come the most complete catalogue available of the various designs made by English potters and engravers for use on wares destined for the American market. Mr. McCauley has said, however, that it would be 'manifestly impossible' to 'distinguish between pottery made in the Liverpool district and pottery produced in other parts of England'* and we do not altogether agree with this statement for it has been possible to identify with certainty a fair number of these pots as having been made at Herculaneum. This is equally true as far as the very extensive collections at the Peabody Museum are concerned, where about a hundred and ninety pieces may be seen, many of which are exceptionally fine. There is scarcely a museum on the eastern seaboard of the United States without at least a few examples of transfer-printed creamware, to say nothing of such important collections as those at the Art Institute of Chicago, the Henry Ford Museum at Dearborn or the William Rockhill Nelson Gallery of Art in Kansas City.

Identification of Herculaneum wares made for America has been achieved in two principal ways, firstly by carefully noting the engraved designs used on *marked* Herculaneum pieces and secondly by comparing prints on marked pieces made for the English market, with unmarked examples in America. Where line-for-line identity of prints can be established this method is clearly valid, for although similar designs were used in various English factories early in the nineteenth century, and many designs were engraved several times as the plates wore out, one can safely assume that no two potteries would have used *the same copper plate*, particularly as the Staffordshire potteries were geographically a considerable distance from Liverpool. At the same time we have seen that all the possible competitors in Liverpool who could have produced such wares were finished by about 1805, and may

* R. H. McCauley, *Liverpool Transfer Designs on Anglo-American Pottery*, Portland, Maine, 1942. Preface, page viii.

therefore be disregarded in the case of the many pieces made after this date. There is still, of course, the chance that Staffordshire creamwares could have been sent to Herculaneum for the application of printed decoration, but this is very unlikely because by the last few years of the eighteenth century the Staffordshire potters had begun to print their own pottery, and creamware was one of the staple products of Herculaneum in its early days. By all this we do not mean to imply that *all* the American wares were made at Herculaneum, but we can show that all those illustrated here, and many others in American collections not illustrated, were from our Toxteth factory.

The range of prints produced for the American market by Herculaneum was very large indeed and examples may be seen in Plates 43, 44, 45, 46, 47, 49, 50, 52, 53, 54, 55, 56, 57, 58, 59, 60, 61, 63, 64, 65. It is interesting to see how our English potters, in the interests of trade, produced designs which were politically almost treasonable! There was, for example, the large range of prints commemorating Washington's death in 1799 which include such legends as 'In Memory of the Immortal Washington whose Patriotism and Military Exploits in the service of his Country will be admired by Posterity' (Plate 43) or another commemorating the patriotism of those Americans who 'Nobly dared to assert their rights and succeeded in emancipating their country from the tyranny of its oppressors and laid the foundation of a great EMPIRE on its natural bassis [sic] LIBERTY'. Nothing could be more anti-British than the print, bearing the legend 'By Virtue and Valour we have freed our country, extended our commerce and laid the foundation of a great Empire', in which an American soldier is seen standing with his foot on the head of the British Lion (Plate 44).

In the Mattatuck Museum at Waterbury, Connecticut, and in the Henry Francis du Pont Museum at Winterthur, Delaware, there are some splendid large jugs which can be identified as from Herculaneum by matching the floral prints and a decorative cartouche with other known pieces. Their principal decoration is a print recording the defence of Stonington, Connecticut, in 1814, the full inscription of which reads 'The Gallant Defence of Stonington, August 9th, 1814. Stonington is free whilst her Heroes have one gun left.' The history of this particular action is that the town was attacked by the British Navy in 1814 and the defenders successfully resisted and sank one British ship. The jugs themselves are splendid examples of creamware (Plate 65) and the application of such an anti-British subject did not, apparently, upset the Herculaneum potters at all when it was imperative to re-capture the overseas market at the end of the War of 1812.

Another Herculaneum jug bearing prints with political overtones is one in the Smithsonian Institution (Plates 45A and B) decorated with the 'Farmers Arms', the 'Farmyard' (see page 24) and a cartoon relating to the difficulties of the embargo on American trade during the wars between England and France. It will be remembered that the American reply to the British embargo, decreed by President Jefferson (1801–1809), was to forbid all American trade with Britain and France, and the cartoon is directed against Jefferson, showing him milking an American cow (of commerce) while John Bull holds its horns

and Buonaparte pulls its tail! This cartoon was originally produced by the engraver James Akin who was born about 1773 in South Carolina and eventually worked in Philadelphia, Salem and Newburyport. A biography of this artist and an account of his work may be seen in Nina Fletcher Little's article published in 1938;* another Akin cartoon which she describes at length appears on a Herculaneum jug in the Peabody Museum, Salem.

The cartoon by James Akin referred to here (Plate 46) is entitled 'Infuriated Despondency—A Droll Scene in Newbury Port', and this print is worth mentioning in some detail partly because of the amusing subject matter and partly because it appears on this jug in the company of prints connected with *English* historical events and institutions. Beneath the spout is a fine rendering of the 'Coopers Arms' which is matched by exactly the same print on a Herculaneum marked jug in the Smithsonian Institution in Washington (Plate 56). Another of the prints shows Nelson's victory at the Battle of the Nile in 1798 and on the other side is a ship print of the vessel *Merremack*. Inserted underneath the Nile print, lying on its side instead of upright is the figure of Edmund March Blunt in the act of hurling a skillet (saucepan). Edmund M. Blunt was an important mathematician, nautical instrument maker, printer and author, who quarrelled with Akin over the payment for some maps which Akin had engraved for him. When Akin slapped Blunt's face the latter snatched the nearest weapon available and threw it at Akin's head. As luck would have it the skillet missed Akin but went through the window of the shop and hit one Nicholas Brown, a prominent Newburyport citizen, as he was walking by. This 'droll scene' inspired Akin not only to publish a broadsheet song describing the event but also to engrave the ludicrous figure of Blunt which we see on the jug. To make sure that the print and story would be well circulated Akin's friend Nicholas Brown, when he next went to England, had it printed on jugs, bowls and 'vessels of less esteem'† which were then sent back to Newburyport to be sold in large numbers. Blunt, of course, was outraged by this insult and he and his friends broke these pots whenever they found them. The one illustrated here was able to escape this treatment because it was that made especially for Nicholas Brown's own use; it bore the print of the ship *Merremack* of which his uncle, Moses Brown, was the Master.

Both the Merremack jug and the marked Herculaneum one at Washington (linked with the Coopers Arms print) were elaborately decorated with 'cold' gilding as well as being copiously embellished with prints. This treatment seems frequently to have been added to pieces made for America (see also Plate 60) but has rarely been noted on purely 'English' wares. The cheap use of gilding in this way, by applying gold on a cold glue size instead of firing and burnishing it in the usual way was a most unsatisfactory and impermanent method, and the gold on most of these pieces is now badly damaged by wear

---

* Nina Fletcher Little, *The Cartoons of James Akin upon Liverpool Ware* published in *The Bulletin of the Society for the Preservation of New England Antiquities*, Vol. XXVIII, No. 3, January 1938.

† Nina Fletcher Little, *ibid*.

and has also gone dark or even black in some cases. It was, however, cheap and speedy to produce and was sufficiently bright and gaudy to appeal to the purchasers of those times. In fairness to the potters we must add that these jugs were almost certainly intended as decorative and presentation pieces and therefore not subject to the rigours of everyday use, and when Herculaneum potters wished to produce good gilding, fired and burnished, they could do it to perfection, as may be seen on the 'Defence of Stonington' jug at Waterbury mentioned earlier.

Although printing on Herculaneum creamware for the American market has been stressed inasmuch as most pieces were decorated in this way, excellent examples of *hand-enamelled* decoration may be found from time to time. We have already noted the fine jug in Chicago (Chapter II, page 25) and very splendid examples survive in such specimens as the Herculaneum marked pitcher in the Peabody Museum, Salem, on which the ship 'OROZIMBO of BALTIMORE' is completely enamelled, not printed as might be thought at first glance (Plate 47). This might, indeed, be thought of as an individual ship portrait rather than a run-of-the-mill print appropriately named. The jug is decorated also with a fine enamelled border round the neck, similar to that on the jug inscribed 'Success to Mold Cotton Mill'* which is in Liverpool Museum (Plate 48), as well as completely enamelled decoration on other pieces elsewhere. Such enamelled specimens are remarkable achievements whatever their aesthetic merits may be, and we would go so far as to say that no other English pottery produced better work of this type than Herculaneum.

The identification of unmarked pieces by exactly matching prints has been stressed in this chapter because it is an important field of research which, for the period of Herculaneum, has been relatively neglected. In Chapter III we have already met a fine large jug in Liverpool Museum with multiple prints (Plates 36A and B, page 39) which may be used as a 'catalogue' for further research. In the Philadelphia Museum of Art, Pennsylvania, there is another such jug, of proved Herculaneum origin, in which the prints used are to be found on wares made for both the English and American markets (Plates 49 and 52). This magnificent specimen is immediately linked to the marked Herculaneum jug at Liverpool (Plates 30A and B) through the matching flower sprays, one of which may be found on the 'Robert Roberts' jug in conjunction with the Joseph Johnson signed 'Farmyard' print (Plate 68B). At the same time a well-known cartouche on other Herculaneum jugs (see Plates 51 and 65) surrounds the inscription 'Presented to the Cumberland Engine Society No. 8 by Wm. Loring', and we have a portrait of James Maddison, a version of the American Eagle, three memorial prints to Washington, a map of the United States and the figures of Faith, Hope and Charity. This is a superb jug, 15 inches high, of ample proportions and splendidly decorated. It reflects the confidence of the Herculaneum potters in the early years of the factory's life.

---

* Mold is a small town in the North Wales county of Flintshire, within easy reach of Liverpool. Much Liverpool pottery was sold in North Wales.

A list of subjects used for decoration on pottery for the American market would be too long to itemise here and the reader may be referred to R. H. McCauley's book for comparative pieces.* Briefly we might mention at least eight prints dedicated to the memory of the immortal Washington, several portraits of other American presidents and heroes, maps of Newburyport Harbour and Lafayette's plan of the new capital of Washington (Plate 55), various emblems of America, subjects symbolising 'Liberty' in the new republic, patriotic prints of all kinds and designs dedicated to 'Peace', 'Prosperity', 'Independence' and 'Commerce'. This was a rewarding field for the Herculaneum engravers who did their utmost to keep in touch with the social and political events of the day, and they did so to a much greater extent as far as America was concerned than for the home market.

Compared with the vast quantities of creamware made at Herculaneum which are to be found in American collections there is very little or nothing of the other branches of the potting trade in which we know Herculaneum was involved. Some pearlware decorated with underglaze painting of birds and sponged decoration, almost always blue-edged, is found here and there (Plate 186). It probably came from our factory and developed into the 'gaudy Dutch' which is so characteristic of later English wares made for America. Blue-printed wares are found and occasional specimens of porcelain, but there is no significant difference between these and the wares made for home consumption, and they are dealt with elsewhere in this book. It is entirely in the field of transfer-printed creamwares that the Herculaneum potters made their unique contribution across the Atlantic, and the best examples of these are very fine indeed.

* R. H. McCauley, *ibid*.

Chapter V

Problems and Change 1820–1833

In spite of the difficulties of the Napoleonic Wars, the American embargo and consequent interruption to overseas trade, the years at Herculaneum between 1806 and about 1820 were characterised by steady growth and development, and the output of good quality wares. Towards the early 1820s, however, a shadow began to fall on the factory's affairs and evidence of this is contained in various documents, the most important of which is the *Minute Book of the Committee.** Unfortunately this book ends in 1822 and the whereabouts of the following volume, if indeed it still exists, is unknown; but the evidence of the early 1820s, in the last two years of the record, is enough to show that all was not well.

The first victim of the problems which overtook our factory in these troubled years was the manager William Smith, whose promising career at Toxteth came to a sudden end in 1821. The first we hear of him was his appointment on May 14th, 1807 as Cash and Book Keeper, at a salary of £105 per year, increased in 1809 to £120. In that year he gave his notice to leave but another advance in his salary to £140 must have made him change his mind, and by June 5th, 1810 he was promoted to Acting Manager in the place of Ralph Mansfield who had just died. In 1813 he made an agreement with the Committee for an engagement of seven years at £300 per year and was by then in a very trustworthy position and made a journey to London the following year to engage additional assistants. On December 5th, 1815 the Committee resolved '. . . that 20 guineas be paid to him as a reward for his extra services and as a testimony of the high opinion the Committee entertain for his zeal and attention', and his rising star reached its zenith in 1817 when he made a new agreement to remain as Manager until 1826, at the very high salary of £450 per year. Our next record in his career is not, however, so bright, for on November 26th, 1821 he handed in his resignation.

The resignation of William Smith, was due to a fundamental difference of opinion between himself and the Proprietors on the subject of the share-

* Liverpool Public Record Office, *Herculaneum Pottery, Resolutions of the Committee 1806–22.* H380 MD47 KF295.

holders' dividends. For several years these payments had stood at 4 per cent half-yearly. This was still the case in May 1821 when the Secretary recorded '. . . that in consequence of the increased expenses which the company now sustain in having lately provided an additional number of persons to conduct and superintend the operation of the works . . . ordered that Mr. Smith do lay before the Committee . . . a particular account of all the salaries and remunerations for services performed by the several persons employed . . . specifying their respective names, and the particular services so performed.'

Two months later it was also resolved that 'Mr. Smith do make out an account of the real net cost of each leading article made for sale in the Manufactory' and in November 1821 Mr. Smith '. . . reported to the Committee that in his judgment (as Manager of the concern) the Committee will not be justified in paying the full amount of the usual half-yearly Dividend of 4 per cent out of the profits of the Concern this year.' In view of this opinion the dividends were, in fact, reduced to 3 per cent. But this was not the end of the matter, for a special meeting was shortly called to hear the manager's report, and William Smith's career at Herculaneum ended when he announced to that meeting '. . . that with their acceptance of that report he wished them to understand that he tendered his resignation.'

The quarrel had clearly been hard and bitter, and it is impossible to believe otherwise than that he, as a wise manager, had been fighting the greed of the shareholders from a financial position which was daily becoming more difficult. Nor was the parting pleasant, for an argument dragged on for two or three months over the value and compensation for Mr. Smith's two shares. By a resolution of the meeting held only three days after that just mentioned, Mr. Joseph Tomkinson was appointed to act as manager in his place until further notice. Nothing further is known of William Smith after he left the factory, and perhaps he left the district. The last record we have is the birth of his ninth child at Toxteth in 1822, but as he was married to Phoebe Roper about 1805 it is likely that he was still in the prime of his life.

Joseph Tomkinson was only asked to take up the managership as a temporary measure and Mr. Archibald Mansfield was appointed to the permanent post one month later. At this time things were not too good at the works and it is of interest to read part of a report of January 1st, 1822:

> The Committee this day called in James Ibbs who is the Biscuit Foreman and Superintendent of the Biscuit Warehouse, who stated that he was in November last applied to by Mr. Barlow to account to him for the ware that had been broken—that in consequence of such application he took Mr. Barlow into a room were [sic] the Seconds are usually put, which room a few months after Mr. Barlow first came he also shewed Mr. Barlow—that he then observed to Mr. Barlow the difference of the quantity of ware that there was then at that time and when he first shewed him the room. Ibbs stated that the rest had been broken by the order of Mr. Smith and thrown to the Heap, that he and Hannah Winckle were so employed for several days and on being asked the reason for

such breakage he stated that the ware was so bad in consequence of the defective state of the Moulds and tools, and the slovenly habits of the workmen that it was not fit for use. The quantity of ware so broken he says he cannot now ascertain but he says it was at least from 500 to 1000 dozen. He was then asked as to the proportion of Breakages of ware made since Mr. Barlow came he replied that the proportion was much less in Breakage than ever was before to his knowledge.

John Barlow had come to the works as foreman from Hanley only a year before William Smith's resignation and had obviously not found things as well as they might have been!

Joseph Tomkinson's appointment as manager was only temporary as we have seen; his real responsibility was that of Cash and Book Keeper. A note on his career has been given in Chapter II (page 23) and his departure for America shows that his attempts to remedy deteriorating conditions had not been altogether successful. His pocket book and various other papers, now in Liverpool Museum,* give us hints here and there of the problems with which he was faced, but mostly they show the efforts of a man who was anxious to improve the wares of his factory and at the same time to bring down costs. The Tomkinson papers contain hundreds of recipes for glazes, bodies and frits, some of which are listed in Appendix III, and there is some evidence that either he or one of his colleagues even went to France to seek new ideas on management and costs. In his personal pocket book Joseph Tomkinson wrote the following notes, as though he had been making some comparisons:

France
<hr>

Banks of the Allier—Labourers can live comfortably for 4 or 5 sous a day.

Lyons
<hr>

16 sous a day is reckoned an ample allowance.

Only a few pages before he had scribbled, in now-fading pencil:

1. What am't of capital wd be sufficient to enable us to carry on the Blue business with Credit & Profit.
2. What wd be the probable am't pr year of the sale of blue in the Potteries.
3. What is a fair average of the profits upon the manufactory of blue.
4. What servants do you think you sh'd want in the business.

The date of these entries is 1825 but comparisons with the Staffordshire trade had already been made, even before William Smith's departure, for on August 7th, 1821 it was resolved that:

'Mr. Barlow be directed to take a journey to the Potteries (in Staffordshire) in order to enquire into the prices given there to the various

* For details of the *Tomkinson Papers* see Chapter II, page 23.

V. PLATE. Coalport porcelain, decorated at Herculaneum by Samuel Williams after Thomas Griffiths. No mark. c.1815. Diameter 8¾″. *Courtesy of The City of Liverpool Museums.*

Artists and workmen and also as to what artists and workmen may be proper to engage. . . .'

and after Tomkinson's arrival another such journey was once more taken:

'Resolved that Mr. Holden and Mr. Mansfield do take a journey into Staffordshire to order two sets of copper plates of teaware, to enquire as to Table Services of Blue Ware and to make such observations and obtain the best information of the general manufactories there in their power and report their observations. . . .'

Joseph Tomkinson, as far as we can tell, was a good and conscientious accountant and financial adviser, but the difficulties must have seemed too great for him; swayed also by his religious leanings and aspirations he departed, as we have seen, in 1826. We do not know who succeeded him as Cash and Book Keeper but it might have been his kinsman Benjamin Tomkinson,* whose name appears as the author of a 28 page notebook amongst the papers of Joseph. This notebook, full of pottery and porcelain recipes (including several amusing ones of no particular concern to potters) is dated 1828, two years after Joseph had gone, and is on French notepaper. Several passages and recipes are in French which might indicate an exploratory journey to France and a continuing search for new ideas.

We cannot by any means say that the factory was on the brink of disaster, but the manager and committee clearly had considerable problems at this time. Joseph Tomkinson's records show that in 1824 the profit on the joint accounts of the Herculaneum Pottery and the Duke Street Warehouse was £4,393 14s. 6d. on a total balance sheet (including the invested capital of £30,000) of £56,404 8s. 10d., while in 1825 the profits were £2,500 13s. 7d. on a total balance of £43,505 15s. 5d. These figures for 1824 and 1825 represent a profit of about 8 per cent and nearly 6 per cent respectively, but they do not necessarily show a firm credit of cash in hand because in a portion of the balance sheet of 1824 which has survived we find that *the debts owing to the concern* totalled £21,517 12s. 4d. (£13,773 0s. 5d. at the Duke Street Warehouse and £7,744 11s. 11d. at the Pottery in Toxteth)—an extremely uncomfortable proportion of the assets shown.

The period was indeed one of heart-searching for the shareholders and committee. Both before and after the change of managers in 1821 there had been very detailed investigations into the accounting and staffing of the factory's departments which would appear to have been an attempt to control a situation which had become somewhat out of hand. In the minutes of January 1st, 1822 we can see all the evidence we need of the tightening-up process:

'The Committee having taken into consideration the means requisite to be adopted so as in the most effectual manner to promote the Interest of

---

* The relationship between Joseph and Benjamin Tomkinson is not known but it is not likely that they were father and son. They may have been brothers.

F

the concern . . . resolved that the management be divided into the five following distinct departments, the manager of each to be accountable to the Committee for the due performance of the duties attaching thereto as well as for the conduct of all those acting under him.

1st. Mr. Holden to be the corresponding and Commercial Agent to receive and negotiate for all orders and to manage the sales—to convey to Mr. Mansfield for execution at the Manufactory all contracts and orders—to direct generally as to the quality and patterns of goods requisite to be made for the supply of orders received and also of the Sale Room in Duke Street and to receive thro' Mr. Mansfield orders for such materials as may be requisite for carrying on the Manufactory.

2nd. Mr. Barlow to receive the orders from Mr. Mansfield for goods to be manufactured and to inform him what materials may be wanted—to direct the Potters and the whole process of manufacture, to communicate the cost of every article produced by him to Mr. Mansfield to enable him to state the same to Mr. Holden and the Committee—to keep the time of the Potters and also an exact account of all goods manufactured by him together with any breakage or loss sustained in his department.

3rd. Mr. Tomkinson to act as Book-keeper and Cash Keeper to collect the outstanding debts of the concern for goods sold at the manufactory and to pay the Men's wages and do the Counting House business at the Works.

4ly. Mr. Mansfield to receive from Mr. Holden the orders for goods manufactured and packed, to superintend the Manufactory in all its branches, to dissect the different charges of materials used and work done so as to calculate and communicate to Mr. Holden the cost of goods made, to direct the Crate Makers the receipt and delivery of goods, Materials &c. to adjust the wages before payment to direct the whole Warehouse department and such workmen (not being potters and painters) as are employed on the premises and to be the medium of report and communication as regarding the manufactory to the Committee at their Monthly Meeting.

5ly. Mr. Taylor to direct and superintend the painters, to keep an account of their time and furnish the same to Mr. Mansfield and to receive from him orders for work executed.

From paragraph number 4 we know the manager was now Mr. Mansfield and this appointment is confirmed by other references to his position in later minutes of the Committee. He did not, however, occupy the managerial office for very long, and in 1824, Archibald Mansfield left Herculaneum and started a potworks on his own account in Canning Street off Bevington Bush, Liverpool. Archibald was the son of Ralph Mansfield whom we have met before, and appears to have been born by Ralph's first wife Anne, about

1797. He had certainly left Herculaneum by 1825, for Joseph Tomkinson wrote in his notebook on March 16th of that year:

> 'Spoke to Mr. Roper ab't going to Mr. Mansfield's building and leaving ours he saying he was sick.'

The distance involved would have taken Mr. Roper about forty minutes of very brisk walking so perhaps he, too, was looking for fresh employment.

That Archibald Mansfield should have chosen this period to branch out for himself, is an indication that things were unsettled at Herculaneum. Little is known about this factory in Canning Street apart from certain details to be found in an advertisement which appeared in *The Staffordshire Advertiser* of December 26th, 1840, after his death. The following extract from this at least establishes the scale of the enterprise, though nothing has ever been found which can be safely said to have been made there.

> To be sold by Auction . . . the FEE SIMPLE and INHERITANCE of and in all that Piece of LAND situate on the south side of Canning Street, in Liverpool aforesaid, with the Warehouse and other erections thereon, called the CANNING STREET POTTERY, lately carried on by the late Archibald Mansfield, comprising workshops for two throwers, five turners, four printers, and suitable conveniences, and workshops for all other branches of the business.

Joseph Mayer* tells us that there was also a grinding mill, a twenty horse-power engine, three glost and one biscuit oven, and that 'the articles made were of an ordinary description, such as were suitable for hawkers in the country trade, and for export'. One can assume that they were a relatively cheap underglazed-blue type and somewhat inferior to the products of Herculaneum. Mansfield's defection probably meant that he had become dissatisfied with conditions at Toxteth, and saw no future for himself. He was a good workman who, as a boy, had been twice commended by the Proprietors at Herculaneum for his skill and good services, and in 1822 his salary stood at £100 with 'the accommodation of a House to live in and to be found with Coals at the expense of the Concern'.†

For about five or six years then, conditions had been very unsettled at Herculaneum. One manager resigned, the cash and book keeper emigrated after a few years of struggling to keep things going, the newly-appointed manager left to found a works of his own, trading figures revealed large unpaid debts to the factory and there was the Committee resolution showing a clear recognition of its need to put its house in order. Herculaneum was probably not alone in its predicament, for the national economy was then far from sound and stability had been unsettled by years of war. It is cheering to

---

* Joseph Mayer, *History of the Progress of the Art of Pottery in Liverpool*, Liverpool 1855 and 1873.
† *Resolutions of the Committee, ibid.* January 1st, 1822. No. 220.

note that in the late 1820s things seemed to be improving and in 1827 we have a clear picture of a once-more thriving community in *The Liverpool Albion* account on July 9th in that year. This report is quoted in full at the end of Chapter VII.

The Wares

Before considering in detail the wares produced in the period 1820–1833 we must refer to a minute which was passed by the Herculaneum Company Committee on August 6th, 1822 which has often been quoted and needs some clarification here. The full resolution in the Minute Book reads as follows:

> 'Resolved that in order to give publicity and Identity to the China and Earthenware manufactured by the Herculaneum Pottery Co. the words "Herculaneum Pottery" be stamped or marked on some conspicuous part of all china and earthenware hereafter made and manufactured at this manufactory.'

Practically every reference to the Herculaneum Pottery in books on ceramics from Mayer onwards, (where the tradition began) quotes or refers to this resolution, but it must here be stated that the author has never seen a single piece marked with these *two* words, apart from several creamware jugs made for the American market which have 'Herculaneum Pottery Liverpool' as part of the decoration underneath the American Eagle (Plate 59), and, in any case, these jugs were all made many years before the resolution of 1822. There are, moreover, many Herculaneum pieces known to have been made after 1822, which bear no mark at all. One can only interpret the decision, therefore, as one which was made to suit the exigencies of that date, when trade was difficult and publicity important, but which was never carried out. Marks including the name Herculaneum, however, continued to be used and two new ones (Plates 164B and 166B) were introduced in the 1820s. The crown is a feature of each and this innovation must be regarded as an attempt to change with the times, to keep in the fashion when many other potteries were employing the crown as a device, to overcome the lack of self-confidence and to capture new markets. Mayer quotes, erroneously, another mark and his error has been copied by other authors. This is the mark of 'LIVERPOOL' inscribed in a semi-circle over an anchor in the way that Davenports of Longport, Staffordshire, used their name curved over an anchor and Mayer actually illustrated a mark of 'Liverpool' over an anchor. This mark, however, does not exist; we can only trace the error to wishful thinking in interpreting a rather blurred impressed mark on a gigantic *Davenport* lustre jug in the museum at Liverpool. That this interpretation gave considerable trouble to later curators in that institution is indicated by the wording of an old museum label which reads 'Manufactured by Davenport, Liverpool.'!!

During the period discussed in this chapter there would seem, therefore,

to have been no less than four different marks used: the old form of the word HERCULANEUM in capital letters; the two incorporating a crown and a crown and garter; and yet another based on that mythical creature from the Liverpool Coat of Arms known as the 'Liver Bird'. The Liver Bird occurs on both the shield and crest of the official arms of Liverpool, an emblem which was presented to Liverpool by the Charter of 1207 in the reign of King John. There has been much speculation about the origin of the bird which has in its beak a piece of weed known as 'Liverwort', but for our purposes it is enough to say that the bird is a cormorant, drawn in a heraldic or stylised manner. The device was used on Herculaneum pottery as an impression in the soft clay before firing, and sometimes the mark is difficult to recognise, particularly when it is filled with glaze and rather blurred (Plates 80, 81).

It is difficult to be sure when the Liver Bird was first used on pottery, and one might be tempted to speculate that this coincided with the incorporation of Toxteth into the City of Liverpool in 1835. Several marked pieces exist, however, which show that this was not the case, for they were certainly made before that date. In view of the attempts made by the Committee to remedy a declining trade it would be reasonable to suppose that the earliest date for the Liver Bird would be about 1825, appearing perhaps immediately after the use of the impressed crown marks. By 1825 Liverpool had increased greatly in size and importance and had become well known as the largest seaport in the north of England; a familiar Liverpool emblem would add much greater prestige to the wares of the factory than the relatively unknown name of Toxteth or the continued use of 'Herculaneum'—a successful trade name which had served well in its day but which by the 1820s was out of fashion. In addition to the use of two more marks from the closing years of the factory (pages 75 and 88), therefore, the Liver Bird, whenever it is found, would indicate a date from about 1825 onwards.

It is surprising to find that transfer-printed creamwares continued to be made in the late 1820s, but a ship printed plate impressed with the Liver Bird proves that this was so, and a very fine jug in the Henry Ford Museum, Dearborn, is inscribed with the date 1823. The transfer-printing on the plate is of a quality which suggests that the end of this great tradition had been reached, but the jug is a splendid specimen on which prints from the early 1800s are still used. Blue-printed wares were, however, the stock-in-trade and many fine pieces of this type from the 1820s are still to be found. Sporting prints in rich dark blue with a floral border are typical of the vogue (Plate 167A) and religious themes such as 'The Flight into Egypt' (Plate 166A) in an *intensely* dark blue were fashionable subjects. Rural scenes with peasants and cattle such as we see on a pierced-edged plate (Plate 164A) were also known, but most important of all perhaps, were the views of English towns. Three of these, in the museum at Liverpool, are decorated with pictures of Cambridge, Shrewsbury and Oxford (Plates 169, 162 and 165). It is not difficult to imagine why prints like these appealed to emigrants in foreign countries, where the Herculaneum trade was largely directed. The subjects would remind them of home, and their warm, rich, decorative

rococo borders would give comfort and cheer when arranged on the kitchen dresser. It is a very curious fact that the Herculaneum factory does not appear to have made any of the blue-printed American views which are so much sought after in that country and which were made in large quantities by such Staffordshire firms as James and Ralph Clews, William Adams, J. and W. Ridgway, Enoch Wood and Sons, Ralph Stevenson and T. Mayer. Of all the Staffordshire factories, however, making blue-printed wares there are none whose products, in this particular field, could be said to be better than those of our Toxteth factory, and the competition which existed between the two has already been mentioned from Tomkinson's papers (page 64). Blue was also used for vast quantities of feathered-edged plates, vases and other wares, but these were the cheaper varieties. Examples from fine blue-printed tea services are known, of which we have the cups and saucers at Liverpool Museum and in the Art Institute of Chicago (Plate 163).

Whether or not Herculaneum ever made lustre ware we shall perhaps never know, for lustre is hardly ever marked and no firm documentary evidence for its manufacture at Toxteth has ever come to light. The only mention it has been possible to find is an account with Lockett and Co. of Lane End, Staffordshire, for 'Figures and Lustre' and it is reasonable to accept that the Duke Street warehouse in Liverpool dealt with such goods from outside. On the whole it would seem strange to imagine that Herculaneum did *not* make lustre, for they apparently made everything else! In this connection we must therefore mention a splendid silver lustre jug bearing the name of the Coffee House at Everton (a well-known institution in the Liverpool locality) and a similar sized specimen in the Henry Francis du Pont Museum at Winterthur, Delaware, which has reserve panels with prints of the Butchers Arms, a Masonic subject and a map of Washington (Plates 183 and 185). If these are from the Herculaneum factory then there must be many other lustre pieces which are now masquerading as Staffordshire.

To maintain a large output as cheaply as would be consistent with the maintenance of quality, we find, as one would expect, that a considerably narrower range of materials was employed than in former years, if not of types and shapes of ware. Bas-relief decoration in stoneware had gone and there appear to have been fewer, if any, modelled figures produced. Cheaper goods such as the typically English 'mocha' ware was made to meet the needs of the poorer table and the tavern, and a graphic account of slip-banding on earthenwares is quoted on page 100 from the *Albion* report of 1827. Mocha is specifically mentioned in Tomkinson's papers where we find that the wages paid for 'turning' in 'mocha' were 6s. 8d. per score, while 'bowls band'd' were 5s. for the same quantity, and 'jugs and mugs' only 4s. 2d. It must be emphasised that 'score' refers to 'a score of dozens' and the number in a dozen could vary according to the nature of the operation being performed and the 'piece-rate' decided upon. Such were the methods of labour and production control in early nineteenth-century factories. Slip-decorated earthenwares were the cheap or common lines which must have formed a

very large part of the output, an anonymous group which will never, in all probability, be identified because all factories made them.

Some idea of the range of goods made at the factory may be gauged from the following list taken from various entries amongst the Tomkinson papers, where the details of the manufacturing prices are given. Most of the types in this list are not represented amongst collections of known Herculaneum wares, partly because they were sold unmarked and partly because it was only the elaborately decorated pieces of attractive appearance which have survived the passage of time. The author has only once seen rough, common domestic wares marked; these were a pair of jelly moulds.

> PLATES (in sizes Royal, Bath, Grass, Paris, Octagonal); MUFFINS; DISHES; GRAVIES; MILK PANS; BAKING DISHES; SALADS (octagonal, deep, scollopt, round,); BIDDY PANS; TUREENS; SAUCE TUREENS; STANDS; COVERS; COMPOTEERS; SHELLS; TOOTH TRAYS; CHEESE DISHES; CHEESE TOASTERS; BAKERS; SOAP BOXES; URINALS; CREAM VAZES; GOOSE POTS; EWERS; COACH POTS; EGGSTANDS; CHEESE STANDS; PICKLE SETS; CANDLESTICKS; BUTTER TUBS; CRUIT FRAMES; STEWPOTS; CREAM BOWLS; FOOT BATHS; BARBERS BASONS; TEAPOTS; SUGARS; CREAMS; MUGS; JUGS; CANS; CHAMBERS; PEPPERS; PORRINGERS; COFFEE POTS; MUSTARDS; SAUCE LADLES; STONE JUGS; SOUP LADLES; BOWLS; TUMBLERS.

Where are all these things to be found today and how shall we know them if we see them?

Although the manufacture of high quality blue-printed wares was of great importance in the factory's economy, porcelain-making still continued. A fine large porcelain bowl (Plate 141) decorated with enamelled flowers and gilding in conjunction with an under-glaze blue ground is certainly from our factory. We have this positive information from Mrs. C. B. Farr, late of Blackburn, whose grandfather Henry Buxton painted the piece. Mrs. Farr presented the bowl to Liverpool Museum along with the Edward Buxton plaque (Plate 131, page 47) and also provided the information that Henry Buxton of Toxteth was born in 1793, died at Salford in 1872 and was buried at St. James' Cemetery, Liverpool. It is not a perfect piece, but it is very vigorously enamelled, as is a cup and saucer presented to Liverpool Museum in 1867 by Joseph Mayer (Plate 140). This piece is unmarked but we can be sure it came from Herculaneum from Mayer's attribution which must be taken seriously. Mayer certainly made several errors concerning the early years of the factory, but it must be remembered that during the 1820s he was a young man keenly interested in Liverpool wares and did a fine water-colour painting of the works from the shore of the River Mersey in 1825 (Plate 2). Just as on-glaze transfer-printing survived into the 1820s on earthenware, so it did on porcelain, and several pieces are illustrated (Plates 144 and 145)

which are decorated in this manner. Herculaneum porcelain of this period is invariably unmarked and it is extremely difficult to know in all cases whether the porcelain is from Herculaneum or from one of the Staffordshire firms for which the factory and warehouse acted as agents. The pieces illustrated have been chosen partly because they have a long and authentic Liverpool lineage and partly because they do not resemble in various details wares which are known to be from other factories. Printing on many of the porcelain pieces was by the 'bat' method, a system in which the print is taken from the copper plate in a special oil directly onto the surface of a piece of gelatine or 'bat'. The pliable gelatine can then be applied to the curved surface of the article to be decorated and the impression in oil is left on the ware. This is then dusted with the required ceramic enamel which sticks to the oil and the design is fixed by firing. Mention of this method will be found in the *Albion* account in Chapter VII (page 106). The porcelain service illustrated with prints of British animals in sepia tint and gilding (Plate 144) must represent more or less the last of such Herculaneum wares, for we have no evidence that porcelain was made after the change of management in 1833.

It is difficult to make generalisations about the products of a pottery of whose wares, quantitively speaking, we know so little and where surviving specimens are relatively few compared with the hundreds of thousands of pieces which the factory must have made. From this brief review of identifiable pieces, however, one feels that the *quality* was there but somehow the individual *character* had gone. The golden age of Herculaneum had ended; the spark which shone brightly in the early years had gone out by the end of this difficult decade. The qualities which make Herculaneum specimens different from those of Staffordshire and elsewhere are no longer to be found. Instead we have a conformity of design and craftsmanship bred of competition with other manufacturers—a merging of identity which, to a greater or lesser extent was universally the case. Herculaneum only raised its head again in one final flourish before the end, a revival concerned with fine under-glaze printing which we shall discuss in the following chapter.

VI. VASE from a mantelpiece garniture. Porcelain, polychrome decoration and gilding. Mark HERCULANEUM. c.1815. Height 11″. *Courtesy of The City of Liverpool Museums.*

Chapter VI

The End of the Road 1833–1840

From the establishment of the Herculaneum Company in 1806 the affairs and business of the concern were controlled by a Committee of Proprietors. This committee consisted of a Chairman, Secretary, Solicitor, the Manager of the factory and two other shareholders, with occasionally an additional honorary member. The members were elected annually at a General Meeting, usually convened towards the end of November and chose their own chairman and secretary.

This system had worked very well from the first meeting held in the special committee room at the works on November 28th, 1806, and, by and large, the factory's affairs were well supervised and protected. In 1833 however, following that difficult era we have described in the last chapter, the old proprietorship was dissolved and the works were offered for sale. It is a great loss for the present record that the Committee Minute Books immediately prior to this sale have not been discovered and we can only hazard an opinion as to why the old establishment broke up. From the problems we have seen in the 1820s the most probable reason is that the shareholders became increasingly dissatisfied with the diminishing returns on their investments, particularly as they knew where their money would yield much greater profits in other Liverpool industries. They were wise to withdraw when they did, for by 1833 the factory had only another seven years to go before it was closed completely.

The state and size of the factory in 1833 may be judged from an advertisement which appeared in *The Staffordshire Advertiser* of March 16 in that year, and in various Liverpool papers. Paragraph five makes it clear that the vendors were contemplating the sale of the works for manufacturing processes *other than pottery*, and in the following paragraph the space between the buildings and the river is particularly mentioned for timber and shipbuilding needs.

HERCULANEUM POTTERY, LIVERPOOL

To be let or sold

All that valuable Freehold and improving PROPERTY known as the

73

HERCULANEUM POTTERY, Earthenware and China Manufactory; together with Ovens, Kilns, Steam Engine, Mill, Workshops, Crate Sheds, Manager's House, and 62 Cottages and Houses, now tenanted by the workmen, and occupying 30,900 square yards of land.

Also the Copper-plate Engravings, Blocks, Moulds, &c. and all other utensils complete for carrying on the Earthenware and China Manufacture, all in excellent working condition.

A large and useful Dock, with a powerful Crane and other appurtenances for loading and unloading of Goods, &c. comprising 1089 square yards of land.

The whole situated on the south shore of the River Mersey, within half a mile of Brunswick Dock, and adjoining the improvements now making by the Trustees of the Liverpool Dock Estate.

The Premises are in a good state of repair, and well calculated by their local facilities to carry on the manufacture of Earthenware and China to considerable advantage, as well as any other Manufactory where space and easy access to the river are required.

By a recent admeasurement, this eligible Property contains a total of 54,245 square yards of Land, including 22,222 square yards, being the Strand of the River Mersey down to low water mark, which may be made available for Timber Yards, Ship-Building, and other purposes.

For further information, apply to Thomas Case Esq., Exchange Street East; Mr. W. T. Keightley, Solicitor, Hanover Street, and at the Manufactory, Toxteth Park, Liverpool, where Plans of the Property may be seen.

In the event the purchaser of the factory was a gentleman called Ambrose Lace, and by the details of the sale agreement we can see that the shareholders at least made sure of the £25,000 basic capital representing the never increased standing holding in fifty separate shares. The present whereabouts of the sale agreement are unknown, but by a very fortunate circumstance the details have survived in the papers of the late Peter Entwistle of Liverpool.* The Agreement was entered into on March 23rd, 1833.

... between Thomas Case, Charles Horsfall, Robert Gladstone, James Bourne and Charles Stewart Parker, Esquires, all of Liverpool in the County of Lancaster, the Committee of the Herculaneum Pottery Co.,

---

* R. J. Charleston at the Victoria and Albert Museum very kindly provided Entwistle's papers on Herculaneum following their discovery in the estate of the late Professor Garner.

of the one part, and Ambrose Lace of Liverpool aforesaid Gentleman of the other part

The said Thomas Case, Charles Horsfall, Robert Gladstone, James Bourne and Charles Stewart Parker, on behalf of themselves and others the proprietors of shares of and in the Herculaneum Pottery Co. agree to sell to the said Ambrose Lace for himself his heirs &c. the land, buildings, steam engine, cottages and fixtures in the dwelling houses belonging to the said Herculaneum Pottery, situate in Toxteth Park near Liverpool aforesaid on the shore of the River Mersey &c. for the sum of twenty-five thousand pounds, with a marketable title freehold of Inheritance free from all incumbrances (except the land tax) from the Earl of Sefton.

To pay £4,000 down as a deposit, and to come in possession on 1st. November next and pay the rest except otherwise agreed.

Signed   Ambrose Lace   Thomas Case.
                                              Charles Horsfall.
                                              Robert Gladstone.
                                              James Bourne.
                                              Charles S. Parker.

It is of some interest to note that by the time this sale was made the property was free of all rents due to the original owner of the site, Lord Sefton, for between October 1820 and final agreement in January 1822, the Committee had negotiated the purchase of Lord Sefton's rights in the factory for the sum of £2,000 when, apparently, Lord Sefton was in need of ready capital.

As soon as Lace had purchased the property and the old shareholders had gone, he evidently decided to continue it as a pottery concern and thereupon leased it to two experts in the pottery processes: Thomas Case and James Mort. Thomas Case had been chairman of the old committee from as early as December 1814 and understood the financial and administrative side of the business, while we can think of James Mort as the practical man with an intimate knowledge of potting. During this period a pottery mark was used which is very rare indeed and has only been found on one specimen (Plate 188B), a finely-made jug with a sage green body and gilding.

By 1836 Thomas Case had retired from business and a new lease was issued for a continuance of the concern in the hands of James Mort and John Simpson, and they were the final proprietors of the factory. John Simpson is recorded as a potter at Herculaneum as early as 1826 when a child was born to his wife Charlotte on October 28. We do not know when he came to Toxteth, but he could well have been the son of Joshua (1771–1826) and Mary Simpson who came with the original Staffordshire immigrants in 1796. James Mort came from a north Staffordshire family, the details of which have been provided by Mr. Reginald Haggar. Mr. Haggar records one John Mort as being a master potter at Herculaneum, the son of the Reverend James Mort, a Methodist preacher who died in Liverpool in 1827. There is a slight possibility that a confusion has been made between James and John,

but since Entwistle quotes James from the agreements with Ambrose Lace, and also since Joseph Mayer independently mentions James, this is unlikely. The lease from Ambrose Lace and his son Joshua, together with others detailed in the agreement, was to run for seven years, a period which was not to be completed. The full details of this agreement, also taken from Entwistle's manuscript, are as follows:

> 'This indenture made the 23rd day of February 1836 between Ambrose Lace and Joshua Lace the younger, both of Liverpool in the County of Lancaster, Gentlemen, John Tomkinson of the same place, stonemason, Samuel Holmes and James Holmes the younger, both of the same place, Builders, of the one part and James Mort and John Simpson, both of Toxteth Park, Earthenware Manufacturers of the other part Witnesseth that in consideration of the rents and covenants hereinafter contained, they the said Ambrose Lace and Joshua Lace the younger, have demised and leased to the said James Mort and John Simpson all those several plots of piece of land delineated on the plan hereto annexed situated in Toxteth Park near and upon the Strand of the River Mersey together with several messuages or Dwelling Houses, buildings, wharfs &c. lately used by the Herculaneum Pottery Co.
>
> To have and hold from the date hereof for and during the term of seven years from the first of December last year paying a rent of £910 yearly for the first three years and the remaining four years at the rate of £960 yearly.'

Unfortunately the plan is lost, but there is additional evidence to suggest that the pottery workers were not occupying the complete set of buildings formerly used by the pottery, at least during the last two years of the establishment. This is clear from the details of an endorsement on the back of the indenture just quoted which is too long to include here. It shows that the rent had been reduced to the potters consequent upon the loss of 17 of the cottages due to the continuance of Sefton Street, and also because the 'Furnace, Kiln and Shed standing on part of the premises lately surrendered' had also had to go. The old works were gradually being encroached upon by the building of houses and other manufactories, one of which was an iron works. There is some evidence to show that a forge for iron-working had been installed *within* the pottery buildings as early as the late 1820s, for in the last ten years of the pottery's life we find William Bevins, Joel Dykes, John Goodall, John Griffiths, David, John and Robert Hood and John Whittaker, all described as forgemen or engineers working at the Herculaneum Pottery! As the number of potters decreased at the Toxteth works it is not unlikely that the ironworkers would have rented a workshop or two amongst the old buildings to supply iron fittings for the neighbouring shipyards. Even today the old name is retained by the Herculaneum Steel Fabrication Works on a nearby site.

By 1836 the other manufacturing and mercantile developments which had

gradually been surrounding the factory almost succeeded in squeezing it out, the owners of the site Ambrose and Joshua Lace having attempted to close the pottery and re-develop the area in that year. Full details of their scheme have survived and the following extracts show clearly what the owners had in mind:

> It has been resolved by the Proprietors (Ambrose and Joshua Lace) of this Estate, that it should be offered to the Public on somewhat similar terms to those by which the Harrington Dock Company have become possessed of the adjoining land.
> The Estate consists of the Pottery and the Dock belonging to it, in lease to Messrs. Mort and Simpson, the Ship Building Yard to Mr. Duncan Gibb; an excellent landing Slip and Pier equal to any on the River; Eight houses forming Park Terrace; about Sixty Cottages, and a large quantity of unenclosed Beach and Land to the Eastward. . . .
> The great extent and compactness of this Property render it capable of being turned to most profitable account; and for Wharfs, Ship-Builders Yards, Forwarding Agents, Depot for Goods requiring trans-shipment, Yards requiring great space connected with the Shipping Station, or any of the general purposes of a Commercial Town, this Estate offers advantages now no longer to be met with. . . .
> Numerous applications for the Land both to rent and purchase Lots have been made, and from its proximity to the Docks, and the Seat of the Timber Trade, it will be occupied as fast as it can be prepared. . .
> It is intended, therefore, that a Company be formed for the purchase and management of this Estate, having a Capital of £22,000 in 2,200 shares, of £100 each, which include a contemplated outlay, according to the Estimates made for finishing the Works of £40,000.
>
> May 10th, 1836*

This particular application to develop the land on a larger and more profitable scale did not succeed, but coming as it did only 15 days after Lace's agreement with Mort and Simpson it shows us that Lace had no faith in them being in a position to carry on much longer, a circumstance not surprising when we learn that a Herculaneum Dock Bill was being mooted in powerful quarters.

James Mort and John Simpson managed to keep going until 1840, when industrial pressures from outside caused them finally to close. We can visualise them having carried on, perhaps dispirited with a closure hanging over them and probably with a much reduced staff, but when the closing sale came at last there was sufficient stock and tools on hand to make it worth their while to advertise in both Liverpool and Staffordshire papers. Many sale advertisements and notices were published which are all more or less the same; the three following ones indicate the nature of the proceedings:

> The Warehouse in Duke Street lately occupied by the Herculaneum

* Liverpool Public Record Office, *Binns Collection*, Vol. 28, pp. 40, 41.

Pottery Company has been purchased by the Government and is to be converted into a Barracks.*

Notice. The Herculaneum Company begs to inform their friends and the Public that in consequence of the Herculaneum Dock Bill being likely to terminate their continuance at the present manufactory in Toxteth Park, they have to offer their valuable stock for immediate sale at reduced prices.

To Merchants, Dealers, Exporters, Captains of Ships, and others in the wholesale and shipping business, and to Hotel Keepers, Boarding House Establishments, and Families, such an opportunity of procuring needful articles at low rates, in Earthenware and Stoneware, may not occur again.

The stock is to be viewed at their manufactory Toxteth Park, or patterns at their offices, Clarendon Rooms, South John Street.

Their manufactory at St. Helens is still continued.†

IMPORTANT SALE

AT THE HERCULANEUM POTTERY, LIVERPOOL
(Now about to be pulled down for the erection of docks)

EXTENSIVE and valuable STOCK of EARTHENWARE, consisting of printed table, tea and toilette ware; and painted, edged, dipt, and cream colour ware, of all descriptions; potters' FIXTURES, MATERIALS, valuable copper plate ENGRAVINGS, being of choice patterns and shapes, blocks and moulds, superior draught HORSES, gearing, carts, lorry, and other miscellaneous effects.

Also the mill work, &c. which will be found suitable for manufacturers, engineers, millwrights, grinders of plaster, barytes &c., consists of two flint pans of 13 feet diameter, three ditto of nine feet, two ditto of five feet, and six colour pans, each $1\frac{1}{2}$ feet diameter, plaster mill, a pair of rollers 20 inches wide, clay mill three feet eight inches by two feet one inch, a large cistern with water pumps, pipes &c., hoisting tackle, a large wash tub, and fan nine feet six inches in diameter, a pump, connecting rods, uprights, &c., with all the needful machinery, crown spur, driving and cog wheels, shafts and collars, arms and drivers in connection with a THIRTY HORSE POWER ENGINE, with everything requisite for working the above.

* *Liverpool Mercury*, September 25th, 1840.
† *Liverpool Mercury*, October 2nd, 1840.

WILL BE SUBMITTED TO SALE BY AUCTION
by Mr. JOHNSON

On the premises, at the Herculaneum Pottery, Liverpool, On Tuesday, December 15th, 1840, and following days until all is sold.

Descriptive catalogues of sale are now in circulation, and may be had on application of the HERCULANEUM POTTERY COMPANY, Liverpool, or from the Auctioneer, Burslem.

Sale each morning at eleven o'clock precisely.

ORDER OF SALE

Sale of finished stock to commence on Tuesday, December 15th at eleven o'clock, and to be on view with the articles enumerated in the catalogue, on Saturday, the 12th and Monday, the 14th December. The earthenware will be offered in bulk together, or by one warehouse at a time, or by quantities of single patterns, or in lots to suit purchasers. The materials and engravings, with blocks and moulds, to be sold on Thursday, the 17th December, and the utensils peculiar to potters' use, to follow.

The horses, carts &c. to be sold on Friday, the 18th December, exactly at one o'clock.

Auction Office, Sytch House, Burslem, Staffordshire Potteries.*

In Peter Entwistle's time, when he was curator at Liverpool Museum, from the early 1900s to about 1936 when he retired, a copy of the catalogue was in his hands, but is now lost and perhaps perished in the bombing of the museum in 1941. This catalogue was listed as an item in the Liverpool Sept-Centenary Exhibition at the Walker Art Gallery in 1907 and fortunately for us Entwistle made some notes from it, though not a complete copy. The catalogue was apparently divided into sections which are worth listing since they give us a very clear idea of the extent of the works and the processes carried on there:

THE MILL	SAUCE MAKERS' PLACE
2 SLIP HOUSES	PLATE MAKERS' PLACE
BLACK SHED	FLAG HOUSE
CLAY BANK	DISH MAKERS' PLACE
(containing 50 tons of blue clay)	SAUCER MAKERS' PLACE
PASSAGE TO VAULT	SQUEEZING ROOM
CLAY VAULT	PLATE MAKERS' ROOMS
CLAY HOUSE	2 MOULD ROOMS
SETTLING ARKS	BISCUIT SAGGAR HOUSE
MUFFIN MAKERS' PLACE	3 BISCUIT WAREHOUSES

* *Staffordshire Advertiser*, December 5th and 12th, 1840.

ENGRAVERS' SHOP

CRATE SHOP

MOULD MAKERS' ROOM

PRESSERS' PLACE

HOT HOUSE

THROWING HOUSE

PASSAGE

CELLAR

SMALL THROWING HOUSE

CLAY BANK

TURNING HOUSE

3 UPSTAIRS ROOMS

PRESSERS ROOM

CESSING HOUSE

PASSAGE TO PRINTING SHOP

EDGING ROOM

2 GLOST SAGGAR HOUSES

NEXT SAGGAR HOUSE

2 SAGGAR MAKERS' PLACES

DRYING ROOM

COLOUR ROOM

ENAMELLING SHOP

NEXT ROOM

WORK SHOP

FRONT OFFICE

BACK OFFICE

FOREMAN'S ROOM

BLACK PRINTING SHOP

FIRECLAY HOUSE

HARDENING HOUSE

3 PRINTING SHOPS and STOVES

BLUE SAGGAR HOUSE

FRET PLACE (Frit)

COPPER PLATE WAREHOUSE

CORDON'S PLACE

(manager)

EDGE WAREHOUSE

CREAM COLOUR WAREHOUSE

SORTING HOUSE

PAINTED WAREHOUSE

OLD BLUE WAREHOUSE

CHINA ROOM

PATTERN ROOM

BROWN WAREHOUSE

NEW BLUE WAREHOUSE

PACKING HOUSE

STABLE & GIG HOUSE

BLACKSMITH'S SHOP

Amongst the sundries also listed in the catalogue are the following interesting items:

70 tons China Clay 60 tons Fayles Blue Clay 14 cwt. Manganese
1 ton Welsh Umber 14 lb. Antimony 10 tons Red Clay
A large and excellent lot of Tiles 6 inches square for lining baths &c.

The list of engraved plates, blocks and cases (from which the pots were made to match the size of the engravings) is quite prodigious, but it is not at all clear, in every case, whether the lists available refer to engraved copper plates or finished wares decorated with copper plate prints. This being the case it is perhaps safer to refer simply to the subjects mentioned, those in list (a) being mainly early patterns, and those in lists (b) and (c) dating, in all probability, from the 1820s and 1830s.

(a) Tile   Figure   American
  Crest   Portrait   Maps
  Arms   Ship   Caricatures
  Jug   Compass   Verses
  Cypher   Ruins   Birds
  Flower   Landscapes Domestic Industry
  Shell   Sporting Subjects

(b) French Scenery   Archery   British Views
     Shell   Liverpool Views   Flower Vases
     Butterfly   Cross Rose   Herculaneum Vase
     Bird Cage   Groundwork   Temple
     Swiss Cottage   Cattle   Cascade
     Chinese Birds   Elephant   Flowers
     Louvre   Field Sports   Spanish
                   Charioteers

(c) Patterns identified for tea wares:
     Chinese   Strawberry   Archery
     Cock & Fox   American Rose   Eagle & Crown
     Mushroom   Scenery   Border
     Chinese Boat   Verandah   Leaf & Scroll
     and Flowers
     Swan & Flowers   Beehive   Royal Star
     Swan   Cascade   Varieties
     Cross Rose   Basket

Particular reference has been made to 'Cordon's Place' in the list of rooms and workshops and by this we can infer that the last manager was one of the Cordon family (page 22). The fact that Ralph Cordon was dead by 1834 means that in all probability it was Sampson Cordon (b. 1797) the son of Ralph, who followed his father as manager; between them they might have looked after the managership from about 1824 when Archibald Mansfield left, until the closure in 1840. We have already remarked on the blue-printed mug (page 22, Plate 158) which was made to celebrate the marriage of Sampson to his wife Myrah in 1817, and since he took over the position of Clerk of St. Michael's-in-the-Hamlet Church, on the death of his father, he would seem to be the most likely candidate for the office of manager.

The extent and scale of the works at the time of the closure causes us to wonder about the amount of manufacturing which was being done at the end, but we can be fairly sure that it was a steadily declining quantity. This is not merely a probable inference from the conditions we have just reviewed, but is strongly supported by the fact that the names of the potters and their children decline sharply in number in the registers of the local churches.

The sale of the building materials, milling machinery, stock on hand, horses and carts etc. took place in Toxteth in 1840, but certain of the potters' materials and tools were removed from the premises and taken to Burslem to be sold there for potters' use in 1841. The details of this secondary sale are to be found in an advertisement which appeared in *The North Staffordshire Mercury* of January 23rd, 1841:

UNRESERVED SALE OF
VALUABLE COPPER PLATE ENGRAVINGS, BLOCKS and
CASES, superior Figure MOULDS, a quantity of COLOURS,

FACED SLATES, PRINTING PRESSES, new LATHE, with
chocks; 500 Workhouse Boards, six feet long, &c. &c. the property
of the HERCULANEUM POTTERY COMPANY, Liverpool,
which will be submitted to SALE BY AUCTION,

By Mr. Johnson

At the Leopard Hotel, Burslem, in the Staffordshire Potteries.
Particulars and time of sale, will appear in a future paper and
catalogues.

Auction Office, Sytch House, Burslem.

It is more than likely that many of the engraved plates, blocks, cases and
moulds continued to be used by the Staffordshire potters who bought them,
providing us with extra difficulties in terms of identification. It would be
fascinating to know the subjects of the 'figure moulds' for no Herculaneum
figures have ever been identified except those made during the early years
and which have been reviewed in Chapter III (pages 43 and 44).

The sale advertisement from *The Liverpool Mercury* of October 2nd, 1840
tells us that a satellite concern was still in operation at St. Helens. St. Helens
is a town only a few miles from Liverpool in south-west Lancashire, noted
in the past for its copper-smelting, coal, chemicals and glass, and glass-
making is still its most important industry.* The crate-making yard of
Messrs. Pilkington Brothers now covers the site of what was the Herculaneum Company's works, in an area known as Greenbank. In 1833 the
pottery was said to have been in existence for many years, the property of
one Thomas Harley whose will was proved at Chester on February 4th, 1833.
James Mort and John Simpson appear to have taken over control in 1836
and although we have found no record to prove it, it seems very likely that
the Herculaneum potters moved in on the death of Harley three years earlier.
The fact that the Herculaneum potters were interested in a St. Helens works
at all only underlines the pressures which they were feeling in Toxteth, but at
Greenbank also they did not last long. An advertisement in *The Staffordshire
Advertiser* of August 7th, 14th and 21st, 1841 shows that this concern was up
for sale within a few months of the parent works, though it apparently did not
cease as a pottery at that time, and was carried on by Doulton and Co., perhaps
for the making of salt-glazed stoneware bottles and jars.

FREEHOLD PROPERTY, ST. HELENS
LANCASHIRE

TO BE LET OR SOLD
With possession in November next

All that compact and well established EARTHENWARE MANU-
FACTORY, with the utensils and fixtures complete, situate and adjoin-

* See T. C. Barker and J. R. Harris, *A Merseyside Town in the Industrial Revolution*,
Liverpool, 1954.

ing the towing path of the Sankey Canal, in the rapidly increasing and populous trading town of St. Helens, a distance of about eleven miles from Liverpool, and now in the occupation of the Herculaneum Company. The premises consist of one large biscuit oven, and two gloss ovens, and all other requisite and convenient buildings for the manufacture of earthenware or china, with a constant supply of good water, and plenty of coal, saggar clay, and other clays, near the manufactory. The St. Helens Railway, which joins the Liverpool and Manchester, the Grand Junction, and several other railways, is at a distance of about 300 yards from the manufactory; this, with the Sankey canal, which communicates with the River Mersey, form a very convenient and easy conveyance for materials and manufactured goods to all parts of the country. There is sufficient vacant land to enlarge the works considerably, or for the erection of other commodious buildings.

Persons desirous of treating for the above, are requested to apply to Mrs. Harley, Longton; Messrs. F. & R. Pratt, Fenton, Staffordshire Potteries; or to Mr. Richard Woodward, of St. Helens, who will show the premises.

The factory, known as 'The Greenbank Pottery' or, on other maps as 'The Liverpool Pottery' may be seen on the plan, sandwiched between Pottery Street, a chemical works and the canal. The canal is now filled in, the line it occupied being today Canal Street, and on the site itself there is nothing of the old works to be seen, though in recent years the author has collected a few biscuit shards of transfer-printed earthenware. The manager of the St. Helens factory was Alderman James Bayley, a much respected citizen of the town, whose obituary is recorded in *The St. Helens Standard* of June 6th, 1874. It is stated in this account that Mr. Bayley 'was born in 1799, near to the town of Burslem in North Staffordshire, and was brought up to the manufacture of pottery, then, as now, largely carried on in his native place. Forty-one years ago he came to St. Helens to assume the management of the Greenbank Pottery, the property of Messrs. Simpson & Co.' If this last statement is true it would seem that John Simpson was working the concern as early as 1833 on the death of Thomas Harley, and perhaps James Mort was with him as has been suggested earlier. At all events the St. Helens works did not last long under Liverpool proprietorship, and to judge by the shards on the site the products were similar to those of the factory at Toxteth. A particularly interesting reference to the installation of the steam engine for grinding flints at the St. Helens works will be dealt with in Chapter VII (page 96).

The Wares

Surviving identifiable specimens of Herculaneum wares in the last seven years of its life are by no means abundant, and in the case of many late pieces it is not easy to decide whether they were made before the change of

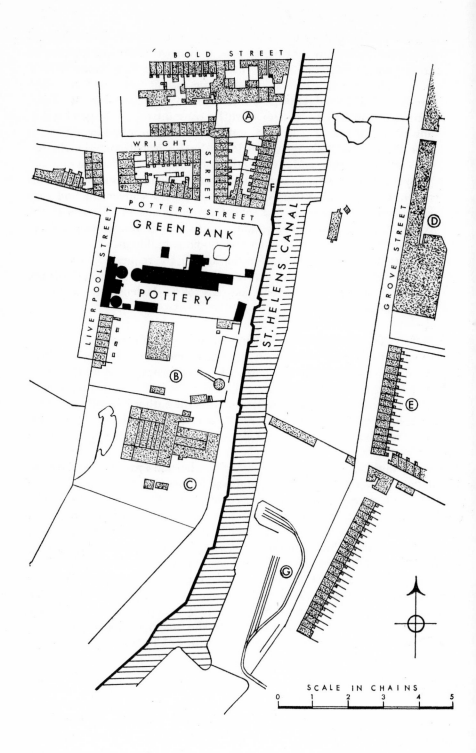

BOLD STREET

WRIGHT STREET

POTTERY STREET

LIVERPOOL STREET

GREEN BANK

POTTERY

ST. HELENS CANAL

GROVE STREET

A

B

C

D

E

F

G

SCALE IN CHAINS

0   1   2   3   4   5

MAP OF PART OF ST. HELENS, LANCASHIRE, SHOWING THE GREEN
BANK POTTERY AND ADJOINING PREMISES.

Drawn from the Ordnance Survey map of 1849.

A. FOUNDRY YARD.
B. CHEMICAL WORKS.
C. GREEN BANK TAN YARD.
D. ST. HELENS CROWN GLASS WORKS.
E. PILKINGTON ROW.
F. CANAL PLACE.
G. RAILWAY SIDINGS.

SCALE: 1 chain = 66 feet.

proprietorship in 1833, or afterwards. One group of very fine pieces, however, can certainly be dated post 1833 and these are the ones decorated with views of Liverpool.

A collection of large meat dishes, plates, tureens and other items, all marked with the Liver Bird (see Chapter V, page 69) and printed with views of Liverpool may be seen in the city's museum. The scenes are taken from an illustrated volume, published in 1832 in London, under the title of *Lancashire Illustrated*. The book is a miscellaneous collection of articles on the important buildings and streets in the major Lancashire cities of Manchester and Liverpool, together with notes on ancient halls, country mansions, castles, ruins and picturesque vistas. The illustrations consist of engravings after the works of S. Austin, T. Harwood and G. and C. Pyne, and are typical of many such topographical works from the early nineteenth century. The engravings in the book were carefully copied, almost line-for-line, and transferred to the surface of pots as under-glaze prints, in black, sepia and occasionally in blue, though in the last case less successfully since the cobalt print lacked definition as the oxide spread into the glaze. One of the finest of these prints is that of Castle Street, Liverpool, examples of which are known in all three colours on 20-inch dishes. The only change in the print from the original is the introduction of several figures in the foreground of the picture to help the composition of the design to fit the oval shape of the dish (Plate 179). The floral borders round the edges of these plates are splendidly arranged, decorative and robust yet not over-elaborate to conflict with the print. Another unique jug shows the same Castle Street view round its curved sides (Plate 175), a technical feat of incredible dexterity, while the same piece has a number of prints *inside*, of caricatures and comic verses in addition to a late copy of a much earlier printed subject, 'Returning Hopes'. No other jug could be more clearly identified than this, for *incised* on the base in neat 'copper plate' handwriting, is the inscription:

> February 14th, 1837 Charles Dale Maker, Herculaneum Pottery near Liverpool.

Charles Dale lived in Wellington Road, Toxteth, a few yards up the hill from the pottery, and is listed in the registers of St. James' Church as a 'Potters' thrower'. His parents Samuel and Mary came from Staffordshire, having been married at Astbury Church, and he was born on August 12th, 1801.

Another smaller oval dish is illustrated here (Plate 178) with a view of shipping entitled 'Liverpool from the Mersey' and a blue-printed bowl in the Williamson Art Gallery, Birkenhead, has local Liverpool views both inside and out (Plate 182). The former is a perspective of Colquitt Street, with the Liverpool Institution (founded by William Roscoe and now part of Liverpool University) on the left-hand side, while the latter print is a view of Birkenhead Ferry. Although views such as this varied little from the original apart from composing the picture to fit the shape of the pot, it is interesting to note that in this one a working derrick crane has been left out, while a

ferry boat not in the original has been inserted. On the whole the pictures used were well selected with an eye to suitability and decoration, but one can only speculate on the admonitory effects of a view of the House of Correction at Kirkdale, printed on the cover of a tureen!

The items thus far mentioned are all impressed with the Liver Bird but two most interesting mugs have recently been discovered, both unmarked, which show that our factory produced 'Railway' subjects. The world-famous Manchester–Liverpool Railway—the first passenger railway to be opened—began its life in 1830, though champions of the Stockton and Darlington line would make this claim to fame. Pioneered by George Stephenson, the line was built to compete with the Bridgewater Canal which by 1772 had linked Manchester with Liverpool, and the engineering feats which were performed to accomplish this project were the wonders of the world in their time. One event which particularly excited the popular imagination was the speed trial held at Rainhill before the railway service opened, on October 6th, 1829. Two of the engines taking part in the contest were the 'Rocket' by Robert Stephenson and the 'Novelty' by Braithwaite and Ericsson, and these provided a wonderful subject for the decorator of pots. A frog-mug and a shaving mug, now in Liverpool Museum (Plates 176 and 177), were made at Herculaneum which commemorate these interesting machines. In addition to the engines and carriages one has a print of Exchange Flags, Liverpool, with the Nelson monument at the centre, taken straight from *Lancashire Illustrated*. Both the mugs have portraits of that early royal champion of the rails, Queen Adelaide, but she is only partly visible on the shaving mug interior. It is of particular interest to note that the handle of the shaving mug has simulated screw heads where it is attached to the body of the pot, a feature we have seen in the early 1800s (see page 41).

Not all the later Herculaneum prints are of as good a quality as the ones just reviewed, though some have a naive charm. An example in this category is a tureen in Colonel Blewitt's collection (Plate 172) printed with a view of that architectural splendour of the Liverpool Docks, The Duke of Bridgewater's Warehouse, which has now shamefully been demolished. Built as the Liverpool goods terminal of the Bridgewater Canal in 1811 it stood in all its Georgian dignity across the waterways, with arches to allow the barges to enter for unloading. Surrounded by ships and a dockyard crane a print of this building embellishes the outer surface of the tureen four times. The printer had great difficulty in making the transfer 'take' and the creasing and cutting of the transfer-paper on the sharply convex surface has distorted the architecture in an alarming way!

It is curious that practically all the surviving pieces of the Case and Mort and Mort and Simpson periods seem to be from large table services, but such is the case. The stand, dish and tureen (Plate 171) are decorated with examples of idealised French views in under-glaze sepia, combined with floral prints on an undulating form and with a gadrooned edge. A dining plate shows this style more clearly still (Plate 174) with its charming rural landscape in the centre, its flower sprays round the edges, its rococo scrollwork and gilded

gadroons. This excellent piece comes from the Sadler collection at Stoke, and in addition to the mark of the Liver Bird it has printed on the reverse 'French Scenery' in a splendid rococo cartouche. It is a remarkable feature of these wares of the 1830s, and a tribute to their designers, that the pattern name was designed with the same attention and care as the print itself, unlike the harsh and work-a-day marks of later years. Two examples will illustrate this point, shown with their appropriate marks (Plates 173A and B, 170A and B). Both are stands for tureens with scrollwork handles at each end, the 'Field Sports' being printed in an intense black while the other 'Chinese' design in a soft, underglaze blue, has the attractive mark of 'Pekin Palm' surrounded by a wreath of leaves and surmounted by the Liver Bird as a crest.

Whatever one might feel about the weight and size and elaborate ornament of these later Herculaneum pieces one cannot but respect the self-confident pride they display, with their well-developed curves and boldly applied designs. An example which might symbolise the whole group is the tureen and stand (Colour plate VII), decorated in under-glaze blue and with enamelled flowers and butterflies. One can so clearly visualise a pair of these, proudly dominating the table of a wealthy Liverpool merchant or ship-owner, a symbol of stability and worldly success.

What else was made in the final years of the factory? If porcelain was produced no examples have been recognised and the advertisements of 1840 only mention earthenware. Even the '70 tons of china clay' in the final sale catalogue was probably the kaolin used for 'stone china' bodies, and the 'China Room' could easily be the traditional name for an apartment used for such wares in the earlier years of the concern. *The Liverpool Mercury* of October 2nd, 1840 (see page 78) refers to stoneware, and one possible line of production could well have been the ubiquitous inkwells, bottles and jars which were in great demand by the clerks and the shippers. If this was the case a salt-glaze kiln would have been in use at the works. There can be no doubt that a large range of cheaply produced tablewares and useful domestic pieces of all types continued to be made, but it is unlikely that we shall ever recognise them now.

One final enigma must be mentioned in this record of late Herculaneum products, and that is a curious range of decorative vases with the printed mark 'Herculaneum' within a garter. The style and character of the pieces known would have suggested a *much* later date than 1840 (Plates 189A and B) and perhaps these designs were, in fact, from a Staffordshire factory employing the name to distinguish a particular style or form they manufactured. It is curious, however, that several of these pieces have come to light in the Liverpool area, and even more curious that a *painted* mark ÷, like the arithmetical division sign, should be found not only on all these specimens, but also on the Pratt-type teapot from many years earlier!(Colour plate III.) Is this, we wonder, a complete coincidence, or have we here the last surviving work of an old Herculaneum potter, old enough to have taken his trade to Staffordshire and worked there for many years, after the Toxteth factory was gone?

VII. COVERED TUREEN AND STAND. Earthenware, underglaze blue printed with polychrome hand enamelling. Impressed with the 'Liver Bird'. c.1835. Height 11", overall length 16". *Courtesy of The City of Liverpool Museums.*

Chapter VII

Methods and Management

The general management of the Herculaneum Company was conducted, as we have already shown, by a small committee of shareholders who usually met monthly (more often in emergencies) to look into the accounts of the pottery, to make appointments and to take other administrative decisions. The day-to-day running of the factory was, however, the concern of the manager who had a place on the committee, and he in turn had a salesman at the Duke Street Warehouse and a cash and book-keeper at the works in Toxteth. Accounts were audited regularly following the drawing-up of the books each year-end and the auditors were, apparently, members of the committee, no outside auditors being appointed for this purpose. The Duke Street accounts were kept separately from those of the manufactory, particularly as goods other than those made at Herculaneum were being bought and retailed. The cottages surrounding the factory were the property of the Proprietors and let to the workmen under varying conditions, the accommodation often being regarded as part of their remuneration. Apprentices were the responsibility of the workmen who took them on and this also involved the provision of their housing. It is clear that many of the junior hands were paid from the wages of the senior craftsmen for whom they worked, and not by the factory management, a pernicious system which operated in other industrial trades at the time. As the factory grew larger each department was controlled by a foreman, but in its early days when it was relatively small there appear to have been only one or two such officials, one being in charge of the kilns. This latter post was one of great responsibility, for experience and skill were needed to manage the ovens and vast quantities of work could be ruined by a careless firing. Most of the labour except for heavy manual tasks and processes requiring great expertise, was provided by women and children.

The proprietors seem to have taken a reasonably enlightened view of the well-being of their employees, particularly as far as the children were concerned, and we have discovered no evidence of the cruelty and degradation which was to be found in many of the Lancashire cotton mills and coal

mines of the time. Negative evidence can, of course, be misleading, and there is no doubt that life was hard and discipline severe. We do know, however, that the proprietors paid a regular subscription towards the maintenance of the Sunday School at the works, and that in 1813 agreed to increase an annual subscription from 6 guineas to 10 guineas towards the school for the workmen's children. In addition, from 1815 onwards, a donation was regularly made of 5 guineas to The Harrington Free School, in Stanhope Street, only ten minutes walk from the pottery; this had been established on a non-denominational basis by the Reverend John Yates, and it is likely that many of the children of the potters attended. In the history of education in Liverpool this particular school is of some importance as one of the earliest in the area to be organised on a liberal and humanitarian basis. Michael Humble, one of the original founders of Herculaneum, was on its Committee and his daughter, Miss Susannah Humble, was one of the 'visitors' for the girls' department; William Smith, the manager of the factory until 1821, was also a 'visitor' for the boys' department. These 'visitors' were public-spirited people who regularly attended to examine the state of the teaching and the progress of the pupils. There is other evidence to show that the proprietors concerned themselves in the social life of the area. On November 25th, 1815, the Committee was empowered to subscribe to the funds of a 'Society in Toxteth Park for the prosecution of Felons' and the manager William Smith was instructed to provide one guinea for this purpose. Three years later, from a minute of September 1st, 1818, we learn that Samuel Worthington had personally undertaken, in 1798, to be responsible for the maintenance of the poor people employed at the factory and to indemnify the 'Overseers of the Poor of Toxteth Park' from such responsibility. In 1818 Worthington was wishing to be released from his obligations (perhaps about the time he was withdrawing his interests in the concern) and it is clear that the members of the Committee took it upon themselves to shoulder them.

Such personal and humanitarian interests in the workpeople at the factory appear to have been entirely altruistic, and there are several examples to show that good conduct and enterprise were rewarded when deserved. We have already seen how Ralph and Archibald Mansfield were encouraged in their early efforts and it is pleasant to record that on August 1st, 1809, Mr. James Woods was presented with 'two handsome jugs' in return for his 'exertions and great attention for the interest of the Proprietors in recovering a debt of £68'. In December 1813, on the occasion of the 'General Illumination' (probably to celebrate the defeat of the French Army under Napoleon which took place at Leipzig in October of that year) it was ordered that the warehouse at Duke Street should be illuminated outside with lamps and a transparency placed in one of the windows, and that the men at the works should receive bread, cheese and a barrel of ale at the expense of the proprietors.

Perhaps the most convincing evidence of the shareholders' interest in the lives of their workers was the establishment of a Chapel and Sunday School, built within the factory premises. This chapel, already referred

to in Chapter III (page 29), was founded to meet the needs of a predominantly Methodist community. The Liverpool historian, J. A. Picton,* refers to the fact that the potters, coming from Staffordshire, 'long continued a separate and isolated people, preserving their own manners and customs and still retaining their Mercian dialect. Being principally of Wesleyan Methodist persuasion, a small chapel was erected for their use by the proprietors, where Dr. Adam Clarke, Jabez Bunting, Robert Newton and many other eminent men of the denomination have occasionally officiated.' Our manager Joseph Tomkinson was evidently a strong adherent of this faith, and emigrated, as we have seen, to devote his life to its ministry. A manuscript notebook which belonged to him, dating from 1815, has been preserved, in which there are many entries showing his services in this field and referring almost weekly to the 'class' which he organised.† Expenses for Bibles, Sacramental Wine, cleaning the Chapel, seat rents for the same and so forth are mixed with such interesting items as:

By Salary paid	Hair Cutting	3d.
,, ,, ,,	Linniments	10d.
,, ,, ,,	cloathing Society	1s.
,, ,, ,,	Boat Hire & Medecine	5s.
,, ,, ,,	getting in coals	1s.
,, ,, ,,	Schooling	10s.
,, ,, ,,	Sick Club	7s. 6d.
,, ,, ,,	Leeches	3s.
,, ,, ,,	Female Society	1s.
,, ,, ,,	Lovefeast	5s. 3d.

We wonder whose the 'lovefeast' was, for which he paid from his salary 5s. 3d. and on behalf of which he collected from others the sum of 18s. shown in the opposite column of the book? His milk bills, incidentally, were all paid to the manager William Smith, which was not unusual in the days when the manager organised the provisioning of his workers as one of his duties! No trading tokens from the factory have ever come to light but they may have been issued in keeping with the current practice of those times.

Excepting occasional dismissals for bad conduct or neglect of duty the records from Herculaneum are remarkably free from any evidence of industrial disputes, which was certainly *not* the case in the shipbuilding industry of the town where labour strikes were sufficiently well organised to bring the yards to a complete standstill.‡ That some mutual benefit society, however, gradually evolved at the factory is proved by the existence in later years of 'The Herculaneum Friendly Society'. This was a well-established concern by the late 1830s and three finely-printed statements of accounts have survived for the years 1836, 1837 and 1838, when the funds held by the secretary reached over £365. These accounts were carefully kept and show that

* J. A. Picton: *Memorials of Liverpool*, London & Liverpool, 1875. Vol. II, p. 466.
† *The Tomkinson Papers*, Liverpool Museum.
‡ R. Stewart-Browne: *Liverpool Ships in the Eighteenth Century*, London, 1932.

the income was derived from subscriptions from the workers, visitors' gifts, interest from the Herculaneum Company from capital loaned, and loans from elsewhere. In the right-hand columns of the account sheets we find superannuation payments being made and sums to cover the expenses of sickness and death. On one evening each month the members of the Society held a 'Club Night', a social function for the benefit of the workers, and it seems that the affairs of the Society were closely linked with those of the chapel. Since non-conformist chapels at that time were not licensed for marriages and the Herculaneum Chapel was not suitable for burials the records of these events are to be found in the registers of the nearest Anglican churches, and in that famous Liverpool Dissenting Meeting House 'The Ancient Chapel of Toxteth'. The earliest references to the beginnings of the Herculaneum Friendly Society are in the records of this chapel for the years 1803 and 1805 when the Society was respectively called 'The Herculanium [sic] Pottery Association' and 'The Herculaneum Club'. On a stone slab in the chapel graveyard the following inscription remains, quoted exactly as it appears:

> The Herculaneum
> Pottery Benefit Soci
> ety[s] Burial Ground
> Four Graves Breath   (breadth)

It is a matter of much regret that a printed pamphlet entitled *The Articles of the Herculaneum Pottery Society, Established 9th June 1804* and published in 1807 is no longer to be found.

The pottery works buildings at Herculaneum were, as may be seen in the plan, arranged round a central yard with the factory dock along one side (D). In the early days, when the plan was drawn, the main road reached the factory on the line of the present Wellington Road (A), which ran approximately from east to west, past the workers' cottages (M). But later when Sefton Street was extended it became the main road, from north to south on the east side of the factory enclosure, engulfing part of the triangular group of cottages. At the factory gates (E) materials arriving either by road or sea would be conveniently placed for weighing in at the 'front office' and those materials requiring crushing (bones), grinding (calcined bones and flints) and blunging (clay) would be processed near the mill (C) which will be described later. No doubt the throwing, moulding and glazing rooms would be on the eastern and northern ranges of the group (P), while the printing and enamelling shops may have occupied the western side of the yard, away from the dust and noise of the opposite range (O). Approaching the dock the three final buildings would have been the packing and pattern rooms and the 'back office', close to the dock to facilitate loading into waiting ships (Q). Large vessels would stand out in the middle of the river to receive their cargoes from small boats, but the dock was large enough to take the Mersey

'flats' which traded in coastal traffic and the Irish Sea. Crate-makers' work-shops, the blacksmith's shop and the stables were probably housed in the buildings outside the main complex to the west and north (R), and the chapel and other domestic buildings such as the bakehouse also stood in isolation (F). A small tidal reservoir (S) was used to scour the silt from the dock from time to time and the reservoirs (H) provided fresh water. The kilns (B) total five in this plan which was made in about 1800, but by the time Codling's en-graving was published on the share certificates (Plate 1) an extra one had been built (T). Mayer's painting of 1825 (Plate 2) shows that further ovens had been constructed on the spare ground on the river side (U), and his view also shows the chimney of the engine and boiler house, built in the early months of 1818.

Power for grinding materials in the early years was provided by a windmill clearly visible, near the dock, in Codling's view (Plate 1), a timber structure of the 'post' type. This kind of windmill would only have been sufficient to grind small quantities of materials, probably glazes and colours. Flint in the early days was purchased already ground from Worthington's mills in North Wales (page 21), but by 1817 this procedure was found quite un-satisfactory, as we can see from the following entries in the Minute Book of the Committee:

> *April 14 1817*
> a special meeting was convened 'for the purpose of meeting Mr. Worthington to investigate the deficiency of the weight of cargoes of Flint which appeared in several cargoes measured by Mr. Smith on behalf of the Proprietors of the Herculaneum Pottery.'

> *September 1 1817*
> 'The Company having sustained considerable inconvenience from the want of a regular supply of the ground materials, the Committee deem it their duty to authorise Mr. Smith the manager jointly with the Chairman to procure estimates of the expense of erecting a steam engine and the uses to which the same may be applied.'

The building of the engine and flint mills mentioned in the second extract above was expected to take about eight months and by the end of 1818 the in-stallation had been completed.

From detailed descriptions in both the sale advertisement of 1840 (page 78) and *The Liverpool Albion* account (page 99) it may be seen that the machinery installed was a beam engine of the conventional form employed in factories until the introduction of the horizontal steam engine in the 1840s. We are indebted to Mr. R. Platt of Widnes, an authority in these matters, for the information that the cylinder of this 30 horse power engine would have measured about 18 inches in diameter, operating a piston of about 4- to 5-feet stroke. The flywheel was no doubt similar in size to that still working (1969) at the Bone Mills of Messrs, Jesse Shirley and Son Ltd. in Etruria, Stoke-on-Trent, which is about 15 feet in diameter. The flywheel would

PLAN OF THE HERCULANEUM POTTERY, ABOUT 1800

Drawn from a damaged map amongst the *Molyneux Muniments, Lancashire Record Office, Preston*

A. WELLINGTON ROAD.
B. KILNS.
C. THE MILL.
D. THE DOCK.
E. FACTORY GATES AND FRONT OFFICE.
F. THE CHAPEL.
G. RAISED AND EXTENDED SHORELINE.
H. RESERVOIRS.
I. GREAT SEA HEY.
J. HIGHER CROFT.
K. LOWER CROFT.
L. THE ROUGHS.
M. POTTERS' DWELLINGS.
N. FACTORY YARD.
O. PRINTING AND ENAMELLING SHOPS.
P. THROWING, MOULDING AND GLAZING ROOMS.
Q. PACKING, PATTERN-ROOM AND BACK OFFICE.
R. CRATE SHOP, BLACKSMITH'S SHOP AND STABLES.
S. TIDAL RESERVOIR FOR SCOURING THE DOCK.
T. SITE OF KILN BUILT BY 1806.
U. SITE OF KILNS BUILT BY 1825.

SCALE: 1 chain = 66 feet

Compare with plan of the Copper Works of Charles Roe and Company, Chapter II, pages 16, 17.

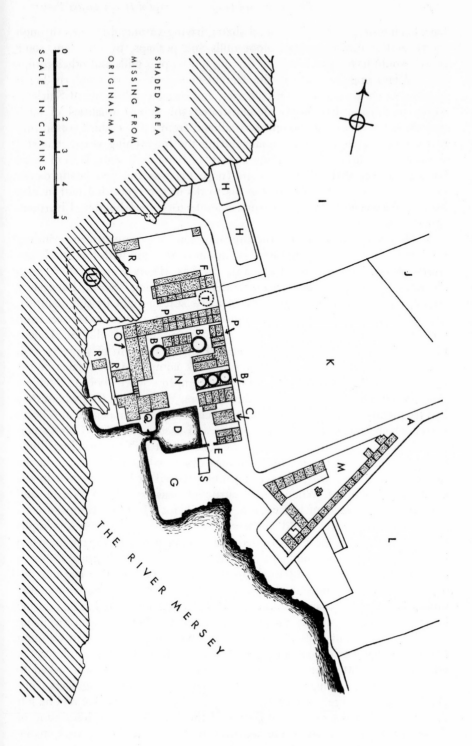

SHADED AREA
MISSING FROM
ORIGINAL MAP

SCALE IN CHAINS
0 1 2 3 4 5

THE RIVER MERSEY

have been geared to two horizontal shafts driving various flint pans through crown and spur wheels, the colour mills and perhaps, by this date, some power would have been taken for driving hoists, pug mills and other equipment. Beam engines such as the Herculaneum one were regularly being installed in cotton mills and at collieries, and the one still in use at Shirley's works in Etruria has amply demonstrated the robust qualities of such machines, for theirs was bought secondhand from a Lancashire cotton mill in 1857 and, with very few repairs during the intervening years, it is still working two shifts a day grinding 25 cwt. of bone each shift. It is of some interest to note that Thomas Wolfe (page 13) was the first Staffordshire potter to employ a steam engine at his works in the 1790s and that he also had similar machinery in his china manufactory in Islington, Liverpool, installed in 1795.

A fascinating account of the introduction of steam-driven grinding machinery for the pottery industry occurs in connection with the St. Helens works of the Herculaneum Company. In *The Wigan Gazette & General Advertiser* for April 12th, 1839, under the heading 'South Lancashire Assizes', a long description is given of a law suit brought by the plaintiffs, Messrs. Watson and Co., engine manufacturers of St. Helens, to recover from the defendants Messrs. Mort and Co., proprietors of the St. Helens Pottery Works, and of the Herculaneum Pottery, the sum of £375 8s. 11d. being the value of goods delivered and work completed. The facts of the matter were that in 1836 Messrs. Mort and Simpson, when about to establish their pottery in St. Helens, approached Messrs. Watson and Co., whom they had frequently employed before, to sell them, for £220, an engine of 6 horse power which had been built by Watsons and used at one Mr. Orrell's colliery. They also asked the plaintiffs to construct a mill for grinding flints, to be driven by the engine, but to a new design wherein the stones in the mill (runners) were *dragged* over the flints instead of being pushed in the conventional manner. When the construction was completed Watson and Co. put in their account but were never paid, for Mort and Simpson contended that the engine would not work. Mr. Simpson in person was implicated in the dispute, for it was argued that he personally saw the engine when it was at Mr. Orrell's mine in July or August 1836, and had agreed to buy it on being told that it would work up to 10 horse power. The account describes how the engine was moved to the pottery, given trials without the mills attached, tried again with the mill work in gear and found to be wanting in power. As the argument warmed Mr. Archibald Mansfield who was using a similar engine and mills for the same purpose at his pottery in Canning Place (page 67) was called to give evidence, and later the flint grinder at the Herculaneum Pottery in Toxteth, Mr. David Ashcroft, was also asked to give his opinion. During long trials of the engine one of the engineers complained that too large a weight was being put on the safety valve and he left the site fearing disaster! In the course of the investigation a description of the engine at Toxteth was presented showing that its 30 horse power engine could work two flint pans of 12 feet 6 inches diameter, 5 glaze pans, 6 colour

pans, 1 plaster mill, a clay mill, a pair of rollers and an apparatus for raising the materials. The opinion recorded at the trials of the St Helens engine was that it was being required to do too large a load of work and that the milling machinery was too heavy for it. The defendants lost their case and were ordered to pay the plaintiffs, Messrs. Watson and Co. the sum of £420 in damages.

This is not the place to attempt to explain the intricacies of the techniques used to test the engine, revealed by the newspaper account, but the basic engineering requirements for the grinding of flints and the construction of mills are more than adequately represented in the account of this action. The financial losses incurred over the law suit and the unsatisfactory nature of the machinery finally installed may well have been one of the reasons for the sale of the St. Helens Pottery by Mort and Simpson in 1841.

The materials used by the Herculaneum potters came from several parts of the country and a reference to their source and suppliers will help us to realise the wide scale on which the manufacturers in our early nineteenth-century pottery worked. Coal and fireclay (normally found together) were purchased from John Clare and Co. of Sankey and John Eccles of Sutton, both in the south Lancashire coalfields, and other collieries in the same area such as James Frazer of St. Helens and Blackburne Claughton and Co. of Ashton Green, also contributed supplies. The coal was brought to the works down the Sankey Canal from St. Helens and thence on the Mersey to the pottery dock. Clay for the pots came from several places far afield, from Dickens and Warwick of Plymouth, Devonshire, William Pyke of Corfe Castle, Dorsetshire, George Yates of Sutton Heath, Lancashire, H. L. Templer and Co. of Teignmouth and Whiteway and Hatherley of Kings-teignton, Newton Abbot, both in Devonshire. Many goods required by the potters were only available through the pottery trade in Staffordshire and its neighbouring areas, and the following list of supplies will illustrate this point:

BLUE: from William Marsh and William Booth, both of Hanley

CALX: from Shorthose & Heath, Hanley

COLOURS: from Robert Keay, Burslem

COLOURS: from Thomas Maydew & Co., Burslem

COLOURS, MOULDS, PENCILS, PRINTING PAPER: from Machin & Baggaley (Baddeley), Burslem

COLOURS, BLUE CALX, PRINTING PRESSES, PRINTING PAPER, CLAY: from Joseph Machin, Burslem

COPPER PLATES: from Andrew Eardsley, Newcastle

ENGRAVINGS: from William Parker, Hanley

ENGRAVINGS and COPPER PLATES: from James Kennedy, Burslem

FLANNEL: (used in the copper-plate printing presses) from Thomas Hulme & Son, Burslem

FLINT: from James Steele, Tunstall

GOLD LEAF: from Richard Shaw, Stoke

H

LAWNS: (used for sieving ground materials and clay) from George Twigg, Burslem

LEAD and CALX: from James Smith and J. K. Picard, Hanley

LEAD: from Burton & Holbrook, Derby

PAPER: from Machin & Baddeley, Burslem

PRINTING PAPER: from James Smith, Newcastle

Crate wood for packing appears to have come from north Lancashire and the Lake District, while many materials necessary for the buildings, machinery and general purposes were purchased from local contractors.

Nothing now remains on the site of the Herculaneum Pottery to remind us of its existence, except the name. In Wellington Road the Herculaneum Bridge Hotel stands on the sloping ground from which the view engraved by Codling in 1806 must have been taken. The Herculaneum Dock, engineered a few years after the closing of the pottery is now, in its turn, but a shadow of its former self and is still to be seen, quiet, sad and seemingly abandoned, slightly to the south of the actual factory site. The Herculaneum Steel Fabrication Works proclaim the proud and classical name on their somewhat derelict exterior, and the station on the old Liverpool Overhead Railway, dismantled several years ago, also identified itself with the pottery name. A group of once fine and dignified houses, contemporary with the pottery, called Park Terrace still stands on Grafton Street, where, lost in a wilderness of drab thoroughfares and in a dreadful state of decay, it surveys the site, across the Cheshire Lines Railway, where the potters worked. It is a far cry today from the time when cattle grazed in the fields outside the pottery wall, and, with the changing state of Liverpool and the plans which are being laid for the redevelopment of Toxteth, it is likely that the name Herculaneum itself will soon have disappeared from the scene.

We end this account with a contemporary description of the Herculaneum works written by a local reporter on the staff of *The Liverpool Albion*. Its detailed description of the tools and machinery used, the fundamental processes carried on and the prevailing conditions at the works make this passage quite unique among journalistic accounts.

THE LIVERPOOL ALBION
July 9 1827

This extensive manufactory of earthenware and china, which gives employment to from three to four hundred persons, men, women, and children, is carried on in a mass of irregular low brick buildings, close to the river. The buildings are enclosed by a high wall, and are distinguishable by several conical chimneys (as at glass houses), or hovels, as they are technically termed, to convey aloft the smoke from the ovens within them, in which the ware is exposed to the action of the furnaces. There is a commodious basin, or dock, attached, for the convenience of landing the clay and other materials, or

embarking the ware. The site and some of the buildings were, some thirty years ago, used as a copper-work, which was removed, having become a nuissance to the town, from the spot on which now stands the old tobacco warehouse, and was here carried on for upwards of twenty years. Large blocks of copper-dross are still seen about the present buildings and in the neighbourhood, and are used in walls or pavement.

We were admitted at the south gate, and conducted through the whole establishment by an intelligent workman, who, while he was assiduous to point out all that was curious to a stranger, was careful not to divulge any of the real secrets of the craft, which lie in the combinations of the materials, the chemical preparation of the colours, the glazing, etc. By a series of passages we were first taken to the steam-engine. Here cargoes of flint were stored, ready for calcination in two contiguous kilns, from which a quantity had been taken out, burned after the manner of lime, preparatory to its being ground, with water, to a fine substance, which, when dried is as fine as flour. In another yard, are fine china clay, like chalk, and cargoes in large square lumps, as imported, of bluish clay, from Pool, and a coarser sort, from Teignmouth. A limy-looking stone, with sparkling particles, from the Isle of Sheppey, and another sort from (we believe) Dorset, is also used; as well as calcined bones, in the composition for the china and finer wares. The ground story of the engine-house is occupied by a number of noisy cog-wheels, turned by a common beam, and giving motion to several strong perpendicular spindles, connected with the grinding apparatus in the story above. The visitor, on ascending to the latter, is struck by the simplicity and the magnitude of the works, which may be briefly explained. Ranged along the floor are several immense round tubs, of perhaps 12–15 feet diameter. The spindles rise through the bottoms of these, which are paved with a hard flinty stone, brought from Chirk. Attached to the spindles, and crossing the tubs, perpendicularly, like the flies of a churn, are open wooden frames, like stout railings, that the liquid may run through them. Against these are placed huge irregular blocks of the stone noticed; the flint, stone, or bones to be ground, is thrown in, and bedded with water; the circular motion of the spindles hurstles the stones along, round and round, with rapidity, and the material sinking constantly to the bottom, by its own gravity, is, of course, ground and mixed with the water, till it becomes as fine as paint fit for the brush. This operation was formerly performed by hand labour, in barrels, with a spindle in the middle and two small stones at the bottom, turned by a crank handle, but the superiority of steam has superceded this practice. The engine, which is of thirty-two horse power, also turns a variety of spindles, in pots, which grind the several colours for the painting and printing of the ware, and is serviceable in other branches of the business. The mixing room is above, to which we were not, of course, admitted.

We next entered the slip-house, an apartment in which the several qualities of clay, etc. are combined. From the stiffness of the clay, it is found necessary to dissolve it with water, in large vats, in which the stubborn lumps are worked up with long paddles, or 'blungers'. It is thence passed, in a thin

state, into a receiver, from which it is tapped off, and purified through seives. There are several of these vats for the different kinds of clay, and, when prepared, it is passed along spouts to the drying-kiln, a long apartment, through which extend a number of fire-proof troughs, that will hold from eight to ten inches, in depth, of the liquid clay. Furnaces are set to work below, and the whole bubbles and boils till, the water being evaporated, the clay is taken up in smoking lumps, and carried off to be finally mellowed by another operation. The manner of carrying those huge lump [sic] is curious; they are placed as low down on the back as possible, and the bearer, holding the load up with a hand on each side, moves along in a stooping posture. We next entered a small vault cut out in the rock: thither the clay is carried, and passes through an iron cylinder having a spindle through it, armed with knives. This has a connexion with the engine: and, being but in gear, it sucks in its rather indigestible bellyfull at the top, cuts and works it, and finally discharges it, reluctantly, below, by a square aperture, at which it is cut off by a wire in convenient lumps for carriage to the hands of those who model it into the various domestic utensils.

We next saw the operation of 'throwing' or forming the several articles, jugs, basins, and round vessels. One man was making jugs of a Roman shape. The operation is performed on an horizontal flat wheel, or 'block', turned rapidly by means of a larger wheel and cord, like a common lathe. The workman seizes a piece of clay, the size regulated by constant practice, and, throwing it on the centre of the horizontal wheel, turns it with his hands, hollows it out, thinning it up in a straightish form, and, with his fingers, gives it the required bulge or shape. The operation is performed in a few moments; and it is cut from the block by a piece of wire, and placed carefully upon boards, to be carried to the drying-house. Other round articles are formed with equal rapidity, and a piece of thin horn is used to give them the proper polish or shape where the hand is not applicable.

The finer jugs, cups, bowls, and other articles are, when sufficiently dried, though still in a very fragile state, turned on common lathes with iron tools; and it is curious to observe the clay shavings curling off. They are afterwards polished. Coarse jugs and other articles are coloured in stripes and irregular ornaments while on the lathe. The colouring is put into pots with two spouts, one of them having a very small aperture. The workman blows through the other, directing the stream to the article, which is instantly encircled by the colouring liquid. Some of these pots have divisions, and will eject a mixture of colours for coarse ornaments.

The plate and dish makers next attracted our attention. The mould, or block, upon which these are turned is exactly of the shape of the inside of the article, with notched, waved, or plain edges, as required. The clay is beated, till like a pancake, on a tablet of plaster of Paris with a flat block of the same material, having an iron handle in it, and placed on the mould, which is fixed on a spindle: a twirl of the hand sends it round, and it is smoothed over the mould, and finished with a bit of horn. Oval or round cornered dish-making is a more difficult art; it is performed in the same manner, with a

delicate jerking of the elbow to meet the shape as it turns, and render the article of equal thickness throughout. When they are taken from the mould, to which they do not stick, from its spongy nature, the inside of the plate or dish is very smooth; yet these are all, after drying a little, repolished by boys.

The next object of curiosity is the operation of the pressers, or moulders of hollow and finer table ware, which cannot be formed by the throwers; such as oval tureens, tubbs, vases, oval sugar-basins, articles having relieve mouldings or ornaments, etc. These are all formed in plaster moulds, opening in the centre, and when finished are, many of them, very beautiful and rich. Handles of common articles are cut from long lengths of clay, and turned by hand; finer embossed or ornamental handles are formed in the moulds; and the fixing of these and spouts, etc. to the pieces, is a neat branch of the trade. Here every class of workmen has a peculiar and exclusive department, and has little or no experience in other branches.

When the articles are formed, they are carried on boards to what is termed the green-house, to be dried, and there are stoves to accelerate the operation. They are then packed with more or less care into 'jaggers' (saggars) or cylindrical vessels, made of fire clay or marl, with lids, not unlike band-boxes. These are piled one on the other in the ovens, which are of considerable height, and the fires below are put in force, to a white heat, for many hours. Tea-cups and other slender-edged articles are protected from warping, or becoming crooked, by a ring of crockery ware, shaped like a quoit, being placed on the top. The china is much thicker and larger when put into the oven first than when it comes out, and, that it may shrink evenly, it is carefully packed in calcined flint, which has the quality of resisting vitrification.

The copperplate engravers next called our attention; retouching plates already used, and drawing out new patterns. The plates are numerous, and there are some very fine landscapes, views, and rich borderings, of all sizes.

The biscuit-warehouses, or stores for the reception of the articles not yet printed, painted, or glazed, are extensive: the articles are each arranged separately; and the quantity of ware is truly astonishing. These are finished as orders are received, for exportation or home use. There are warehouses for the finished articles, but these seldom remain long on hand.

We next visited the 'blue painting' shop, where the ware is painted chiefly by girls, after the several patterns, and in various colours. There is here a judicious division of labour, which greatly accelerates the work. One girl paints, for instance, the ground-work of the flowers; another, that of the leaves; and others shade and streak them. Some of the finer ware is painted after being glazed.

The printing-rooms are the busiest and most crowded in the whole premises. Here are stoves to keep the copper-plates warm, and a number of men who print them off on a kind of silk paper, in the usual manner of engravers. The ink, or printing material for the blue ware, which is, by far, the most in request, is a sort of dirty purple colour in its raw state; it is glutinous. The paper is of a nature not to imbibe it. As soon as the centre-piece and border of a plate is printed on one piece of it, little girls clip off the border

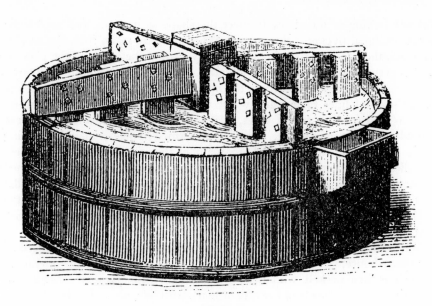

A FLINT PAN

BLUNGING THE CLAY

SIEVING THE CLAY

THROWING

APPLYING THE TRANSFER PRINTS

HANDLE MAKING

PACKING THE KILN

PLASTER MOULDS

and the superflous paper to its edge. A number of women and girls, seated on long benches, lay the centre-pieces carefully on the unglazed plates, and, afterwards, place round the borders, with as few wrinkles as possible. The article is then held in the left hand upon a piece of thick leather on the bench, and the paper is rubbed and smoothed stoutly upon it, with an instrument made of flannel, and rolled round with cord till it is as hard as a stick, a portion of the flannel being left loose at the end. This is applied to the right shoulder, the plate is turned under the rubber, as the friction smooths on the paper, and, when finished, the paper is scarcely perceptible. The article is afterwards plunged into large tubs of water; the paper comes off 'maché', and the colouring matter remains on. Operations somewhat modified are used with other articles. The prints upon small jugs, in black and other colours, are done by filling the copperplate with a sort of oil. The impress is then taken upon slices of a substance like India rubber, probably a composition of glue. These are wrapped round little jugs, or put upon flat surfaces; after which, the colouring matter is dusted on with a cushion, and adheres to the oil. Many of these prints are remarkably clear and fine. After printing, the ware is put into the oven, to dry out the oil, and the print of the blue becomes, in this stage, of a green colour. Other colours are also changed by the chemical action of the furnace, which renders the printing and painting of the ware a nice and difficult art. When thus prepared for the glazing, the articles are dipped into a fine thin composition, like whitewash; in which, ground glass, flint, etc. form ingredients, and this completely conceals the colours. They are then put into the glazing, or finishing ovens, where they are brought to a great heat for some hours; the fires are then withdrawn, they are gradually cooled, and come out the proper colour required, with a beautiful gloss, and, in all respects, suitable for the table.

Progressing to witness the higher branches of the trade, we were conducted to the china-painting or enamelling room. Here we found a clever young artist painting fine showy ware (fruit plates), for the American market, after some elegant new patterns. He had, with a fine pencil, being [sic] laying on the gold upon a superb tea-service, of china, destined to swell out the splendour of the sumptuous civic feasts given by our worthy Mayor. The workmanship is rich, yet chaste. Each piece has the Liverpool coat of arms on each side, in gold; and, when completed, they will do honour to the purchasers as encouragers of the fine arts, as well as to the furnishers as a creditable specimen of their skill and taste. The gold, when laid on the china, with a pencil, looks like dirty brown paint; it comes from the oven of a dead or frosted-gold colour, and is afterwards burnished with agates to the lustre of the genuine metal.

We concluded our inspection by visiting the pattern-room, which is plenished with a number of beautiful specimens of the skill of the potter, chiefly in china. We observed many landscapes and fancy pieces, in glowing colours, on the enamelled chimney ornaments, baskets, plates, etc. but, as these may be seen at the ware-rooms of the establishment, in Duke Street, we shall not detain our readers with further particulars.

We must not, however, close our sketch, without noticing the great regularity and order that prevail throughout the establishment, and the great cheerfulness and civility of the people. All of them seem too busy for debate or conversation, and silently attend to their several vocations. The females employed apparently exceed in number the males; and, amongst them, are many who are not without considerable personal attractions. There is within the walls a neat little chapel, where sermons are preached every Sunday; and here there is a Sunday School, attended by about 100 scholars. The females, by their attendance at the chapel and their being together, are many of them good singers, both of church music and of songs. We heard their voices several times as they joined in glees over their work. The people mostly live in cottages on the hill behind.

In the last apartment which we visited, there is placed a box, for the reception of donations, to the Benefit Society of the workmen and their families, from those who visit the works, no one being allowed to receive a gratuity. We should be glad, if this hasty and imperfect account of their labours should be the means of increasing the little fund set apart for the sick and infirm of this interesting community.

The above account is reprinted from the only copy of this issue of *The Liverpool Albion* which is known to exist. It is in the British Museum. All copies originally preserved in Liverpool were destroyed by bombing in 1941.

The line illustrations used in this extract are taken from *The Cyclopaedia of Useful Arts and Manufactures* published in 1853.

Herculaneum Pottery; Factory Marks

The practice of marking Herculaneum wares with the name of the factory began in 1796 and continued throughout the life of the pottery until 1840. Only a certain number of pieces were, however, marked and it is difficult to understand why this should have been so, but perhaps marking was regulated by the wishes of the retailing agents who may not have wanted the wares they sold to be identifiable as to origin. In certain cases only one or two pieces of a table service were marked to identify the whole; when odd pieces come to light now, therefore, they have no marks. The *quality* of the wares produced bears no relationship, generally speaking, to whether or not pieces were marked, for some extremely fine specimens are found unmarked yet at the same time some very humble ones bear the factory impress.

The following list of marks, with corresponding Plate numbers for reference amongst the illustrations, may be used to identify pottery from Herculaneum and to date the specimens approximately. The actual sizes of some of the marks will be found on the captions to the Plates.

1. *Impressed mark HERCULANEUM using printers' type (Plates 33c, 84, 105B and 129).*
   This mark occurs in several sizes, from very small about $\frac{1}{16}$ inch in height, to the largest size about $\frac{1}{8}$ inch in height. The very small marks belong to the period from 1796 to 1810, while the larger sizes were in use until about 1825–1830. In some cases there is a numeral combined with the mark, e.g. HERCULANEUM $\frac{}{12}$ which might denote the year of manufacture after 1800, but this cannot be relied upon in every case. In a few rare cases the mark appears as H P 1809 but this mark has not been found for any other year. On one very rare piece (Plate 99) the mark is fully dated and appears as HERCULANEUM. 1808

2. *Impressed mark HERCULANEUM in Gothic printers' type (Plate 76).*
   This is a very rare mark which in one case is found on a commemorative stoneware bust of Nelson (Plate 114). It is suggested that this was briefly used to identify itself with the general mourning following the death of Nelson in 1805.

3. *Impressed mark of HERCULANEUM in a semi-circle over a crown (Plate 164b).*

4. *Impressed mark on a garter surrounding a crown (Plate 166b).*
   Marks 3 and 4 appear to have been used for a few years during the mid 1820s

when trading had become highly competitive and other factories were employing the crown device (see page 68). Pieces marked in this way are fairly rare and are invariably used on blue-printed earthenware. It is likely that mark 3 pre-dates mark 4.

5. *Impressed mark of the 'Liver Bird' (Plates 81 and 167B).*
This mark was derived from the heraldic bird used on the Liverpool Corporation Coat of Arms (granted to Liverpool in 1207) and appears to have been used at the factory from the late 1820s, perhaps until the very end in 1840 (see page 69).

6. *Under-glaze printed marks (Plates 170B and 173B).*
Various printed marks incorporating pattern names were used in the 1820s and 1830s but the one reproduced containing the pattern name 'Pekin Palm' is the only one noted which includes the Liver Bird. The 'Field Sports' mark is shown printed over the impressed Liver Bird.

7. *Over-glaze printed mark (Plate 135).*
This delicate and elegant transfer-printed mark is found in puce on pieces of high quality porcelain dating from about 1810–1815. It is a rare mark and includes the Liver Bird and the name of the town of Liverpool.

8. *Moulded mark of the Case and Mort period (Plate 188B).*
This is a very rare mark indeed being only known on one specimen. The initials C M refer to Thomas Case and James Mort, managers of the factory between 1833 and 1836 (see page 75). Unlike the previous marks it was not applied separately from the manufacture of the pot by impressing or printing, but was an integral part of the mould from which the jug was cast.

9. *Printed mark in dark brown of HERCULANEUM within a garter (Plate 189B).*
This is by no means a proven Herculaneum mark since it appears on wares which would suggest a much later date than the period of the Herculaneum factory, and it may be a pattern name only, used by a later nineteenth-century Staffordshire pottery. Since it appears in conjunction with a particular decorator's mark which *is* associated with a Herculaneum Pratt-type teapot of about 1810 (Colour plate III) it is included here and is specially referred to in the text (page 88).

10. *Transfer-printed mark used on American wares (Plate 59).*
This mark HERCULANEUM POTTERY LIVERPOOL, printed in capitals underneath the American Eagle, occurs on several jugs in American collections, but no comparable mark is found on any other wares. The jugs on which it is found date from about 1800–1810 and it is associated in several examples with a print entitled 'Commodore Preble's squadron attacking the City of Tripoli, August 3rd, 1804'.

Herculaneum Pottery; Resolutions of the Committee

The following brief extracts are taken from the *Minute Book of the Committee of Proprietors* from 1806 to 1822.

November 24 1806
First meeting held at the Star and Garter Tavern in Paradise Street.
Those present were: Samuel Holland, John Menzies, Robert Jones, Edward Blackstock, Samuel Berey, William Harding, John Harding, Richard Sutton, Samuel Worthington, George Orred, William Fawcett, Adam Steuart, William French, William Cartwright, Lathan Hanmer, Ralph Mansfield.
Archibald Keightley in the chair.

November 28 1806
Appointed Ralph Mansfield to be acting Manager and Superintendent of the Pottery concern for the ensuing year with a salary of £150, occupation of house free and use of coals.
Ordered that the bank account of the concern be continued at the Bank of Arthur Heywood, Esq., & Co. as heretofore.
Ordered that a board be put up in the warehouse 'No goods to be sold here by retail, but for ready money only' inscribed or printed thereon.

March 3 1807
Reported that Mr. Gregson's house at the bottom of Duke Street is more desirable for a warehouse; taken same for a period of 21 years.

March 10 1807
Immediate necessity for the addition of a number of cottages for the artists and workmen, an estimate for 10 such cottages being submitted by Mr. Ireland accepted at the sum of £470.

March 18 1807
Resolved alteration to Ware Rooms in Duke Street . . . as soon as possible and furnished with a proper assortment of China and Earthenware—that an advertisement be inserted in Gore's Liverpool Advertiser, London Daily Advertiser and Worcester Weekly Paper for a proper person qualified as salesman at a suitable salary.

May 5 1807
Contract with Mr. William Reeves to fill appointment for Warehouseman at a salary of £100 per annum and also occupation of rooms in Duke Street rent free for one year.

May 25 1807
Resolved that the following advertisement be inserted in the Liverpool newspapers: 'The Proprietors of the Herculaneum Pottery beg leave to respectfully inform the Public that they have opened a Warehouse at the bottom of Duke Street for the sale of China and Earthenware for Home use, where orders for Exportation will be received at and executed with Punctuality and Despatch. Herculaneum Pottery'. Resolved that the Bill Heading plate be engraved. . . . (Plate 190).

July 28 1807
Resolved that a good stock of coals be kept at the Pottery, say not less than 50 or 100 tons.
Resolved that in future all Bills of Parcels of goods and wares purchased by the Herculaneum Pottery Company from Staffordshire or elsewhere, be immediately sent to Mr. Mansfield. . . .

November 3 1807
Resolved that £500 be insured on stock in Warerooms, Duke Street
        £200 on 10 new cottages
        £100 on new saggar house
        £200 on stock therein.

January 15 1808
Special meeting to take into account the conduct and impropriety of Mr. William Reeves, their clerk and salesman, admonishment having had no effect.
Resolved to terminate his appointment after existing contract had expired. . . .

March 8 1808
Balance of cash at the Bank nearly all drawn out and several debts remain uncollected. . . . List of debts to be laid before the committee.

May 2 1808
Resolved that the following advertisement be inserted twice in the succeeding weeks in Gore's, Merritt & Wright's and Billinge's newspapers:

HERCULANEUM POTTERY
The proprietors respectfully inform their friends and the public that they have on sale, for home use, at their Ware Rooms in Duke Street a large and elegant assortment of China and Earthenware, of the most new and approved patterns. Orders for Exportation sent to the rooms will be forwarded to the Works, and executed with punctuality and despatch.

May 6 1808
Read a letter from Mr. Holden re appointment as clerk. Offered him the post at 60 guineas per annum from time of commencing employment until he shall fix his residence and begin to occupy a House in the Park near the Pottery, and from that time to be allowed after the rate of £80 per year as salary.
Understood that he shall attend at the Pottery before breakfast and during the same hours as the other clerks. . . .
Considered application by Mr. Edward Buxton and resolved that he be appointed as salesman in Duke Street in place of Mr. Reeves, at a salary of £80 per annum. . . .

Resolved that the following circular letter be sent to the Proprietors accompanied with the cards:

Sir. The Committee have taken the liberty of sending you herewith a few cards, and request you will have the goodness to circulate them among your friends.

They also beg leave to impress upon your mind the necessity of every Proprietor (in these precarious times) using his utmost endeavour to promote the interest of the concern.

September 6 1808

The meeting noticed the increase of small debts through pottery sales at Duke Street. Resolved therefore no purchase to be made on credit for goods less than 2 guineas unless purchaser has an open account in the books of the Herculaneum Pottery Company, or be of known respectability and resident in Liverpool. . . .

November 25 1808

Resolved that Mr. Archibald Keightley continue as solicitor and that Mr. Samuel Worthington be continued an Honorary Member of the Committee and be thanked for his services.

December 14 1808

Considered cash and expenditure and resolved to make application to each proprietor to make an advance of £50 on each share held—amounting to £2,500 . . . and that Mr. Mansfield curtail the weekly expenditure by reduction of the wages to the artists and workmen employed and of such other part of the weekly expenditure as he shall see most proper.

April 3 1809

Insurance on Duke Street stock of Earthenware be extended from £500 to £1,000 and that the Albion Insurance Office be informed.

June 6 1809

Resolved in future no goods to be sent out upon an adventure to any part out of Great Britain without insurance being previously effected.

August 1 1809

At Mr. Mansfield's suggestion resolved that the present china oven be taken down and enlarged and that the same be done as expeditiously as possible.

June 5 1810

Mr. William Smith be henceforth considered and he is hereby appointed the Acting Manager of this concern in the room of the late Mr. Mansfield deceased, and that his annual salary be advanced to the sum of £220 per year. . . .

November 26 1810

This meeting, feeling sensible of the great loss which Mrs. Mansfield and her family have sustained by the death of the late Mr. Mansfield, they do vote the sum of 40 guineas to be presented to his widow as a token of respect which the proprietors bear to his memory.

December 4 1810

The Committee having been applied to by Mr. Edward Buxton, and in consideration of his faithful services and growing increase of his family, have resolved . . . that the said Edward Buxton's salary be advanced to £100 per year. . . .

February 5 1811

The Committee having taken into consideration the propriety of erecting a Steam

Engine at the Works, for the purpose of grinding the Flint, Glazes and Colours . . . are of opinion that a very considerable saving would be produced. . . . They also find that to enable them to carry such a plan completely into effect, a loan of £2,500 would be required, which they propose to raise by an advance of £50 per share from each Partner; but as they are aware that some of the Partners might object to a further advance of capital until they find the beneficial effect of such a plan, they propose that if any Partner or Partners will advance such loan they shall have credit . . . in their Share Account in the Ledger and shall be paid five pounds per centum per annum upon such sum advanced. (N.B. this proposition did not go through and no steam engine was erected at the works until 1817—see April 14th 1817 and following minutes.)

July 2 1811
Mr. Smith reported to the Committee that he had appreciated the services of Mr. Archibald Mansfield for the last two years and was of opinion that £35 was what he ought to be paid for his services.
Resolved that the above £35 be paid to Mrs. Mansfield in discharge of the demand due from the Herculaneum Company for her son's services to this day and in full.

November 25 1811
Resolved that power is granted to the Committee to make such allowance to the Sunday School as they shall, in their discretion, from time to time see fit and think reasonable and proper.

February 4 1812
Resolved that it would be advantageous to open a warehouse for the sale of earthenware in Liverpool and that the warehouse situate on the East Side of the Dry Dock at the bottom of Redcross Street appears most eligible.

January 5 1813
Resolved that Mr. Tomkinson shall have the occupation free from payment of any rent of the house he now holds, so long as he continues to hold his present situation as Clerk to the Proprietors, he paying all such taxes as the house may be charged with.

March 2 1813
Resolved that a new Flatt be built for carrying coals for the use of the Concern and Mr. Mercer having offered to build and complete a Flatt suitable for the sum of One Thousand Pounds including all materials ready for sea . . . they agree to enter into contract with Mr. Mercer accordingly.

May 11 1813
Resolved that Mr. Smith be requested to wait on Mrs. Briggs and fix the terms of her engagement at the rooms in Duke Street, and he is authorised to engage her in that situation at a salary or wages of sixty pounds per year.

November 25 1813
Resolved that the Annual Subscription of £6 6s. od. heretofore given by the Proprietors to the school established at the Pottery for the workmen's children be augmented to ten guineas per annum.

December 3 1813
Resolved (for the evening of the General Illumination) that the warehouse in Duke Street be illuminated on the outside with lamps and transparency in one of the windows and that Mr. Smith and Mr. Holden have hereby authority to see this order carried into execution, the expense not to exceed Twenty Pounds.
Resolved also that the men at the Works have bread and cheese and a Barrel of Ale at the expense of the Proprietors on Saturday after the general illumination.

I

February 1 1814
Resolved that Mr. Smith do take a journey to London as early in the month of March next as convenient to obtain information and to engage additional assistants for the advantage of the concern.

February 8 1814
At a special meeting of the Committee this day to take into consideration the propriety of disposing of a quantity of (unsaleable) stock of Earthenware and China accumulated in the last seven years.
Resolved that the above stock be shipped in two or more parcels as may be most convenient for the Lisbon market or any other that may be thought advisable—and that Mr. Smith has a discretionary power in the disposal of the above goods for the advantage of the concern.

May 3 1814
Resolved two additional cottages be erected on the vacant plott of ground adjoining the other cottages, the same being much wanted for the accommodation of the workmen. . . .

June 7 1814
Mr. Smith having reported to the Committee that a modeller is much wanted at the Works—resolved that Mr. Smith do make such application as he may think fit in order to engage one as soon as possible.

November 1 1814
Resolved . . . the difference between the actual cost of the manufactured goods on hand and the cash prices is about 20%.
That the following mode in re-valuing the stock at the ensuing balance be adopted viz: from the long or credit prices 15% be deducted (which will reduce the amount to the *cash* prices) from which cash price 20% shall also be deducted thus bringing the value of the manufactured stock to about its original cost.

December 6 1814
Resolved that Mr. Smith be authorised to make such extension in manufacturing the Blue Ware as he shall think necessary and proper for the advantage of the concern.

January 3 1815
Mr. Smith reported to the Committee that in consequence of his suggestion to them at their last monthly meeting of a supposed deficiency in the account of the stock in Duke Street, that he has caused a fresh account to be since taken, and that the same now appears to be correct.
It appearing to the Committee that a reduction of the expenses in the management of the Rooms in Duke Street may be made by reducing the number of persons attending at those rooms and that the services of Edward Buxton be dispensed with. Resolved that Mr. Smith do give notice to Ed. Buxton to provide for himself another situation in 3 months or sooner if he can so provide for himself.

June 6 1815
Mr. Smith having laid before the Committee an estimate of the expense of taking down and rebuilding the Packing Room and Straw Loft over same amounting to £160 including all the materials &c. and also expense of building three new cottages for the sum of £172 10s. 0d.
Resolved that the said buildings and cottages be erected and completed with all convenient expedition.

Resolved also that an additional Hovel and Oven be erected . . . the estimate of the expense of which will not exceed sixty pounds.

November 23 1815
Committee audited accounts and found that there is a surplus of capital arising from profits more than sufficient to meet the current exigencies for the ensuing year.
Resolved that it be recommended to the Proprietors that £1,500 (being £30 on each Proprietor's share) be paid out of the cash now in hand as a bonus.
Resolved also that it be recommended to the Proprietors that the Dividends for the ensuing year 1816 be 8 per cent on the amount of the consolidated capital £30,000 being the same as the preceding year.

April 2 1816
It appearing that the terms of insurance offered by the Norwich Union Fire Office are more advantageous to the insured than the proposals held out by the other insurance offices. . . .

£	
500	on Warehouse, Shew Room & Counting Houses
2,500	on Utensils and Stock therein
150	on Manager's House
200	on Throwing House, Hot House, Turning House and Rooms over
200	on Stock and Utensils therein
200	on Plate Makers Stoves and Rooms over
300	on Stock and Utensils therein
200	on Dish Makers Stove, Flagg'd House, dipping House, Saggar House (and Rooms over)
400	on Stock and Utensils therein
100	on Enamelling Shops and Rooms under
200	on Stock and Utensils therein
120	on seven cottages and a Printing Room under one roof
200	on Stock and Utensils in Printing Room
100	on Slip House
250	on Chapel
50	on Mould Makers Stove and Rooms over
80	on Stables and Buildings adjoining
50	on Live Stock therein
150	on China Saggar House and Rooms over
300	on Stock and Utensils therein
50	on Carters House and Two sheds adjoining
200	on Biscuit Saggar House and rooms over
50	on Plate Makers Stove and Green Ware Room and rooms over
1,000	on Fifty cottages in equal proportions
100	on Wind Mill in the Yard
100	on Saggar House and printing shop over
50	on Utensils and Stock therein
30	on Cottage at the Gates
100	on Packing House and Sheds in Back Yard
200	on Stock therein
20	on Mill and Cottage in the field
2,000	on Stock of China and Earthenware in Warehouse situate in No. 3 Duke Street, Liverpool, and fixtures therein
100	on four cottages on the Lower Road to Liverpool under the reservoirs
£10,250	
500	= Insured on Engine & Mill 1818

That the insurance on the buildings and stock of utensils belonging to the Herculaneum Company now insured in the Albion Fire Office be discontinued and a policy of insurance be taken out in the said Norwich Union Fire Office amounting in the whole to the sum of £10,150 as per specification particulars . . . and that Thomas Case Esq. and Sam'l Berey Esq. be requested to see this Policy of Insurance properly effected.

May 7 1816
Resolved that Dividends be paid at 4%.

April 14 1817
. . . convened for the purpose of meeting Mr. Worthington to investigate the deficiency of the weight of the cargoes of Flint which appeared in several cargoes measured by Mr. Smith on behalf of the Proprietors of the Herculaneum Pottery.

September 1 1817
The Company having sustained considerable inconvenience from the want of a regular supply of the ground materials, the Committee deem it their duty to authorise Mr. Smith . . . to procure estimates of the expense of erecting a steam engine and the uses to which the same may be applied.

November 25 1817
Resolved that the Committee to be this day chosen have full power and authority to erect a Steam Engine for grinding of Flint and other useful purposes to which the same may be applicable and to enter into a contract with Mr. Kirk or some other competent engineer for building and completing the same. . . .

December 2 1817
The Committee having taken into consideration Mr. Worthington's letter of 28 November last. . . .
Resolved that it is their wish to have the ground material ascertained as correctly as possible and as Mr. Worthington has a conviction that it cannot be done without Blunging the whole of a cargo, to a standard weight, it is their desire that Mr. Worthington do either come over or send a person on whom he can rely to Blunge the next cargo, conceiving as they do that the delivery is at their works consequently the accuracy to be ascertained there; and if Mr. W. has any casks or tubs that will facilitate the operation they suggest the propriety of his sending them for that purpose.
And the Committee take the liberty of stating that it is their intention to act on the resolution of the General Meeting and until they are in a situation to supply themselves they have no objection to take the ground material from Mr. Worthington which probably will be for the space of eight months at least, and beg Mr. Worthington's immediate reply relating to the supply—but the Committee decline entering into any agreement for a continuance to the end of Mr. Worthington's term.

January 6 1818
Mr. Kirk having produced a plan and estimate for the erection of the intended Steam Engine—Resolved that the plan be approved and the erection of the engine be proceeded in without delay.

May 1 1818
Special meeting of the Committee convened for the purpose of taking into consideration the propriety of altering the old road adjoining the Herculaneum works and opening a new road of 30 feet wide agreeably to a plan now produced. . . .

Resolved that a letter be written to Mr. Foster . . . submitting the intended plan . . . to be laid before the Rt. Hon. Lord Sefton for his approbation . . .

J. Foster Esq., Sir,
I beg leave to state to you that the Herculaneum Pottery Company are desirous of bringing the whole of their manufactory within one enclosure. In order to effect this it will be needful for them to have the present road from the north to the south end of their works entirely closed, and they are willing to open another one in lieu thereof. With this object in view they beg leave to submit to you on behalf of the Rt. Hon. the Earl of Sefton the plan accompanying this letter in which is traced out (in dotted lines) the line of road they propose to open. . . .
Upon receiving his Lordship's consent hereto the Herculaneum Pottery Company will immediately open the Road as here laid down and make the same with proper materials at their own expense to the satisfaction of the magistrates without any charge to his Lordship.
Requesting you will have the Goodness to lay the matter before his Lordship and to obtain his reply as soon as convenient.

I am, on behalf of the Committee of the Herculaneum
Pottery Company,   Yours very respectfully
Thomas Case.

(N.B. The alteration of the roads mentioned in the above application to Lord Sefton was carried out and the full details of the signed agreement between the H.P.C. and Lord Sefton may be seen in the Lancashire Record Office, Preston. Ref: QSB/1 1819.)

January 5 1819
Messrs. James & Co.'s application for taking the land opposite the Pottery Dock as a yard for ship building having been taken into consideration: resolved that the matter be defer'd for the present.

July 6 1819
Mr. Holland having applied for permission to make a tunnel out of the reservoir for the purpose of supplying a Watering Place in his fields for his cattle; the Committee think that by granting such permission it may lead to disputes in future. Resolved that such application be rejected.

May 2 1820
Mr. Case and Mr. Keightley being deputed at the last meeting of the Committee to enter into an agreement with Mr. Thomas Hawkes & Co. of Dudley, near Worcester, Glass Manufacturers, for the sale of Glass manufactured by said Messrs. Hawkes & Co. by the Herculaneum Company at their ware rooms in Duke Street, Liverpool under certain restrictions on Commission. Mr. Case and Mr. Keightley now report to the Committee that they had entered into a contract in writing with said Mr. Hawkes & Co. for the above purpose.

August 1 1820
Mr. Smith reported to the Committee (agreeable to their orders at the last meeting) he had been at the Potteries in Staffordshire and has finally agreed with Mr. Benjamin Bentley (at present residing there) as a Modeller for the Herculaneum Works.

October 19 1820
At a meeting . . . convened for taking into consideration certain proposals contained in a letter dated the 25th. September last addressed to Thomas Case Esq., . . . from John Foster Esq., Agent to the Earl of Sefton, respecting the purchase of

of the reversion and ground rents of the Company's premises in Toxteth Park and also in respect of payment for the same if it should be thought eligible to make such purchase. Copy of the letter referred to in the preceding minutes:

Liverpool   25th. September 1820

Sir,

I beg leave to acquaint you I have received authority from the Earl of Sefton to offer to sell to the proprietors of the Herculaneum Pottery near this town, all his Lordship's interest in the land and premises in their possession, including the reserved annual rent paid by the said proprietors, for the sum of Two Thousand Pounds, 10 per cent to be paid within two months from this date, and the remainder in six months from this date hereof; The deposit of 10 per cent to be forfeited if the remainder of the purchase money be not paid at the time mentioned. It being understood that this offer is made subject to the agreement dated the 12th. May 1818 for opening a New Road and closing the old ones, and for rounding the corner of a garden or enclosure near the south-west corner of the said premises.

This offer will be considered null and void if not accepted in two months from its date.

	I am, Sir,
Thomas Case Esq.,	Your obedient humble servant,
Chairman of the Committee of	John Foster
Proprietors of the Herculaneum	
Pottery.	

(N.B. This offer was agreed to initially, then at another meeting in November 1820 it was decided to decline it. On February 27th. 1821, however, it was again discussed and this time unanimously agreed to accept the offer.)

May 1 1821
Resolved . . . that no coals be brought to these works in future but by way of the Sankey Canal; the Committee having made a calculation of the Expense of supplying the works with coals, do find the difference so great as to warrent them in coming to the foregoing resolution.

June 5 1821
Resolved for the future the charges for freight of the two Flatts Argo & Phoebe (N.B. so-named after William Smith's wife) be 2/4 p. ton only and that the Captain of the Argo be paid 1/3 and the owners 1/1 p. ton for each trip for the carriage of Coals for the Herculaneum Company.

August 7 1821
Resolved that Mr. Barlow be directed to take a journey to the Potteries (in Staffordshire) in order to enquire into the prices given there to the various Artists and workmen and also as to what artists and workmen may be proper to engage, and to consult and arrange with Mr. Smith as to that object. . . .

November 6 1821
Mr. Smith having reported to the Committee that in his judgement (as Manager of the Concern) the Committee will not be justified in paying the full amount of the usual half-yearly Dividend of 4 per cent out of the profits of the Concern this year. Resolved that the half years Dividends due on the 12th. inst. be £900 only instead of £1200 and that the same (being after the rate of 3 per cent.) be paid to the Proprietors accordingly.

Resolved that Mr. Smith do prepare a full statement and Balance sheet of the state of the concern to be laid before the Committee. . . .

November 26 1821
Mr. Smith having stated to this meeting that at the meeting of the Committee when the report on the then state of the manufactory was made to them 'that with their acceptance of that report he wished them to understand that he tendered his resignation' which report and tender with all the other circumstances connected with the causes that have led to such result having now been taken into considera- tion and whilst the Proprietors most sincerely regret the differences of opinion which have necessarily led to the conclusion they are under the necessity of coming to, they feel it incumbent on them and therefore hereby do agree to accept Mr. Smith's resignation, Mr. Smith having acceded to the above on condition of his two shares being taken at £1,500 cash on the 12th. Nov. inst. and the concern taking his share of the Flat Argo at £225 cash the same period.
Resolved that the cordial thanks of this meeting be given to the Chairman for his able and impartial conduct in the Chair.

November 29 1821
It appearing to the Committee that the two shares which were agreed to be pur- chased from Mr. Smith . . . at the sum of £1,500 by (Mr. Case) the Chairman were valued by Mr. Smith at a much greater sum than the shares would under present circumstances sell for and that such offer was made by the Chairman in order to carry into effect Mr. Smith's resignation. Resolved that the authority given by the Chairman . . . 'authorising Mr. Tomkinson to take the superintendence and management of the works' be confirmed and continued until further orders.

January 1 1822
(N.B. Full details of the Minutes of this date are quoted in Chapter V, page 63.)

March 5 1822
Resolved that Mr. Holden and Mr. Mansfield do take a journey into Staffordshire to order two sets of copper plates of teaware to enquire as to Table Services of Blue Ware and to make such observations and obtain the best information of the general manufactories there in their power and report their observations. . . .

April 2 1822
Resolved that Mr. Carson and Mr. Sutton be . . . a select committee to superintend and give their joint directions about the alterations to be made in the house (late occupied by Mr. Smith) and intended for the residence of Mr. Tomkinson and Mr. Mansfield.

May 7 1822
Mr. Mansfield having laid before the Committee an estimate of the expense of erecting an additional Flint pan amounting to about £250 a calculation of the beneficial results in grinding an additional quantity of Flint and which appears to the Committee to be desirable . . .
Resolved that the additional Flint pan &c. be erected and completed with all convenient despatch. . . .

June 4 1822
Resolved that it is highly expedient that Mr. Holden (as salesman at the Rooms in Duke Street) do henceforth give the whole of his time and attendance at the Ware Rooms in order to promote the sales and to attend to all orders as well wholesale as the Retail sales.
The Committee this day entered into an agreement with Mr. Wm. Lovatt as Modeller and Painter for a further term of Six Months at the wages of 45/- per week.

August 6 1822

The Committee this day entered into an engagement with Mr. Jesse Taylor as foreman of the Painters for the term of One year from the 11th. November next at the Wage of Two Pounds Ten Shillings per week. . . .

Resolved that in order to give publicity and Identity to the China and Earthenware manufactured by the Herculaneum Pottery Co. the words 'Herculaneum Pottery' be stamped or marked on some conspicuous part of all china and earthenware hereafter made and manufactured at this Manufactory (see page 68).

October 1 1822

Mr. Barlow having signified to the Committee that he is desirous of renewing his engagement for a further term of three years from the 11th. November next (at which time the term of his present engagement will expire) the Committee have this day agreed with him for a further term of 3 years at his present salary £150 p. year and Mr. Barlow being now present doth agree with the Committee to the terms above stated.

November 5 1822

Resolved that the half year Dividends of 3 p. cent on the consolidated capital of £30,000 be paid on the 12th. Inst. to the Proprietors according to their respective shares.

> The further minutes and proceedings of the Committee are transferred to the new Committee Book at and from the 25th. November 1822.
> Thomas Case—Chairman
> Richd. Sutton—Secretary to the Committee.

The Tomkinson Papers

The Tomkinson papers were the personal documents of Mr. Joseph Tomkinson (1784–1836), (see Chapter II, page 23). They accompanied him to America when he left Herculaneum in about 1826 and were in the hands of his grand-daughters, Miss Martha and Miss Ellen Tomkinson in Harrisburg, Pennsylvania in 1924. They were sent by the Misses Tomkinson to Mr. Peter Entwistle at Liverpool Museum where they may still be seen.

The collection of papers comprises:

1. A small pocket book entitled *'Price Book for the Warehouse from December 8th. 1808.'*
2. A small notebook, without covers, containing many recipes of pottery materials and various disconnected personal notes.
3. A Cash Book for 1818.
4. A notebook, without covers, of 28 pages written by Benjamin Tomkinson.
5. Various loose sheets of papers as follows:

   (a) ⎫
   (b) ⎬ glaze, body and enamel recipes
   (c) ⎪
   (d) ⎭
   (e) Prices paid to workmen for various articles and processes.
   (f) Underglaze colour recipes.
   (g) Factory Balance Sheet for the year 1825.

6. Three letters from Miss M. and Miss E. Tomkinson to Peter Entwistle, Liverpool, 1924.

The following extracts are selected from some of these papers, primarily to provide evidence for the types of bodies, glazes and other materials used, and articles made at the Herculaneum factory. The number of recipes in the documents totals about 350 and since many are repetitive only those of the principal bodies and glazes manufactured are quoted.

I. 1. *PRICE BOOK FOR THE WAREHOUSE FROM DECEMBER 8th. 1808*

Neat Prices as under ('Neat' here means 'net')

		s	d
Common China Enameld Best	12 Cups not handled	3s	3d
	12 Saucers	3	3
	12 Cups handled or Cans	6	–
	1 Teapot small	2	2
	1 do. middle size	2	5
	1 do. large	2	7
	1 Stand		7
	1 Slop Bowl		10
	1 Sugar Bowl		8
	1 Cream		8
	1 Sugar Box	1	3
	1 Toast Plate		10
	12 Bkfast Bowles handled	12	–
	12 do. comn.	6	–
	12 Saucers	6	–
	12 Coffees	6	–
	1 Coffeepot	3	6
White China Best	12 Cups handled	6	9
	12 Saucers	3	9
	12 Coffees	6	–
	1 Teapot	2	8
	1 Stand		9
	1 Slop	1	2
	1 Sugar Box	1	6
	1 Cream	1	2
	2 Plates	2	3
White China Second	12 Cups handled	4	6
	12 Coffees	4	6
	12 Saucers	3	–
	1 Teapot	2	–
	1 Stand		6
	1 Bowl		8
	1 Sugar Box	1	0
	1 Cream		6
	2 Plates	1	4
Neat Prices Cream Coloured Ware	Porrenjes pr. doz.	2	0
	Jugs ,, ,,	2	0
	Mugs ,, ,,	1	6
	Bakers, Comn. 7 inches	1	4
	Bakers, deep 7 inches	1	6
	Salads, 7 inches	1	9
	Oval flat dishes 10 inches	1	9
	Patty Pans pr. doz.	1	8
	Pickle Jars ,, ,,	1	6
	S. Boats, 1st. size	1	0
	S. Boats, 4th. size	2	0
	Plates, Royal	1	3
	Twifflers		11
	Muffins 7 inches		10
	Water Ewers	2	6
	Turtlemugs pr. doz.	2	4
	Water Plates		9

Neat Prices Myrtle Pattern & Rose Common Ware	6 Cups and Saucers	1	6
	1 Teapot Capt.		10
	1 Slop Bowle		$3\frac{1}{4}$
	1 Sugar Bowle		$2\frac{1}{2}$
	1 Cream Ewer		3

		Gross		Neat	
Neat and Gross Prices of a set of china Val. £1 10 0	12 Cups handled	7	0	6	0
	12 Saucers	4	6	4	0
	12 Cans	7	9	6	6
	1 Teapot	3	2	3	0
	1 Stand	1	0		10
	1 Sugar Box	2	0	1	6
	1 Cream		11		10
	2 Plates	2	6	2	4
	1 Slop Bowl	1	2	1	0
		£1 10	0	£1 6	0

(The following recipes are included in the warehouse price book for 1808, but the date of the entries is probably later because Ironstone China was not patented until 1813.)

Body for Iron Stone China	250 Stone
	300 Flint
	260 Blue Clay
	14 oz. Blue Calx.

Black Egyptian	100 Blue Clay
	60 Ochre
	40 Magnass (manganese)
	20 Iron Scales

Cream Coloured Glaze	120 lb. Lead
	48 lb. Stone
	18 lb. Flint

Blue Printed Glaze	126 lb. Lead
	56 lb. Stone
	24 lb. Flint

Green for Edging	$1\frac{1}{2}$ lb. Copper Calcined
	3 lb. Glass
	2 lb. Flint
	2 lb. Stone

A good Jasper Body	14 oz. Stone
	12 oz. China Clay
	$1\frac{1}{4}$ oz. Blue Calx.

Brown for Printing	6 lb. Antimony
	6 lb. Litherage (litharge)
	2 lb. Nitre
	2 lb. Manganese
	$1\frac{1}{2}$ lb. Blue Calx.

A good Green Glaze   12 Red Lead
           5 Flint
           1 Calcined Copper
           1 Borax
           4 Stone

Black Glaze   13 cups Red Lead
           7 cups Flint
          23 cups Slip
           9 cups Manganese
Grind it all together at the Mill and then
sift it through a fine No. 12 Lawn.

Oils for Printing   1 qt. Linseed Oil
           $\frac{1}{2}$ pint Oil sweet almonds
           1 teaspoonful Red Lead

Receipt for preparing gold 12 dwts. gold
H.P.Co.   6 grains lead flux
           4 grains prepared silver
           2 grains copper calcined & ground in water
           1 grain crude antimony

For Brown Line   4 lb. litherage
           3 lb. crude antimony
           1 lb. manganese
           6 oz. blue calx.
Run down in a very easy place. Biscuit oven
For an Hair Brown on the glaze, add $2\frac{1}{2}$ oz. blue
to the above flux.

2. A SMALL NOTE BOOK CONTAINING MANY RECIPES

H.P. China Body   196 lb. Bone
          21 lb. Flint
         128 lb. Clay
          60 lb. Stone
           $1\frac{1}{4}$ lb. Calk
The above reduced (proportions)
          49 Bone
           $5\frac{1}{4}$ Flint
          32 Clay
          15 Stone
say this weighed Four times and
then $1\frac{1}{4}$ oz. stain calk.

4. NOTEBOOK OF 28 PAGES, WRITTEN BY BENJAMIN TOMKINSON

Enamels for Earthenware
Take any quantity of Tin and inclose it in clay or loam, and put it into a
crucible. Place the crucible in the fire that the tin may calcine then break it.
There will be a pound of calx very white and when used for painting on a
white ground the colour will come forth whiter than the ground.

Yellow Glazing

> 3 lb. Red Lead
> 3 lb. Tin
> 3 lb. Antimony
> Calcine the whole. This glaze will run very soon and give a good yellow.
> Take two parts of the above
> Take one part of Copper—fuse them twice and you will have a green.

Olive sponge Dip

> 1 quart Yellow Slip   1 oz. Zaffre

Brown under Glaze

> 8 oz. Glass antimony
> 16 oz. Litharge
> 3 oz. Manganese
> 4 drams Calx.

To make a purple enamel

> Pour a little of the solution of Tin in muriatic acid into a solution of gold in nitro muriatic acid till a purple colour begins to appear and when the coloured precipitate has subsided put it into an earthen vessel to dry.
> (Muriatic acid is an old commercial name for hydrochloric acid.)

Red enamels from Iron

> Mix equal parts of Sulphate of Iron (Copperas) and Sulphate of Alumina (Alum) fuse them together untill perfectly dry. Continue to heat them untill Red Hot. This last operation must be performed in a reverberating Furnace keep the mixture heated till every part assumes a Beautiful Red colour which may be known by taking out a little and allowing it to remain to cool in the air. The more alum applied the paler it becomes.

To prepare a Blue Enamel

> Take a quantity of the oxide of cobalt and fuse it along with a flux of white glass, Borax, Nitre and white oxide of Antimony and a beautiful blue enamel will be obtained.

Observations upon the Bodies

The base of most Bodies is the Ball (clay) from Devonshire, which contains the two important qualities, whiteness and refractoriness in a greater degree than any other British clay. It is the base of all our C.C. (cream colour) Bodies . . . for Common C.C. Bodies flint and Cornish stone are added to increase the hardness and fineness of Texture and to make it ring well, the proportion varies in most Manufactories. Some use 4 flint to 20 of clay others 4 to 15 with a small quantity of Stone to make it enamely (sic), and the Printing Body has china clay added and the proportion of flint and stone increased. The materials are separately made into slip and the weight of a pint of slip is as follows:

> Slip   24 oz. to the pint
> Flint   32 oz. ,, ,,   ,,
> Stone 28 oz. ,, ,,   ,,

Dry Bodies such as are of a Vitrified texture and not fit to receive a glaze, but only a smear, a different course is taken. There are two ways of producing them the first is by using Barytes Earth or Lime, which will act as a flux to the

clays and form enamels, this is the mode of jaspers which require firing with great caution, they drop in the oven if fired too high and if short they do not become enamels.

The preceding mixtures may receive an Infinity of colours from the metallic oxides and earthy ores of metals: of the former there are the principal Black oxides of Manganese for some Purples, Browns or Blacks; oxides of gold precipitated with Tinn for purple and rose colour; Antimony for Orange; Cobalt for Blue; Iron for Browns; Copper for Browns and clear Greens; also Nickle also Umber for Brown and to heighten Blacks. . . .

By a judicious combination of them very fine colours may be made, in short here is a field for Discovery in which but little has been attempted. Of the oxides 1 p. cent. is sufficient for the first trial of its tint.

(In this section there are several 'medical' recipes of which the two following might be quoted.)

Rheumatism

Take Cucumbers when full grown and put them into a pot with a little salt then put the pot over a slow fire where it should remain about an hour then take them and press them the juice of which must be put into bottles cork'd up tight and put into a cellar where they should remain about a week then dip a flannel rag into it and apply it to the part affected.

Tooth ache

A Radical cure for the tooth ache use as a tooth powder the best Spanish snuff or Tobacco ashes and make a point of washing behind your Ears with cold water every morning.

The Remedy is infallible.

[5a and 5b omitted here]

5c. *SHEET OF RECIPES*

The frett is	40 lbs. Stone	
	40 lbs. Glass	
	20 lbs. Lead	
	12 lbs. Soda	Stained to suit the colour
	6 lbs. Nitre	of the Ware in the Warehouse
Soft mixture	260 lbs. Lead	
	70 lbs. Stone	
	60 lbs. Flint	
	40 lbs. Glass	

Hanley   March 9th. 1827
Sir,
The above is the glaze promised to suit you and hope it will answer, anything I can do for you in the Pottery will be a pleasure—your earliest information as regards the trial of the Plate will oblige; no trouble shall be spared on my part to furnish you with a good patt^n. and remain

Your obed^t. St. C. Hall.

Stain	30 lbs. of flint glass
	2 lbs. of White Lead
	1 lb. of Borax
	1 lb. of Common Salt
	8 ozs. Nitre
	10 ozs. Blue Calx

All these articles forming the *stain* to be pounded fine and well mix'd together, then put in a flinted Sagar and calcine it on top of the gloss'd oven.

When it is calcined, chip the flint from it, then pound and send it to the mill to be ground very fine: it is then fit for use. To prevent having blue specks on the ware, weigh the quantity of stain that you want, which, put it in a large basin of water, and after stirring it well up in the basin, run it gently off into the glaze, leaving the sediment all at the bottom which will be free from specks attaching to the wares.

Wash all the Biscuit Sagars with common slip before they are used.

Place all the ware in biscuit with calcined flint, viz. take Dried flint and sift it through a coarse hair sieve; then put the sifted flint into sagars, and calcine them in the gloss'd oven—when calcined, you must sift it over again before it be used.

Wash for the gloss'd sagars   130 lbs. of White Lead
                                 30 lbs. Composition
                                 20 lbs. Flint

all ground & sifted together, wash the sagars every time they are used.

To place the ware upon, in gloss'd sagars. Take calcined flint stone pound and sift it through a small wire riddle: then take the dust from it by sifting through a hair Sieve. Place the ware on the covered part. N.B. The Dresden must be fired in the Earthen ware bisquet oven, in the hottest part, or in the middle of the china bisquet oven.—To be gloss'd in the China oven.

Drab Body No. 1
100 lbs. of Broken ware, or shavings of the Cream Col'd Body
  2 lbs. of Nickle to the above.
The Nickle to be pounded in a mortar and put through a fine wire riddle and spread upon bisquet dishes about $\frac{1}{2}$ inch thick, the dishes put on top of the bungs in the gloss'd oven: when it comes out the Nickle will be of a green-col'd powder, which must be well ground at the mill. When ground, dry it in a plaster mould not too much but about the hardness of clay when the men are working it.

Drab Glaze   220 lbs. of White Lead
                      65 lbs. of Cornwall Stone
                      40 lbs. of Dried flint

Drab Body No. 2.
80 lbs. of Broken ware, or shavings of the Cream Col'd Body.
$2\frac{1}{2}$ lbs. of Manganese.
The manganese must be pounded fine and put through a fine wire riddle— then take 5 lbs. of Manganese and 5 lbs. of Nitre; put the nitre through the same riddle as the manganese, mix them well together, and calcine it upon dishes on the gloss'd oven, same as the nickle is done for No. 1. When this comes out of the oven it will be a flat solid cake; then pound it in a mortar, and afterwards well ground at the mill. Dry it the same as Nickle in No. 1. it is then ready for use.

NB This mixture will produce a drab body similar to Wedgwood's. The glaze for the above, same as No. 1. only a little blue stain is sometimes put to it.

NB These bodies should be fired towards the *middle* of the bisquet oven and be kept *all together* as much as possible.

5d. *SHEETS OF RECIPES*

Fawn or drab body
40 Marle
 4 Cornish Stone
 1 Flint

Superior White Jasper bodies
50 caulk Stone
50 Blue Clay
25 Bones

10 Flint
perfectly adapted for figures
in baso-relievo & to be
fired in E'Ware ovens.

Calcedony Body
32 Yellow Clay
10 Stone
4 Flint

Brown Body
50 Red Clay
7½ Common Clay
1 Manganese
1 Flint

Stone Body
480 Stones
250 Blue Clay
240 China Clay
10 Glass
1 Blue Calx.

Jasper Body
10 Caulk Stone
10 Blue Clay
5 Bones
2 Flint
1¼ Blue Calx
sh'd be all gr'd together

Stone Morter Body (Mortar)
480 Stone
250 Blue Clay
240 China Clay
10 Glass

To Make a fawn porous Body (for Wine Coolers)
40 Argillaceous Clays (white potters' clay)
4 Blue Clay
2 flint
To be ornamented with clay of diff't Colours if desirable.

5e. *SHEET OF PRICES PAID TO WORKMEN FOR VARIOUS ARTICLES AND PROCESSES*

SLIP MAKING 3s. 3d. pr. ton for Making it
1s. 4d. pr. ton for beating it

THROWING† 1s. pr. score dozens
3½d. pr. score Balling (i.e. weighing clay into balls)
3½d. pr. score Turning (i.e. turning the wheel)
Capt. Teapots 1 score is counted for 5 score

TURNING†
(on the lathe)

Qts. & all sizes larger	1s. 6d.	pr. score
pints & all Less Sizes	2s. 2d. ,, ,,
Saucers Backing and faceing	4s. 4d. ,, ,,
Bute Ware	2s. 8d. ,, ,,
Capt. Teapots	8s. 4d. ,, ,,
Cans, Creams & Chocolates	2s. 5d. ,, ,,
Saucers 36s & Dutch Jugs	2s. 8d. ,, ,,
Saucers fluted	8s. 4d. ,, ,,
Cups do.	6s. 8d. ,, ,,

(for this group
application of
bands of slip on
the lathe is
meant.)

Moca Ware	6s. 8d. ,, ,,
Bowls Band'd	5s. ,, ,,
Jugs do.	4s. 2d. ,, ,,
Mugs do.	4s. 2d. ,, ,,

† (In the above cases it is not clear how many dozens are counted in a score, this being variable to suit the nature of the work as in the case below, page 129).

CHINA THROWING	Slop Bowls & Cake Plates	5s. pr. score
	Cups & Saucers	2s. ,, ,,
	Rings (for supporting ware in firing)	6d. ,, ,,

All kinds of Comm'n Ware blocked ready for Turner   2s. 3d. pr. score
For Fluted ware and Egg Cups   2s. 6d. ,, ,,
he paying all necessary expenses out of it.
(He being the Turner who paid for his assistants—see Chapter VII)

To be counted†	Cups & Saucers	22 doz. to score
	Coffees	13 doz. to do.
	Sugar Bowls	13 doz. to do.
	Bft. plates	9 doz. to do.
	Bowls	13 doz. to do.

BLACK PRINTING	Mugs & Jugs	4d. pr. doz.
	all above 6's	3d. pr. doz.
	Bowls all sizes	10d. pr. doz.
	all 24's Jugs & Tumblers	5d. pr. doz.
	Comm'n plates	9d. pr. doz.

1s. 9d. for Every Hundred doz. for looking to the Ware & carrying clay.

5f. *UNDERGLAZE COLOUR RECIPES*   (see Colour Plate III)
Colours under glaze   Good Lineing

Brown No. 2.   Good one W.P.
5 Litherage
3 Antimony
1 Manganess
Calcine in the Buiscet (sic)
oven Near the Middle on a
flatt dish but not Covrd.

Black Green
1 of Common Green
1 of Yellow Calx
1 of Orange
1 of Blue Calx

Orange No. 1
6 Litharage
4 Antimony
3 Tin Ash
1½ of Crocus Martis

Calcine top of Fore bung.

Green
16 oz. Glass
14 oz. yellow Calx.
3½ of Blue Calx
Grind for use this will be a light green
Make it dark
Leving out ⅓ of the Glass &
ading More Blue
Greens may be Made dark or
Light by the ading More or
Less Blue as you wish to your
yellow.

Yellow No. 1.
2 Litherage   this is
2 Tin ash   used for
1 Antimony   yallow Glaze
                    Good one W.P.

Yellow No. 4.
1 Tin   add more Tin or
1 Antimony   Antimony as you
1 litherage   wish it lighter
                    dark.

K

6. *THREE LETTERS FROM MISS M. AND MISS E. TOMKINSON, TO PETER ENTWISTLE, LIVERPOOL*

604 BOAS STREET   JUNE 30, 1924
HARRISBURG, PA.

PETER ENTWISTLE,
DEPUTY CURATOR OF MUSEUMS

Dear Sir,

I take pleasure in sending you another parcel of papers.

We still have a little book with some data. I find that I packed it and sent it to the home to which we are going, later will send it.

Sister and I had the photographs you spoke of made and sent them.

They are china most of which is still in our possession. It is eagerly desired by younger relatives as it was desired by us in the early days.

I am glad you are about to publish the account of the collections, and of the progress of the ceramic art in Liverpool.

I should be glad to possess a copy when it is published.*

Yours sincerely,
MARTHA M. TOMKINSON
FROM THE MISSES TOMKINSON
MARTHA M. & ELLEN F.

P. ENTWISTLE,   [No date or address]
DEPUTY CURATOR OF LIVERPOOL MUSEUM.

Dear Sir,

We are sending you the private book of Joseph Tomkinson, supervisor of Herculaneum Pottery.

It seems to contain price lists that might be of interest. It had been sent with books sent before we came upon the papers sent last.

I think it is the last of the papers.

We should be glad to have your book on the Liverpool China industry.

It does not suit to purchase it now.

I do not think any of our family are willing to part with any of the pieces of the china.

The teapot sent I rescued years ago. It was broken then but patched together, and was in pieces when packed. I was laughed at for sending it.

The vases &c. you have photographs of are watched by our young relatives as the prized possession of the family to sometime come to them as they came to us.

With earnest wishes for your success in perfecting the collections.

We remain   Yours sincerely,
                           THE MISSES TOMKINSON
                           PER MARTHA M. TOMKINSON

[No date, address or other preliminary]

I have packed and am mailing to the Liverpool Museum the remains of a tea pot made in the Herculaneum Pottery where my Grandfather Rev'd Joseph Tomkinson was in charge.†

It had been set aside as worthless; but may be of some use as an example of the sort of ware made.‡

---

* Peter Entwistle's book was, unfortunately, never published.
† See Chapter II page 23, and Chapter V page 64.
‡ This teapot is not known now at Liverpool Museum.

There must once have been a set of this ware in the family.

I have seen other pieces. I am also sending some balance sheets I found among Grandfather's papers.

They show the amount of business done.

There are many papers about bodies and glazes. If they would be of any interest we would send them.

If these papers are not interesting you have a waste basket no doubt.

TO THE CURATOR OF THE MUSEUM, LIVERPOOL, FROM

THE MISSES TOMKINSON, 604 BOAS ST., HARRISBURG, PA.

PER MARTHA M. TOMKINSON.

BIBLIOGRAPHICAL NOTE AND ADVICE TO COLLECTORS

No student of Liverpool ceramics can begin his work without reference to the first writer on this subject, that extraordinary collector and benefactor Joseph Mayer (1803–1886). The paper he read before the Historic Society of Lancashire and Cheshire in 1855 and again in 1871 entitled *The History of the Progress of the Art of Pottery in Liverpool* was published in the Society's *Transactions* and may be consulted in *Vol. VII 1855* and *Vol. XXIII 1871*. The second is a slightly amended version, prefaced by a general introduction *On the Art of Pottery* and was reprinted separately in 1873, while the 1855 version can also sometimes be found as a separate booklet. In spite of the mistakes Mayer undoubtedly made, his work remains a classic, for he was the first man to take the subject seriously, was writing at a time when potting was still active on Merseyside, and he knew and talked to the sons and daughters of the eighteenth-century potters. It should be remembered that Mayer painted a picture of the Herculaneum factory (Plate 2) fifteen years before it closed, when he was twenty-two years of age.

In 1882 the second work on Liverpool wares was published by the scholar and museum curator Charles T. Gatty. His booklet *The Liverpool Potteries* was also reprinted from the *Transactions of the Historic Society of Lancashire and Cheshire*, and unlike Mayer's text it is scholarly and precise and accompanied by a most valuable list of Liverpool wares in the museum of that city in those days, as well as listed details of the sites of the potteries and their proprietors. One of Gatty's colleagues at the museum, was Peter Entwistle, a younger man who spent a lifetime of research on the subject, but unhappily died in 1939 following his retirement in 1930, without his work ever being published. The notes he left, however, remain available to students today as *The Entwistle Papers* in the Liverpool Record Office.

Peter Entwistle, like Gatty, was a museum official but the next author of note was a bank manager in Bootle, H. Boswell Lancaster, and a collector and contributor to journals on antiques. His work *Liverpool and Her Potters* was published by W. B. Jones & Co., 20 South Castle Street, Liverpool in 1936, and although he leaned very heavily on Mayer and is often not to be trusted there is a list of potters and engravers included which is of some value. World War II put an end to any useful work for some years and caused the destruction of Liverpool Museum by bombing in 1941, when many fine documentary Liverpool pieces were lost. In 1948, however, E. Stanley Price published privately a fine monograph entitled *John Sadler, A Liverpool Pottery Printer* which may be said to be the first really detailed and analytical work published on one important aspect of Liverpool's ceramic history. This was printed by Gould's, West Kirby, and is now difficult to obtain.

A collector who did a very great deal to further research into the history of Liverpool pottery and who had an amazing eye for ceramics was the late Ernest Allman of Bootle. A friend of Stanley Price he was well known to other collectors including Dr. Knowles Boney who, in 1957, published his magnum opus *Liverpool Porcelain of the Eighteenth Century and its Makers* (B. T. Batsford, London). This important volume helped perhaps more than any other work to focus attention on Liverpool porcelain, and its influence may be found today as the prices of Liverpool specimens are rising higher than many of the wares of hitherto more famous factories elsewhere.

In recent years the most outstanding contribution to the analysis of Liverpool

porcelains has been the work of Dr. Bernard Watney. Most of what he has had to say has appeared in the *Transactions of the English Ceramic Circle* at various times (see footnotes *§ page 4, Chapter I) and also in his book *English Blue and White Porcelain of the Eighteenth Century*, published by Faber and Faber, London in 1963, while a section by Dr. Watney on Liverpool wares appears in *English Porcelain 1745–1850* (Ernest Benn Ltd., London), edited by R. J. Charleston in 1965. In the same volume the editor Robert Charleston has a valuable contribution on *New Hall and other Nineteenth Century Staffordshire Factories and Herculaneum.*

The porcelains of Liverpool have rightly had much publicity in recent years, but the same cannot be said of its earthenwares of which far more were made than porcelain. Liverpool delftware, however, was first seriously discussed by the late Professor F. H. Garner in his book *English Delftware* (Faber and Faber, London) in 1948, and this has been followed by Anthony Ray's *English Delftware Pottery in the Robert Hall Warren Collection*, published in 1968 by Faber and Faber which is a scholarly and informed publication.

Before the present volume was written no work on the later years of Liverpool potting and the Herculaneum factory had been attempted, apart from several magazine articles, and some contributions to the *English Ceramic Circle Transactions.* All the writing on Herculaneum in the standard works on English pottery and porcelain was based primarily on Joseph Mayer's account, and the details he gave have been copied again and again. Apart, therefore, from such valuable contributions as G. A. Godden's *British Pottery and Porcelain 1780–1850* (Arthur Barker, London, 1963) and his *Illustrated Encyclopaedia of British Pottery and Porcelain* (Herbert Jenkins, London, 1966) there is nothing of any detail to be found published, and the scope of these works is so wide that they can only serve to indicate the general picture of pottery-making in England when Herculaneum was a going concern, as the author (Editor of the present series) would be the first to admit. This book, therefore, has been based entirely on two avenues of research, (a) the investigation of documents and records in the Liverpool area and elsewhere, most of which are mentioned in the footnotes to the text, and (b) a study of Herculaneum wares wherever they are to be found in public and private collections, both in England and in the United States.

As the interest of collectors is now extending further into the nineteenth century than ever before the wares of Herculaneum are increasing in price, particularly when the specimens are marked. In a recent sale (1967) a marked porcelain vase (compare Colour Plate VI) realised well over £60 and it must be expected that this kind of price will rise higher as collections change hands in the coming years. Good examples of transfer-printed creamware jugs are now (1969) realising between £50 and £100 while certain smaller items such as 10 inch plates of the early period will reach between £20 and £30 if they are unusually decorated, though this is not the case for pieces from the 1830s. The field of *unmarked* examples provides an opportunity for the collector of limited means to exercise his judgment at far less cost than marked pieces will command, and there are many hundreds, if not thousands, of humble unmarked pieces on the market today which may be purchased for less than £5. A piece which cannot be firmly identified can often give pleasure in the interest it creates, and it is the exercise of judgment and speculation as to provenance and dating in which most of the pleasure of collecting consists. To attempt to discover Herculaneum pottery and porcelain amongst the masses of contemporary Staffordshire wares which are readily available will bring exciting discoveries in a field which is only just being charted, and the collector therein will reap his own rewards.

INDEX

Index

Abbey, Alice, 18
Abbey, Richard, 3, 15, 18, 19, 23, 29, 35, 38, 41
Abbey, William, 18
Abercromby, General, 44, 45
Adams, William; *Cobridge*, 41, 55
Adelaide, Queen, 87
Akin, James, 59
Albion Insurance Office, 112
Allman, Ernest, 5, 131
America, embargo on trade, 53, 58
  relationships with England, 44, 58
  trade with, 50ff.
  wares produced for, 58ff.
  views printed on pottery, 70
Anglesey, North Wales, 15
Ashcroft, David, 96
Aynsley, John; *Lane End*, 37

Baddeley, J. and E., *Shelton*, 55
Bailey, William and Company, *Lane End*, 55
Ball, William, 4, 7
Bangor, North Wales, 20
  slate from, 21
Barker, John and Company, *Lane End*, 55
Barlow, John, 63, 66, 120
Barnes, Zachariah, 5, 7, 12
Bartolozzi, 34
'bat' printing, 72, 106
Baxter, Thomas, *Worcester*, 46
Bayley, Alderman James, 83
Belfast, clay from, 2
Bentley, Benjamin, 117
Bentley, Thomas, 3
Berey, Samuel, 29
Bevington Bush, *Liverpool*, 22
Bidston Hill, signal flags, 35, 36
Birkenhead, Williamson Art Gallery, 38, 86
black basalt wares, 42

Blundell Street, *Liverpool*, 11
Blunt, Edmund March, 59
Boney, Dr. Knowles, 3, 11, 34, 131
Booth, William, *Hanley*, 97
Bourne, James, 74, 75
Bourne, William and Company, *Burslem*, 55
Bridgewater Canal, 87
Bridgewater, Duke of, 87
Brighton, Museum and Art Gallery, 24
British Museum, *London*, 5, 35, 37, 45
Brooks, Joseph, 7
Brown, John, 31
Brown, Moses, 59
Brown, Nicholas, 59
Brownlow Hill Pottery, *Liverpool*, 4, 7
Bullock, George, 32, 55
Bullock, William, 32
Buonaparte, Napoleon, 44
  defeat at Leipzig, 90
Burton and Holbrook, *Derby*, 98
Burton, William, 1
Buxton, Edward, 47, 71, 111, 112, 114
Buxton, Henry, 71

Cadell, Thomas, publisher, 40
Canal, Leeds–Liverpool, 7
  Mersey–Trent, 9
Canning Street Pottery, *Liverpool*, 7, 22, 66, 67, 96
Carrickfergus, Northern Ireland, 2
Cartwright, William, 30
Case, Thomas, 74, 75, 117, 118
Castle Street, *Liverpool*, 86
Chaffers, Richard, 2, 4, 5, 7
Charleston, R. J., 74 (footnote), 132
Charlotte, North Carolina, Mint Museum of Art, 40
Cheetham and Wooley, *Lane End*, 55
Chicago, Michigan, Art Institute of, 25, 43, 57, 60, 70

Christchurch graveyard, *Liverpool*, 2
Christian, Philip, 3, 4, 7
clay, preparation of, 99, 100
Clieveland Square, *Liverpool*, 7, 18, 47
Coalport, Shropshire, 27, 47
Codling, George, 29, 93, 98
Colonial Williamsburg, Virginia, 18, 35, 37
Colquitt Street, *Liverpool*, 86
Cope, William, 31
Copeland and Garrett, *Stoke*, 44, 45
copper smelting, 15, 28, 99
Copperas Hill Pottery, *Liverpool*, 7
Cordon, Elizabeth, 22
Cordon, Myrah, 22, 81
Cordon, Ralph, 22, 26, 81
Cordon, Sampson, 22, 32, 81
Cotter, James, 7
creamware, 4, 11, 12, 23ff., 38ff.
Cropper, Benson and Company, 50
Crosby, William and Mary, 24

Dale, Charles, 86
Dale Street, *Liverpool*, 2
Dale Street Pottery, *Liverpool*, 7
Dale Street/Preston Street Pottery, *Liverpool*, 7
Davies, William, 31
Dearborn, Michigan, Henry Ford Museum, 57, 69
delftware, 2, 3
Dixon, William, 32, 47
Dodd, A. H., 21
Doulton and Company, 82
Drinkwater, George and Company, 2, 7
Driver, John, 32
Duke Street, *Liverpool*, 2
Duke Street Pottery, *Liverpool*, 7
Dunbibbin, John, 2, 5, 7
Dunbibbin, Samuel, 5
Duncan, Lord, 39, 44, 45

Eardsley, Andrew, *Newcastle*, 97
Eccles, John and Company, 7, 11
Eccleston Parish Church, Douglas Chapel, 36
Edgar, Archibald, 31
Edge Hill, *Liverpool*, 37
Edmondson, J., 29
Edwards, Miss Diane, of *Widnes*, 39
Edwards, John, 32, 39, 46
enamelling on pottery, 25, 45, 60, 106, 124, 125
Entwistle, Peter, 45, 74, 76, 79, 129–31
Etruria, Staffordshire, xiii, 8, 39
'Estruscan' pattern, 49
Evans, Robert, 32
Everton, *Liverpool*, 37
Exchange Flags, *Liverpool*, 87

Fairclough, Joseph, 31
'Farmers Arms' prints, 24, 35, 38, 58

'Farmyard' prints, 24, 33, 35, 37, 38, 58, 60
Faucett, William, 29
Ferrybridge, Yorkshire, 24
firing of pottery, 101, 105
flats, on the Mersey, 9
Flaxman, John, 34, 39
Fletcher, Thomas, *Shelton*, 18, 37
flint, 21, 93, 99, 116, 119
    grinding at *Nant Gwreiddiog, North Wales*, 21
Flint Mug Works, *Liverpool*, 5, 7, 10, 11
Flixton, St. Michael's Church, 20
flowers, use of in prints, 24, 38, 39
Floyd, Abraham, 32
Folly Lane, *Liverpool*, 12
France, information on the French pottery trade, 64, 65
Franceys, S. and J., 32
French, William, 29
Frye, Thomas, 3
Fuseli, Henry, 33, 34, 37

Gainsborough, Thomas, 33
Gardiner, Rachel, 18
Garner, F. H., 132
Gatty, Charles, 11, 131
'gaudy Dutch' patterns, 61
'General Illumination', 90, 113
Gerard, Richard, 13
Gibson, Solomon, 32, 48
Gilbody, Samuel, 2, 4, 7
gilding, 59, 60
Ginder, Samuel and Company, *Lane Delph*, 55
Gladstone, Robert, 74, 75
glazing, 106, 124
    yellow glazing, 38, 40, 125, 129
Godden, G. A., 132
Gore, James, 32
Grafton Street, *Toxteth*, 98
Graham, Andrew, 19
Graham, James, 19
Grant, Mary 19
Green, Guy, 3, 7, 10, 23, 33, 41, 47
Greenbank Pottery, *St. Helens*, 82–5
Gregson, John, 14
Griffiths, Thomas, 48

Hackwood, Dimmock and Company, *Hanley*, 56
Haggar, Reginald, 75
Hanley, Museum and Art Gallery, 12, 26, 42, 46
Hanmer, Latham, 29
Harding, John, 29
Harding, William, 30
Harley, Thomas and Mrs., 82, 83
Harrington, development area of *Toxteth*, 14
    Dock Company, 77
    Free School, 90

Harrington Street, *Liverpool*, 3, 7
Hartley, William, 32
Hawkes, Thomas and Company, *Dudley*, 56, 117
Haymarket Pottery, *Liverpool*, 5, 7, 12
Henshall and Williamson, *Longport*, 56
Herculaneum Dock, 98
  Dock Bill, 77, 78
Herculaneum Pottery, *Toxteth*,
  apprentices, 89
  articles manufactured at, 71, 106
  buildings, 29, 30, 79, 80, 91–5, 99, 114, 115
  chapel and Sunday School, 90, 91, 107, 113
  coastal trade, 50, 54
  Committee Minute Book, 30, 46, 53–5, 62, 73, (see Appendix II)
  Duke Street Warehouse (see Warehouse)
  early advertisements, 20, 111
  emigrants from Staffordshire, 22, 23, 91
  engravers, 31, 39
  formation of Company, 29
  foundation of, 9, 14, 110
  Friendly Society, 47, 91, 92
  insurance of buildings and stock, 112, 115, 116
  iron-working at, 76
  labour conditions, 89–91
  lease of site and buildings, 28
  management of, 89
  marks on pottery, 24, 26, 41, 43, 44, 48, 68, 69, 75, 88, 108, 109, 120
    Liver Bird, 4, 5, 69, 86–8
  materials used, 97–9
  numbers of employees, 32, 98
  'outside' workers, 32
  prices of articles, 38, 122, 123
  prices for manufacturing, 122, 123, 128
  profits, 31, 65
  recipes of bodies and glazes, 123–8
  records of potters, 22, 23
  retail shop, South John Street, 55
  sale advertisements, 44, 45, 73, 77, 78, 79, 81, 82
  school at the works, 90, 113
  share certificates, 29, 30
  speculation account, 50
  steam engine and mill, 78, 93, 96, 99, 112, 116
  trade, American embargo on, 53, 58
  trade overseas, 50, 51, 54, 112, 114
  vessels with cargoes from, 51, 52
  Warehouse, Duke Street, *Liverpool*, 47, 48, 54–6, 65, 66, 77, 78, 89, 90, 110–14, 119
    Redcross Street, *Liverpool*, 30, 54, 113
    Salthouse Dock, *Liverpool*, 20, 54
  windmill, 29, 93

Herculaneum Steel Fabrication Works, 76, 98
Heywood, Arthur Esq. and Company, Bankers, 110
Hicks and Meigh, *Shelton*, 56
Hillary, Richard and Company, 7
Hird, Anna, 30
Holden, Richard, 22, 29, 65, 66, 111, 119
Holgate, David, 26
Holland, John, 30
Holland, Samuel, 19, 21, 22, 29
Holland, Thomas, *Burslem*, 56
Hollins, John, 30
Hollins, Samuel, *Shelton*, 41
Holmes, James and Samuel, 76
Holt, Richard, 2, 7
Horsfall, Charles, 74, 75
Hulme, Thomas and Son, *Burslem*, 97
Humble, Green and Company, *Leeds*, 21
Humble, Michael, 19, 21, 29, 90
Hurry, Nicholas, 21
Hutchinson, William, 30

Ibbs, Isaac, 22
Ibbs, James, 22, 23, 63
Ibbs, Joseph, 22
Ibbs, Ruth, 34
Ibbs, William, 22
'Indian' designs on pottery, 49
Infirmary, *Liverpool*, 5
Ireland, National Museum of, *Dublin*, 23, 26
Islington China Manufactory, *Liverpool*, 5, 7, 12, 13, 96

Jackson's Dam, *Toxteth*, 15
Jefferson, Thomas, President of the U.S., 58
Johnson, James, 34
Johnson, John, 34
Johnson, Joseph, gentleman of *Liverpool*, 34, 37
Johnson, Joseph, potter and decorator, 18, 34–8
Johnson, Joseph, publisher of *London*, 32, 34, 37
Johnson, Nathaniel, 31, 34
Johnson, William, 34
Jones, Robert, 29

Kansas City, Missouri, William Rockhill Nelson Gallery of Art, 35, 39, 57
Kauffman, Angelica, 33
Keay, Robert, *Burslem*, 97
Keeling, James, *Hanley*, 56
Keightley, Archibald, 29, 112
Keightley, Margaret, 22
Kennedy, James, *Burslem*, 97
Kirkdale, Liverpool, House of Correction, 87
Kosciuzko, Count, 44

Lace, Ambrose, 74–7
Lace, Joshua, 76, 77
'Lancashire Illustrated', 86, 87
Lancashire Record Office, *Preston*, 36
Lancaster, H. Boswell, 131
Lawrence, Henry, 30
Lee, Mary, 20
Lege, Frederick, 32, 45
Liverpool, Coat of Arms, 49, 69
    Sept-Centenary Exhibition, 39, 79
    Town Records, 1
    Volunteers, 43, 47
    Warehousing and docks, 14, 77
'Liverpool Albion', description of the
    Herculaneum Pottery, 98–107
Liverpool Museum, 5, 12, 22–6, 32, 34,
    35, 40–3, 45–7, 49, 60, 69–71, 86, 87
Liver Bird, (see under Herculaneum Pot-
    tery—marks)
Livesley, John, 2, 7
Llwynan, near *Bangor, North Wales*, 21
Lockett and Company, *Lane End*, 56, 70
Lord Street Pothouse, *Liverpool*, 2, 7
Lovatt, William, 32, 34, 46, 47, 119
Lucock, John, 5, 7, 13
lustreware, 70
Lyons, Henry, 31

McCauley, Robert H., 57, 61
McCrery, David, 11
Machin and Baggaley, (Baddeley), *Burs-
    lem*, 48, 97, 98
Maddison, James, President of the U.S.,
    60
Manchester, City Art Gallery, 46
Manchester–Liverpool Railway, 83, 87
Mansfield, Anne, 22
Mansfield, Archibald, 7, 22, 63, 65–7, 81,
    90, 96, 113, 119
Mansfield, Ralph, (junior), 22, 90
Mansfield, Ralph, (senior), 22, 30, 62,
    110, 112
maritime subjects in pottery decoration,
    40
marks, (see Herculaneum Pottery—
    marks)
Marsh, William, *Hanley*, 97
Martin, George, 31, 39
Mary, Queen of Scots, 40
Mason, Miles, 5, 7, 13
Mason, Miles and Company, *Lane Delph*,
    56
Maydew, Thomas and Company, *Burs-
    lem*, 97
Mayer, Elijah, *Hanley*, 41
Mayer, Joseph, xiii, 3, 9, 15, 18, 19, 22,
    23, 25, 29, 39, 42, 67, 68, 71, 76, 131
Mears, Thomas and John, 7
Menzies, John, 29
Meredith, Sir William, 5
Miller, Aaron, 26

Milligan, Hugh, 32
Minton and Poulson, *Stoke*, 56
mocha ware, 70
Mold, Flintshire, 60
Moore, John, 30
Morland, George, 48
Mort, James, 75–7, 82, 83, 96
moulds, 100, 101, 105

National Trust, Upton House, 48
Naylor, John, 31
Nelson, Admiral Lord, 39, 44, 87
New Hall, *Shelton*, 26, 48
Newburgh, Lancashire, 36, 37
Newburyport, Massachusetts, 59, 61
North Wales, importance of in the early
    nineteenth century, 21

Okill, James, 10
Okill, John and Company, 7, 10, 11
Ormskirk, Lancashire, 1, 36, 37
Orred, George, 29

Paisley, Museum and Art Gallery, 41
'Paradise Lost', decoration from, 34
Parbold, Lancashire, 36, 37
Paris, Prince of Wales Pottery, 18
Park Lane Pothouse, *Liverpool*, 5, 7, 11
Park Terrace, *Toxteth*, 77, 98
Parker, Charles Stewart, 74, 75
Parker, William, *Hanley*, 97
Parr, James, 30
Part, John, 4, 7, 12
Parys Mines, *Anglesey*, 15
Patrick's Hill Pothouse, *Liverpool*, 2, 7
pearlware, 4, 25, 43, 61
Pendleton, Thomas, 7
Pennington, James, 4, 7, 11, 13
Pennington, Jane, 13
Pennington, John, 4, 7, 13
Pennington, Seth, 4, 7, 12, 13, 26
Penrhyn, Lord, negotiations of leases
    with, 21
Penrhyn Slate Quarries, *Caernarvonshire*,
    21
Philadelphia, Museum of Art, 26, 60
Picton, J. A., 91
Pinxton, Derbyshire, 27
Platt, R., of *Widnes*, 93
Plinth, Charles, 32
Podmore, James, 31
Podmore, Robert, 4
Poole, Josiah, 7
Poole, Samuel, 2, 7
'Poor Jack', 40
porcelain, 3, 4, 26ff., 46ff., 71, 72, 124
Pothouse Lane, *Liverpool*, 2
Pratt, F. and R., *Fenton*, 83
'Pratt' ware, 42, 43, 45, 129
Prescot, Lancashire, 1, 5
'pressing', 101

Preston, Harris Museum, 35
Price, E. S., 131
Prince, William, 32
printing, on pottery, 3, 18, 19, 23–5, 33, 38–41, 48, 49, 57ff., 61, 69, 70, 80, 81, 86ff., 101, 104, 106, 124, 129

Rainhill, Lancashire, 87
Ranelagh Street Pottery, *Liverpool*, 7
Rawson, Benjamin, 30
Ray, Anthony, 132
Reeves, William, 55, 111
Reid, William, 4, 7
Reid's China Works, *Liverpool*, 7, 32
Reynolds, Sir Joshua, 33
Richmond Row Mug Works, *Liverpool*, 7
Ridgway, J. and W., *Shelton*, 56
Rigg and Peacock, 7, 11
Roberts, Edward, 25
Robinson, John, 18
Roe, Charles and Company, 14, 15, 28
Roe and Company, copper smelting, 14, 15, 16, 17
Rogers, John and George, *Longport*, 56
Roscoe, John, and Rigby, James, 3, 7, 32
Roscoe, William, 32–4, 37, 40, 41, 48
Rowe, George, 29
Rowlandson, Thomas, 48
Runcorn, Cheshire, 9

Sadler Collection, Myott Son and Company Limited, *Stoke*, 41, 88
Sadler, John, 3, 7, 18, 41
St. Helens, Lancashire, 82
St. Helens, pottery at, 82
trials of steam engine at, 96, 97
St. James' Church, *Toxteth*, 7, 11, 86
St. Michael's-in-the-Hamlet Church, *Toxteth*, 22, 39, 81
St. Nicholas' Church, *Liverpool*, 7, 18, 19, 24
St. Vincent, Earl of, 39, 44
Salem, Massachusetts, Essex Institute, 43
Peabody Museum, 24, 57, 59, 60
saltglazed pottery, 4, 5, 11
Sandby, Paul, 33
Sankey Canal, 83
Scotland, trading with, 45
Seddon, Joshua, 31
Seel, Thomas, 7
Sefton, Dowager Countess of, 14
Sefton, Earl of, 14, 15, 19, 21, 28, 29, 75, 117, 118
Sefton Street, *Toxteth*, 76
Shaw, Alderman Thomas, 2, 7, 12
Shaw, Richard, *Stoke*, 97
Shaw, Samuel, 7
Shaw's Brow, *Liverpool*, 2, 3, 7, 12
Shirley, Jesse and Son Limited, *Etruria*, 93, 96

Shorthose and Heath, *Hanley*, 56, 97
Simpson, John, 75–7, 82, 83, 96
Simpson, Joseph, 31
slipware, 1, 2
Smith, James, *Newcastle*, 98
Smith, James, and Picard, J. K., *Hanley*, 98
Smith, Jane, of *Chester*, 47
Smith, William, 23, 62, 63, 90, 91, 112
Southwark, potters from, 2
Spode, Josiah, *Stoke*, 27, 44, 49, 56
sponged decoration, 61
Staffordshire, pottery trade, 2, 3, 10, 13, 18, 26, 31, 48, 55, 64, 65, 82, 111, 118
Star and Garter Tavern, Paradise Street, *Liverpool*, 29
Steele, James, *Tunstall*, 97
Steuart, Adam, 29
Stevenson and Goodwin, *Cobridge*, 56
Stewart, Gilbert, 40
stonewares, 39, 41, 42, 44
Stonington, The Gallant Defence of, 38, 58, 60
Stothard, Thomas, 33
Stubbs, George, 33, 34
Sutton, Richard, 29
Swansea, Glynn Vivian Art Gallery, 42
Sykes, John and Company, 7, 11

Tansillo, Luigi, 34, 40
Tarleton, Colonel, 23, 33, 35, 43
Taylor, Jesse, 120
'throwing', 100, 103
Thwaites, Richard and Willcock, Robert and Company, 7, 11
Thyer, Robert, 7
Till, Eli, 22, 42
Till, Elizabeth, 22
Till, Thomas, 22
Tomkinson, Benjamin, 65
Tomkinson, James, 23
Tomkinson, John, 76
Tomkinson, Joseph, 23, 63–7, 91, 113
Tomkinson, Martha and Ellen, 23, 121, 129
Tomkinson Papers, 23, 48, 64, 70, 71, 121ff.
Toxteth, 9, 11, 14, 69, 98
Ancient Chapel of, 22, 92
copper smelting at, 15, 28, 99
Overseers of the Poor at Toxteth Park, 90
Society in Toxteth Park for the Prosecution of Felons, 90
Truro, County Museum and Art Gallery, 5
Turner, John, *Lane End*, 39, 41
Turner, Dr. Matthew, 33
'turning', 100
Twigg, George, *Burslem*, 98

Victoria and Albert Museum, *London*, 18, 24, 40, 41, 45, 46

Walker Art Gallery, *Liverpool*, 79
Walker, Richard, 35
Walls, Thomas, 12
Walton, Parish Church, 15, 18
War of 1812, 53, 58
Warehouse, (see Herculaneum Pottery, Warehouse)
Warrington, Museum and Art Gallery, 45
Washington D.C., Smithsonian Institution, 38, 40, 57–9, 70
Washington, George, President of the U.S., 25, 40, 43, 44, 58, 61
Watchmakers, of *Liverpool*, 4, 19, 33
Waterbury, Connecticut, Mattatuck Museum, 38, 43, 58, 60
Watney, Dr. Bernard, 4, 13, 33, 132
Watson and Company, *St. Helens*, 96, 97
Wedgwood and Company, *Ferrybridge, Yorkshire*, 23, 24

Wedgwood, Josiah, xiii, 3, 8, 9, 33, 34, 45
Wellington Road, *Toxteth*, 98
Wheatley, Francis, 33
Wilcox, Robert and Mrs., 3
Willcock, Robert, (see Richard Thwaites)
William Brown Street, *Liverpool*, 12
Williams, Samuel, 32, 48
Willow pattern, 13, 49
Wilson, Richard, *Hanley*, 23
Winter, Admiral de, 44
Winterthur, Delaware, Henry Francis du Pont Museum, 58, 70
Wolfe, Thomas, 5, 7, 13, 26, 96
Wood and Caldwell, *Burslem*, 56
Woods, James, 90
Worcester, Flight and Barr, 27
Worthington, Samuel, 8–10, 15, 19–22, 28, 29, 90, 93, 112, 116
Wright, Joseph, of Derby, 33

Yates, Reverend John, 90
Yates, John and William, *Shelton*, 56

Zucchiro, 40